"As Pedram Shojai so eloquent~~ly~~ ~~...ts~~ us each to let go and open up to our own true potential, and to come home to ourselves. In these stressful, unpredictable times, he provides an inspiring, user-friendly guide for this essential journey. In this fascinating read, Pedram's brilliant mind and open heart lead you inevitably to your true being, where you will find peace, love and joy—and the inspiration to create planetary change in the process."

—Hyla Cass, M.D., author, *8 Weeks to Vibrant Health*

"Every once in a while you run across a literary gem that is so purely poetic, so lovingly and perfectly crafted, that each word is a tracing at the edges of transcendence. A doorway opens. A new life beckons. Then your soul knows it has come to the source of all longing...

"In that moment you know you have been given a gift beyond measure. *Rise and Shine* is that gift. Pedram Shojai is that voice."

—Paul Rademacher, Executive Director of The Monroe Institute and author of *A Spiritual Hitchhiker's Guide to the Universe: Travel Tips for the Spiritually Perplexed*

"A brilliant book on the alchemy of the Spirit. Revealing the secrets of health and even immortality, Pedram Shojai takes us through an inner journey into the secret teachings of the Taoist Masters. A must-read for any serious student of the healing arts and the alchemy of life."

—Alberto Villoldo PhD, bestselling author of *Shaman, Healer, Sage, and Power Up Your Brain*

RISE AND SHINE

RISE AND SHINE

Awaken your Energy Body with Taoist Alchemy and Qi Gong

PEDRAM SHOJAI

PROCESS

Rise and Shine © 2011 by Pedram Shojai

A Process Media original paperback
ISBN: 978-1-934170-25-0
All rights reserved.

Printed on recycled paper

Process Media
1240 W. Sims Way Suite 124
Port Townsend, WA 98368
www.ProcessMediaInc.com

Design by Bill Smith

Contents

Acknowledgements

I owe everything to my beloved parents, Farhad and Sonbol Shojai, who brought us to America in times of uncertainty. They were seeking a better future for their children and sacrificed everything they had in order to make that future a reality. The degree of selflessness and personal commitment to family, love, and mutual respect always served as the central foundation of my worldview and has helped me become the man I am today. I can never thank them enough for setting their own dreams aside so that we could realize ours. They wanted a better world for me and, in that light, the only way I know how to repay them is to make the world I have stepped into a better place. Thanks to Farhad and Sonbol Shojai, I am committed to shining the light of love and realization through the shadows so that goodness reigns on Earth once again.

I would also like to thank my sister Shery who has lovingly been by my side throughout the years and has always believed in me. Again being surrounded by love and mutual respect is an honor that is not to be taken lightly. Of course there is my beautiful wife Elmira who has supported me and encouraged my work from the beginning. Baby, I love you.

There are also many teachers, masters, doctors, and friends to thank—too many to list them all. One, in particular, deserves a full salute—Grandmaster Carl Totton. He has been my guide, friend, teacher, and mentor for many years. He has served as a major influence in my awakening and continued development. The world owes Sifu Totton immense gratitude for preserving the essence of the Chinese internal arts and so openly sharing these secrets.

I'd like to thank H.H. The Dalai Lama, for his patient instruction and dedication to the enlightenment of humanity. I was fortunate to learn from him in India and his mere presence is a testament to our potential.

The list wouldn't be complete without my meditation master, Yo Hoon. He is a beacon of light and peace in this fast-moving tumultuous world. I thank him for his patience and dedication to his students. I'm proud to have learned from Yo Hoon and am lucky to know him.

Finally, I'd like to thank Jay Weidner, Sharron Rose and Steve Grabowsky for being such great friends and mentors and believing in me. It has been an honor to be in your company and I am proud to know you.

Introduction

At some point in the history of our human development, we fell asleep and forgot about the most amazing miracle in the Universe. Imagine that. The most incredible truth about the essence of our being and the nature of our existence simply slipped under the radar of our knowing. We went from seeing energy and being able to heal ourselves with thought and touch to relying on devices and drugs to save our lives. We slipped out of the realm of multidimensional awareness and fell asleep.

In a not too far-off past, the practice of Alchemy, the ancient spiritual science of the transmutation of lead into gold, was alive and well. In the past few centuries, however, alchemy has become misconstrued by many as being only a literal process. There is another perspective from which to view this process, and it is centered around a powerful metaphor. It is about taking the lead of our human experience and transforming it into the gold of spiritual awareness. It is about refining the essence of our physical bodies into the development of a fully activated Light Body--a luminous sphere that is a reflection of the internal balance and connection of our mind, body, and spirit. Alchemy is about finding the gold inside of ourselves and waking up from the trance that tells us that something "out there" is what we are lacking. It's about snapping out of the delusion of dualistic thinking and becoming aware of our true nature, one that is inherently whole.

It has been a good few hundred years since the western world fell into this culturally-induced hypnosis, one which causes people to walk around like sophisticated zombies, sleepwalking through their lives. Most people are completely unaware of their true nature, the energy flow within their bodies, and their profound connection to the rest of the Universe. It is my conviction, and the wisdom of the ancient Taoist Masters from which I draw that we all must collectively stir from this deep sleep and awaken. We must free ourselves from the dark bonds of our subconscious programming and evolve towards the light of awareness. Then we can appreciate the beauty of who we truly are and take a more active role in manifesting a peaceful world around us. For when we move beyond the dark veil of unconsciousness, we are able to focus the conscious light of awareness back on the present moment and wake up to our inner voice.

For me, this first happened most unexpectedly. I was eight years old and was visiting a powerful spot near a city called Hamadan in modern day Iran. I was with my family and we had taken the trip to see a series of subterranean lakes that had formed inside a network of caves. It was bone-chillingly cold and the deepest darkness I had ever encountered.

The tour guide had a strong flashlight and he was in the first in a series of boats that were linked together like a train; each equipped with bicycle peddles for our feet to propel them along. That cutting beam of light was all we could see in a cocoon of darkness that wrapped all around and was our only thread of connection to the bright world from which we came. We peddled deep into the caves for over two miles before my uncle and the guide decided to play a prank on the group. The flashlight suddenly went out and the guide yelled a series of profanities. He shouted that his batteries were dead and we were trapped two miles underground in rickety boats over freezing cold water.

All the women started screaming and the men yelled as nobody knew what to do, and then someone cried out in the darkness that we were surely going to die! Suddenly, a profound feeling of peace came over me and I heard a voice in my head that was very familiar. I knew that I was going to be okay but was confused about the timing; "Already? Not again!" I caught myself. What do you mean "again"? "I've been here before, actually, many times." Yes, I have. I didn't expect it to come this way but here I go again—dying.

I was so at peace and comfortable at that moment that nothing seemed to matter anymore. Suddenly, just as I found myself at ease with the notion of my own death, the flashlight clicked back on. Realizing it was a joke, the men laughed and the women cried sighs of relief and a happy, nervous chatter swept through the group as is customary for people who bond through adversity. The train of boats slowly turned around and everyone was elated to be getting out of there, but I was quiet. What just happened and what was that voice? Why did I feel so comfortable in that moment of terror and how was I so familiar with dying? I was just an eight-year-old kid with no particular religious or philosophical soundtrack running in my head to guide my experience. Thinking back, this experience was the single event that thrust me upon my spiritual journey. It became the basis of an undeniable familiarity with inner realms that sat in the back of my mind as my own yardstick from then on. I had an early experience to relate to that nobody could take away from me. Simply call it a hallucination or a child's imagination run amok, if you will, but it projected me onto a path that was very different from the one my folks had in mind for me.

I'm not the first person to have his spiritual awakening in a cave but, unlike many of the great masters I have met on my journey, I was only eight years old at the time and I didn't really do any work to get there. Now, however, with experience as my teacher, I consider it a spiritual gift paid in advance to serve as a sort of barometer for future experiences. It is important to note that, unlike many of the fairytale stories about great masters, my awakening was transient at best. I quickly fell back asleep into the deep lull of adolescence and the story lines of the American teenager.

I slumbered on for another seven years until I had another experience when I tasted that feeling again…that feeling of utter peace and freedom. When I was 15 I had a reflective moment where I felt incredible remorse after killing some ants. The action suddenly transported me to a deeply compassionate state where I briefly viewed the world from the ants' perspective and saw the parallels between their colonies and our society- the only difference simply being a matter of scale and size. But again, I naturally fell back into my story lines and returned to the familiar zombie state, plugging away through high school this time until the light came on stronger when I was in college.

Relaxing between classes, I remember having a conversation with a good friend of mine about God, when suddenly, out of nowhere, I felt as if something popped inside my head. That pop ushered in a profound sense of deep connection with all life around me. It was the most peaceful and powerful vibration, like walking around in a soup of people and seeing their energies and thoughts swirl all around. From that day on, I stumbled around UCLA muttering about deeper things that I could not possibly have known about, and everyone noticed. The light had clicked on once more and I had woken up. I had crossed from the night into the day and people noticed. I knew this space somehow from the cave experience but the sheer power of this new state where I found myself was overwhelming. I started to be known as "that deep guy" or "the little Buddha" by my neighbors. This soon became a problem because I was quickly facing a powerful juxtaposition of identities and my self was now being defined by a bunch of loaded terms like "spiritual" and "deep." So what does a spiritual 20-year-old have to do when all he wants is to fit in and meet girls? How can he fill the shoes he's been given and still allow himself to be a kid?

Fortunately, I had the wherewithal to understand that I was in trouble. My ego was loving the attention but I didn't feel right about having people project their notions of piety on me. I recognized that I was falling into a trap and I decided to find some help immediately.

I was walking through my university's research library after having put several hours into a paper, but my mind was constantly involved in the central inquiry of my life at that time, namely, what is going on with me and how can I find some direction? I asked God for guidance. I silently pleaded with Him (for exactly what, I didn't know…) and then the strangest thing happened; a book dropped off of a rack in front of me and fell open to a powerful story. It was about a Taoist (pronounced Daoist) master leading his disciples across a raging river by linking the energy of his lower abdomen to theirs and tugging them along. The story caught my attention and I checked out the book. It was called The Wandering Taoist by Deng Ming Dao, and I read the whole thing that night. Since books don't usually fly, I took it as an omen and I started searching for a Taoist teacher the following day.

I found an accomplished Taoist martial arts master and channeled my energy into a proven system with a solid lineage. I was determined to understand the nature of the energy I was seeing and feeling all around me. I plunged headlong into 30 or more hours per week of training in Kung Fu, Tai Chi, Qi Gong (pronounced chee gong), meditation, and Eastern philosophy. It led me to train with several other masters and eventually becoming a Taoist monk. This happened while I was taking a full load at UCLA and running a summer camp for children. I trained diligently in my martial arts and in 2001, I became an Acupuncturist and master herbalist after four years of study in Oriental Medical school.

The paradox that is my life started at first with two very different lifestyles and trajectories and, over the years, has come to a balance point where all things meet in the middle. This notion of balance will be a recurring theme and the crux of the work we will be doing in this book. After years of suffering an identity crisis, I finally came to understand what it means to be one's self.

Teachers told me that I was going to write a book, but I felt that day to be far off into the future. There was so much to know with endless books still to read and many masters to study under. I had bought into the western model of spiritual capitalism—more is better. I was so busy studying new things and jamming information into my head that I didn't have time to practice all the techniques I had learned. I was getting pretty stressed out about it, as I was hell-bent on changing the world and time was running out. I returned from a sabbatical in the Himalayas and was fully engaged in running an integrative wellness practice in Los Angeles. I finished four difficult years of training as a Taoist monk, as well as studying with some great masters in India and Nepal. And now, finally, I was back to slay the dragon, one patient at a time.

It's easy to feel at peace and connected to everything up in a hermitage in the high Himalayas, but when sitting in rush hour traffic in Los Angeles and you're late to a meeting with a conference call on speakerphone, that peace becomes elusive. I have studied in the East and lived mostly in the West. I have been in a fraternity and have sat at the feet of the Dalai Lama. I have known profound peace. I have also wanted to rip my hair out in board meetings. I've come to learn to accept the highs and lows of life with an open heart. My path has fortunately taken me along the middle path and for that I am grateful. My Taoist teachers have taught me the importance of balance, and that has saved my life more than once.

There is the famous Taoist story of the man who was terrified of his shadow. One day while in the field, he looked over and saw his shadow looming over his shoulder and he began to run in terror. The faster he ran, the more he panicked because his shadow was still right there chasing him. He started to sprint, determined to lose his shadow once and for all and found that no matter what he did, the shadow was always behind him. Exhausted and broken, he collapsed under a tree with an attitude of defeat only to find the shadow was nowhere to be found under the shade of the tree.

I'll never forget the time I was in the holy city of Pushkar, India. I had just finished doing my yoga for the day and was walking down the street with the characteristic glow of a westerner who had escaped to the East to find God. I was feeling great and connected to all life. I was on a natural yoga high and wished my friends could be with me and witness me in my exalted state. Then it happened. Looking across the street I saw a leper who had lost both legs and one arm. Someone had sewn him a leather pouch that protected his trunk and another for his one functioning arm. This was so that he could drag his torso across the dirty roads and somehow get around town. There are many lepers in India but I had never seen one in such seemingly dire straits. He sang a devotional song while dragging himself down the street.

I stopped in my place and was heartbroken. I rushed over to him and pulled a rupee coin out of my pocket and offered it to him. What happened next changed my life forever. This young man looked up at me with the brightest, most beautiful eyes I had ever encountered and gifted me with a smile that could melt a glacier. He softly stated in good English, "No thank you, I have already eaten…" and, signaling with his eyes and a slight nod of his head to the right, "…but my friend over there is hungry so please, give it to him." I dropped to my knees. Tears started pouring out of my eyes uncontrollably. Here I was, "yoga guy", offering my "gracious charity" to an individual who fit my criteria as being the most deserving person for it that I had ever met, and he was more concerned for his friend. I felt like a pauper in his presence. I could not comprehend this level of humanity and it changed my life forever.

His shell of a body radiated the light of compassion and acceptance. His acceptance of his life's lot and his ability to see grace and beauty in the world made him a saint in my eyes. He set the bar for the new criteria I looked for in teachers. I care less about what they say, and look through to who they are and how they live. Are they hypocrites or are they real people?

This chance meeting led me down a path of self-inquiry and reconciliation that I want to follow always.

Up to this point, I have learned that there is no spirituality higher than our own enlightened humanity. The joys of the human experience, once one is awake, are the most incredible gifts we have been given, and this is what I am here to impart.

This book is a juxtaposition of many traditions and cultures; I am here to hold the center. I am here to tell the story of the Light Body and the practice of energy work called Qi Gong. And I am here to do it in plain English.

The reason I've written this book is to share the powerful universal teachings of Taoist Alchemy without esoteric language and complicated manuals. My goal is to have this book serve as a gateway text that demystifies Alchemical principles, and inspires readers to develop a personal practice. I chose to study Taoism because it stands for balance. It teaches us to balance all aspects of our lives, bring harmony to our divisive ways of thinking, allowing us to become whole again.

There are a number of phrases in the current lexicon that point to a forgotten language that centers around energy. We get weird "vibes" from people or are in "high spirits." We get into the "flow" of things and get "flashes" of inspiration. We listen to our "gut" and wish we had more "mojo." We have many words that point to a way of seeing the subtle world, fragments of a body of knowledge that have long been lost to the masses. It's my intention to bring this knowledge down to earth as best I can.

If you practice what you learn in this book, your life will change in ways that you have never imagined. Let me be clear about something though. You are the only one that can wake yourself up. I have provided you with the tools and support. My interest is in your growth and your personal development. I know these techniques work, because they have worked for me and many thousands before me. They will do the same for you, if you practice them.

In Part One of this book, I lay out the philosophy and background you'll need in order to have a basic understanding of the body's energy matrix and the nature of the challenges we currently face. In Part Two, I lay out specific exercises and techniques that are designed to clean our energy fields and wake us up. This includes instruction in diet, exercise, sleep, and basic lifestyle modifications. In Part Three, I offer up more advanced techniques and lay out a formula for you to practice and literally change your life within a hundred days. There are many resources I have pooled together for you in the appendix and online (taoistpath.com). Essentially, I have laid out the baseline knowledge and tools you need in order to clean up your light body and get into the most profound work I have ever experienced in my years of training.

My writing style reveals that I am at once a Monk and at other times, a Monkey. My intention is to humanize this process and make it joyful. At times they might seem strange, but try the exercises and see their value for yourself.

A variety of subjects in this book are drawn from various traditions. Although I am a Taoist teacher primarily, I also have training in Western Esotericism, Buddhism, Kabala, medicine, herbalism, and a whole host of self-help techniques from various schools. I believe that we are living in a time of experimentalism and the postmodern era has led us to deconstruct cultural barriers of the past. You don't have to be Chinese to study Kung Fu and be good at it. Likewise, you don't need to wear a turban to practice yoga.

The title of this book, Rise and Shine, was chosen for its multileveled meanings that occur throughout the different stages of attainment taught in this work. It draws a parallel between the waking human and the rising sun, and rising out of the sleepy dark slumber of the night into a new day with new possibilities and fresh energy. As we wake from the heavy sleep of the trances we are under, we can rise into a new life filled with endless possibilities.

Next, like a Phoenix rising out of the ashes we can rise from the murky waters of our mental and emotional baggage and regain our center of power and focus. In this state we can stop identifying with dramas and stop being slave to the energies trapped in our shadows. The freedom we find in this process is uplifting. We learn to rise out of our story lines and let our true selves shine through.

A third angle of the Rise and Shine title has more to do with the esoteric concept of Alchemy in which ancient Egyptians saw this world as a "Star Seed." Humans have come to this planet to learn about their true nature and to wake up to the magnificence of who they truly are. When this self-discovery happens, a process of illumination ushers more and more light into one's Light Body. Once there is enough connection to the Source, our Light Body ignites and we become the "light unto ourselves" of which Jesus spoke. The Egyptian system teaches that humans who have ignited their Light Bodies rise up and are born as stars in the cosmos, and rise to the next level of evolution. Whether we take this story literally or not, it carries powerful implications for the future of the human race. We will explore this concept further in Part Three of this book.

We are about to embark on a journey. Along the way, we are going to discover facets of ourselves that have been hiding right under our noses. The hardest challenge we'll face in this process is being honest with ourselves and opening up to the reality of our situation. This is the true spiritual work. You cannot refine lead until you pick it up and weigh it. You cannot talk about some far off concept of gold unless you have experienced it within your own flesh. In the course of this book, we are going to walk through a variety of topics and learn a great deal about ourselves. Why should we do this? What's in it for you? Everything. We are the only people that can liberate ourselves from the prison of perceived limitations. There is unlimited peace, power, freedom, money, love, and joy right on the other side of us letting go of our stories and waking up to our true potential. There is no real darkness once you come home to yourself. Tap into your Source energy and wake up to the adventure life has in store for you.

In Loving Light,
Pedram Shojai

PART ONE
Taoist Alchemical Science

CHAPTER ONE

THE FREE FLOW OF ENERGY

All the power that ever was or will be is here now.
—*Hermes Trismegistus,* The Pattern on the Trestleboard

The human mind is infinite. And because of the vastness of our comprehension we all have certain blind spots in our awareness. They may manifest in the unconscious tone we take when our father rings on the phone or maybe in the rush to smoke a cigarette when we feel overwhelmed. Maybe they'll appear as the nervous things we say when put into a challenging situation or even allow us to go through an entire work day and not know what happened; simply moving through the motions all day long. Most of us can also relate to having gotten lost into some TV show, not realizing what time it was and that we were late for something important. Regardless of the item, we have all faced things that emerge from the shadows of our subconscious minds. We don't feel fully in control. Perhaps we can sense a powerful battery of stored-up emotions and grievances that haunt us from our past and remain unexpressed. This has become the condition of most of us human beings every day of our lives. We struggle with our internal dialogues and push through as best we can to get through our days and make our lives go around.

It doesn't have to be this way. There is a way to escape this vicious cycle and break free of our mental and spiritual bondage. It is based in an ancient system of Taoist Alchemy that is designed to clear the energy fields around us and bring balance back to our lives.

Alchemy is the practice of turning our lead into gold. The process of turning the material "lead" of our human experience into the "gold" of spiritual awakening is the essence of this ancient science of spirituality. This sounds interesting in theory, however, to make it a reality requires a deep understanding of energy flow and the internal landscape of the human energy field. This knowledge used to be widely understood by the elders in nearly every culture on this planet but slowly, over the past several hundred years, it contracted into obscure circles in tucked away monasteries or secret societies worldwide. Aboriginal cultures and remote villages have held traces of it but it had mostly been lost to our modern world. We fell asleep to the knowledge of our true nature, and now it is time to wake up. The secret science of Alchemy has been preserved for thousands of years and we are fortunate to be living in a time when we can be a part of the great re-dissemination of this ancient information.

We have entered a period of convergence where many spiritual traditions have released their inner secrets and opened up to help the public, allowing untold numbers to rediscover their inner light. I am here to represent some of the knowledge from the tradition of Taoism, a philosophy of balance and self-inquiry that has its origins in ancient China.

The ancient Taoists were known for their prowess in personal cultivation and their ability to activate their Light Body. They spent thousands of years studying the inner realms of consciousness and mapped out a comprehensive system for training, meditation, and personal evolution. They were some of the first alchemists to discover the gold that could be found within the Self, and they passed their training down through the centuries from teacher to student all the way to the present. I was able to learn from some of the best of the living masters and I am now sharing this knowledge with you.

The Tao that can be spoken is not the eternal Tao.

—Lao Tzu

Much has been said about "that which cannot be spoken" because telepathy and clairvoyance aside, words are the best form of communication we've got. Words have the power to impart concepts, ideas, wisdom, and, most importantly, a new way of thinking. It is my path to teach, using words, pictures, and video as devices, this ancient wisdom that has been passed down through the ages- much of which comes through oral tradition.

Oral tradition is a more holistic form of transmission that not only imparts the concepts and stories of the storyteller, but also allows the beingness or the suchness of being of the person to be conveyed and transmitted. Much of what I have learned over the past several years has come from direct transmission, and more importantly, through direct experience of these concepts with great masters. I have had the fortune of traveling and seeing these individuals and it is my intention to humbly impart my understanding of this wisdom in plain English.

The logical conventions of our written language oftentimes pose problems because of their limited ability to clearly convey esoteric concepts.

This limitation in immaterial, however, for all of the answers you seek lie within you. The journey we are about to take will help unlock this ancient knowledge and challenge growth from within. The Grandmaster of my lineage often said: "Taoist way not forced." As you read these pages, allow your innate wisdom to surface and permit it time to grow and germinate naturally. You are on the path—the destination is coming back to Here and Now.

There is a famous Taoist tale by Chuang Tzu wherein he wakes up having dreamed that he was a butterfly, but then, after some confusion, was not sure whether he was a human dreaming that he was a butterfly, or a butterfly dreaming that he is a human. I say that this story sums up the human experience perfectly. When are we awake and when are we dreaming? How can we really know which is actually real? What does the concept of real imply? If both exist in our conscious awareness as phenomena, then shouldn't they be equally real?

We live in an unprecedented time in recorded human history wherein our left brain sciences are coming full circle with the words and wisdom of the ancients. Notions of reality have been defined, redefined, constructed, deconstructed, scrambled, and served sunny side up since we began thinking about it. Much to the chagrin (or maybe it's relief) of the classical Newtonian physicists, Reality isn't so "cut and dry" when we take our material existence as the frame of reference. In fact, in the wild world of quantum, the only math that computes is the one pointing to the answer that arrives at the whole deal being nothing but consciousness. [Springer Netherlands, 2004]

It's funny to hear our world's most brilliant theoreticians propound such a theory today, because a guy called the Buddha said something like that around 600 BC. Actually, although the Buddha's contribution to humanity was immense (and we'll spend some time with his teachings shortly), he wasn't the first to go there—not by a long shot. People have been coming to this very same conclusion for a long time: the Maoris of New Zealand, the Egyptian Mystery Schools, the Shamans and Shamanesses of Siberia, South America, and Africa, and of course, our more recent Saints who have worked with a much-abused name for "It"—God. The history of the Church is laden with enlightened people trying to explain this phenomena under the safe haven umbrella of their faith's taboos.

So if all is consciousness, then what about my body? I can poke at it, I can fall and hurt myself, I get hungry, tired, and…I eventually die…right?

Sure, but in the shamanic, Hermetic, or Taoist point of view, death is simply our Self's Consciousness leaving the physical plane. When we withdraw from our physical body, then we experience the phenomenon known as death. In life, there are millions of subconscious activities going on under the radar of our conscious awareness in every moment. We don't have to think about breathing or the beating of our heart. These things simply happen on their own without the need of our conscious intervention. The body is actually wholly conscious and simply represents the part of us that is tied to this physical existence. Death is the opposite of birth, not life. All energy and matter are interchangeable and the Law of Conservation of Energy states that energy is neither created nor destroyed—it simply changes form. We may shed our physical bodies but our consciousness is eternal and infinite. So currently, we sit around in our "earth suits" trying to reconcile the perceived gap (or abyss for some) between our material and spiritual states. We try to do enough good here to be rewarded with going there, since Heaven and Earth have always been taught to be separate places. We set aside Sunday mornings or the Saturday Sabbath for this usually, trying to erase our bad deeds from the week, trying to find forgiveness for things we can't forgive ourselves for.

We are self-conscious beings that are a part of a Universal Consciousness which is all-encompassing. Somehow, having taken incarnation in these bodies, we have forgotten the Source from which we have come and have fallen asleep to its ever-present currents right here and now. Feeling disconnected, we have come to perceive our material existence as separate from some notion of eternal spirituality, which is only to be granted in the afterlife.

This split is the fundamental fallacy of our age and given the name of Kali Yuga, or "The Iron Age" in Hindi, which represents the lowest order of consciousness and highest degree of materialism. This marks an era in our history when we are the farthest from understanding our true nature and the most disconnected from Source. It is the time when we have completely forgotten our own personal connection with the Source and instead blindly rely on ministers or "agents" who represent the Source to help us and tell us how to attain enlightenment. The Kali Yuga designates a period where people are sleepwalking deeper than ever before and, as if in a trance, are simply unaware of their incredible potential and the critical role they play individually in the Universe. Being at the end of this cycle, we are now said to be emerging into the next Golden Age, where people begin to wake up, and the spiritual science of using the Light Body enters back into our global consciousness. In the Mayan calendar, it indicates that we are currently at the farthest point from the center of the Milky Way, which coincides with a time of great unrest and discord. The Mayans also forecast that our present time is the end of this epoch when we are finally starting to awaken from the deep sleep of materialism and spiritual separation. In their system, we are to be turning the corner around the end of the year 2012 wherein we, for the first time in eleven thousand years, begin to face the center of the galaxy and slowly move towards it once more. The closer we get to the center, the more we are said to wake up and feel connected with our spirits again. [Arguelles, 2002, p. iv] This date, however, marks an era of change and great transformation of human consciousness. The Hindu Vedic tradition places the end of the Kali Yuga somewhere between 2010 AD and 2442 AD. [Danielou, 1987, p. 197] In my opinon, this timeframe is open-ended because the shift is predicated on the state of our race's mass consciousness. The ancients have said that the nature of this shift will rely on the degree of our awakening. The more people we have that become Self-Realized, the softer the transition. In the past several hundred thousand years, these times have been associated with mass coronal ejections from the sun, increased volcanic activity, pole shifts, tidal waves, desertification, and much more. [Cox, 1997, pp. 1-2] We have had major magnetic shifts through the Cambrian, Devoniam, Permian, Triassic, and Cretaceuous periods of Earth's history which have affected the type and amounts of radiation penetrating our atmosphere. This has caused massive mutations in the genetic material of every species of plant and animal on the planet. [Lawlor, 1991, pp 94-96] It is now time for us all to wake up to the changing of our current cycle and come back into contact with our higher purpose in life.

This awakening brings us back to Unity Consciousness. The fundamental split in our awareness that created a perceived sense of duality is corrected and we return back to an important realization: Spirit and Matter are One. All is One and the reconciliation of this understanding is tantamount to our recovery from the self-inflicted suffering we have been clinging to, both individually and collectively.

So here is the lesson in time: Know where you are at in the cycles of reality, and act accordingly. If you are hiking in the mountains and the sun is beginning to set, what do you do? Naturally, you begin to head home or make shelter; hunkering down for the inevitable fall of light for a set time as dictated by the cycles of nature, until the morning sun arises, freeing you from darkness. For all of us, the night of our materialistic slumber is at an end as we are about to rise with a new cycle of Reality that will usher in our Unity Consciousness.

The ancient Egyptians, Mayans, Hindus, Hopi, Western Alchemists, and Inca have prophesied that this era is the most remarkable time to be alive in all history. They speak of a powerful shift in the consciousness of our planet and in particular, the evolution of our species. They further tell of a challenging time where we are forced to correct the fundamental schism that has dominated our thinking for the past 5000 years. [Braden, 2009 p. 53] This imbalance has led to endless conquest, genocide, and deterioration of our ecosystem while also causing a powerful distraction that has put us all to sleep. This break in our understanding of reality comes from our proverbial "fall" from the Garden and our lapse into Duality Consciousness.

Our infected form of thinking permeates everything, from our relationship with nature, the way we treat each other, and even to our (mis) understanding of Divinity. We are no longer one with the natural environment from which we came. Heaven and Earth are seen as separate places, and strict rules are given to release us from this nasty rock so that we can return to paradise.... We are currently getting through the darkest part of the night while the light of awareness is about to start shining through for all of us.

In order to begin the process of awakening, we need a frame of reference—a starting point from which to launch. I put it to you that your body is the alchemical vehicle and your experience in this world is the proverbial "lead" which will be turned into "gold." Listen to your body. Don't ignore it because you're focusing on some higher spiritual goal, but learn to balance your internal energies and harmonize your emotions. This is a very important step in practical spirituality and in living life. A famous alchemical axiom states that Heaven is within us and not above us, as many have mistaken the axiom to say. The exploration of our own consciousness gives us a glimpse at the Mind of God. The more we come to understand our true nature, the more we will be able to understand reality.

The Taoist perspective of life does not require you to renounce God or get a Yin/Yang tattoo, nor does it insist that you join the "Taoist Club" and start arguing with the Buddhists. It is just a label. Balance is what we strive for and we strive for this in all things, including our religion. To understand the nature of the Universe we need to understand our own nature first and, to do this, we must start with the cultivation of our bodies. This training will guide us along the path to liberation and at that future point, we will simply be enlightened humans—and not Taoists, Christians, Muslims, or Jews. Again, these words mark the Dark Age attachment to titles and separation which we will move beyond, for remember, there is only one chosen people and that is all of us. In fact, even that perspective is limited unless we include all that exists into that definition. Waking up to our deep and intimate connection with all life in the Universe brings us back to our essential nature and liberates us from the bondage of the trance we've been under. The whole "my God is better than yours" mentality is the primitive mark of the Kali Yuga and remains a fundamental sticking point we need to surpass in order to evolve as a species. To do this, we'll need to examine some basic principles in greater depth.

Chaos and Energy Fields

According to modern physicists, chaos is the dominant ruling principle of the Universe. All things move towards it as it governs and tears apart all things that are manifest. Life, in contrast, is an ordered system. In fact, when organic systems start to fall out of order, we begin to experience deterioration, decomposition, mutation (which leads to cancer), and the eventual breakdown of living systems (aging). [Holland, 1998] Our goal as living beings, therefore, is to support, enhance, and harness the power of life and guard it against the annihilation coming from outside. To better understand this, let's look at some basic concepts in biomagnetics. Below is a picture of the planet earth with north and south poles intact.

THE EARTH'S MAGNETIC FIELD

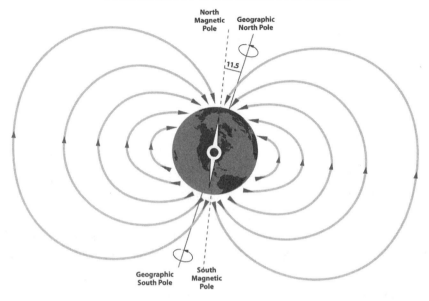

Magnetic Poles of the Planet

The lines coming into each of these poles represent the edges of the magnetic field generated by the polarity of the planet. This dynamic tension is an important interface between the positive (yang) and negative (yin) poles on the planet, which create an energy field wherein all life can be supported. In fact, fluctuations in this field can be very harmful to all life forms on earth. The three dimensional manifestation is call a toroidal field and is the basis of all hyper-dimensional physics and energy work.

Before we continue, it is important for me to briefly speak of the distinction between the electric and magnetic fields. The magnetic field can be measured by forces acting on certain kinds of materials such as the element iron. It is interesting to note that the hemoglobin molecule of our red blood cells is primarily centered around an iron molecule to which the oxygen binds. The electric field can be measured by forces acting on electrically charged particles such as sodium and chloride. The electric charge of an object is the sum of the charges of its particles. All nerve and muscle function in our bodies relies on electrical charge gradients that are constantly shifting. Electrical signaling is therefore the body's internal language of operation. These two fields, electrical and magnetic, always coexist with the same intensity at a given location and instant in time. They are really parts of the same field and are thus called electromagnetic. [Bruyere, 1994, p. 241]

The importance of the electromagnetic field to our bodies can be illustrated by what happens to us in its absence. One of the early problems for our orbiting astronauts was that their biological systems were beginning to break down outside of the magnetic field of the earth and they were feeling sick and weak for no apparent reason. The scientists working on the Soviet space program had figured out why this was happening and they shared their findings with us. We eventually found a way to mimic what is known as the Schumann Resonance, and are now able to create energy field bubbles for our astronauts to exist within when performing outer space missions.

The lowest-frequency (and highest-intensity) mode of the Schumann resonance occurs at a frequency of approximately 7.83 Hz. This is just under eight cycles per second. This happens to coincide with the alpha rhythm of our brainwaves that is closest to the state of meditation and deep connection with our surroundings. [Robbins, 2000, pp. 229-230] Everything tunes to vibrations. In physics we have particles and waves, both of which seem to have an underlying system of communication we are just starting to understand. Our bodies can detect and respond to waves of energy just as our ears can distinguish different sounds from waves in the auditory spectrum.

Bruce Lipton, in his pioneering book titled The Biology of Belief, speaks about the sensitivity of membrane proteins on the surface of a cell to energy. Electromagnetic charge changes a receptor protein to its active configuration and that can be triggered by either chemical or electric signaling. An example of chemical signaling would be estrogen or histamine binding to a specific receptor on a cell. Electrical signaling can happen through light, sound or radio frequencies as the receptor proteins act as little tuning forks for vibration. The speed of a diffusible chemical is less than 1cm/second while light travels at 186,000 miles/second. Cells can respond to both so what's more efficient—regular mail or email?

There is a resonant vibration with all light, sound, and movement and these are some of the energies we can sense with our hands, and within people's fields. These particles, or photons, seem to travel through our bodies and trigger a light-based system of interaction between the DNA molecules in our cells. These light particles apparently have something to do with how the DNA zips and unzips in its trans-coding of information. [Kim, 2009] This new knowledge may give us some hints at how the ancients were able to decipher the language of the "coiled serpents" and hear the song of Creation when looking inwards. The flow of energy becomes the fundamental currency for the field of life, which lives in a perpetual array of fields within fields—all the way up to the scale of the entire Universe down to the smallest subatomic particles we can find.

Dynamo Theory explains that the Earth's magnetic field is caused not by magnetized iron deposits, but mostly by electric currents in the liquid outer core. The Convection of molten iron within the outer liquid core, along with a "Coriolis Effect" caused by the overall planetary rotation, tends to organize these "electric currents" in rolls aligned along the north-south polar axis. (Herndon, 1996) When conducting fluid flows across an existing magnetic field, electric currents are induced, which in turn create another magnetic field, after which a self-sustaining dynamo is created. This Dynamo Theory becomes an important concept in our internal cultivation because the dynamic flow of blood and qi energy within our bodies form a microcosm of this same Dynamo phenomenon. [Demorest, 2001] This explains why the smooth flow of blood within the body is vitally important to the integrity of our energy fields. It is almost as if our blood is a microcosm of the molten core flowing inside the planet—both generate and reinforce the energy field around the external body.

These fields are the foundation of all life. Each living system has its own energy field that supports the living cells within it; all the way down to the subatomic level and, all the way up to a Universal level. We are fields of life within one great field, all dependent upon the other, enhancing the ability of others to grow. [Capra, 1991, p. 209] We affect the field of the earth with our consciousness while the earth's changes in field strength affect us as well. The fields of energy throughout the universe resonate and affect all other energy fields in the entire Universe. This nonlocal influence seems to cross both space and time and is becoming the subject of much debate on the world of physics.

The ancient sages knew this to be true because they experienced it through meditations and their knowledge of how their own energy field operated.

Being able to sense these things became the fundamental mark of a true Gnostic, who finds the answers within himself and, because of this, is able to unlock the secrets of the Universe. The concepts imparted in this book come from a vast body of knowledge that has been confirmed by hundreds of ascended masters over thousands of years. (Ascended masters are humans, just like you and me, who have woken up and become enlightened.) They found these answers internally and were able to agree on the principles that they discovered. They were able to feel the energy running through their bodies and track its flow through the various organs. They represent a living tradition of seekers who have learned to be the very knowledge they we seeking. These masters learned about the secrets of our luminous bodies and developed an understanding of energy fields well before we had developed any instruments to measure such phenomena with our modern technology.

The Human Energy Field

In the Taoist interpretation of energy, you, as a human being, have a positive "yang" pole at the top of your head and a negative "yin" pole in your perineum (base of the spine) as well as smaller yin poles at the bottoms of the feet which dip a couple of feet into the ground. These create an energy field around your body with a number of internal "stars" along the spine contained within. These concentrations of energy cascade down like the descending colors of a prism or a rainbow, beginning with white, moving to violet, then all the way down to red at the base. These internal stars are called chakras in the Indian tradition or dantiens in the Chinese tradition and represent the areas where the energy of all creation is differentiated from the crown, which is the highest vibration, down to the root center, which is the densest or most earthly vibration. The goal of the yogi initiate is not to ignore the base centers and run to the crown, but to bring peace, understanding, awareness, and most importantly balance to each of these centers. In fact, in the Western Alchemical tradition, our "lead" is said to reside at the base of our spine and the refinement process has to do with the transmutation of this energy into the spiritual gold expressed through the higher chakra centers.

HUMAN ENERGY CENTERS (CHAKRAS)

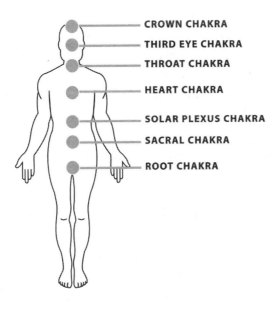

CROWN CHAKRA

THIRD EYE CHAKRA

THROAT CHAKRA

HEART CHAKRA

SOLAR PLEXUS CHAKRA

SACRAL CHAKRA

ROOT CHAKRA

Seven Stars of the Human Energy Field

The harmonious flow of our energy field enhances life and nourishes the brain and internal organs. Any problems with this flow, or "impedance" causes breakdowns in this network and leads to ailments on the physical, mental, emotional, and spiritual levels, as they are all reflections or octaves of the same energy. The chakras each represent different archetypal aspects of the human experience and many of our life lessons are to be learned by harmonizing these centers. We can start by forgiving and healing wounds and perceived assaults that have driven us to create the defense system we refer to as our ego. In our ignorance, we take this primitive defense mechanism and apply it to various aspects of our lives—effectively cutting off the free flow of energy available to us. This vital energy flows through nadi (Indian) or meridians (Chinese) that carry it through the entire body and literally brings life to every cell of the body through a comprehensive network of channels. The scope of this network is beyond this book (and many great books on this subject already exist), but it is important to know that any energetic blockage will be reflected somewhere in the body and it will usually hold a mental and emotional charge with it.

The human energy field is an accurate reflection of the inner workings of the physical body and mental processes. In fact, all emotional, spiritual, and physical phenomena will be reflected somewhere in this field. We will often feel and see lulls and dips in these fields after meals or with the rise of certain emotional content in our lives. In fact, energetic attachments are often trapped in our fields and block the smooth flow of energy throughout our bodies.

Herein rests the core issue.

Unexamined emotions and memories that we are not willing to address are often the cause of these blockages. In Taoism and Chinese medicine, we see blocked emotional energies wreak havoc on the body and block our vitality. So how do they do it? They get stored in our bioelectric field (this includes your physical body which is simply denser energy) and act as a dam, trapping more energy behind. They await a release. This release can be very difficult, however, for it requires our focused attention to them with forgiveness and love. We'll spend a whole chapter on this concept and will work on how to fix this problem, but, suffice it to say for now, these blockages are what we accumulate throughout our lives and these frozen energies are what cause further suffering for us today on a physical, emotional and spiritual level. These are the same blockages we move to resolve in Acupuncture. They cut the vital current of our energy and literally make us weak and sick as the free flow of our energy fields is reduced.

The good news is that we can learn to detect blockages in our fields and to correct the flow of energy with certain exercises and techniques. Once we learn to read the signs in our energy fields, we open ourselves up to a vast inner language of communication within our bodies, that has always been going on under our radar, but which we've been mostly blind to. In fact, once we get into an understanding of this system, we expose ourselves to a subconscious mind that has been anxious to communicate with us for years! It has always been sending us signals in the form of tingling hands, hunches, sudden headaches, the chills—essentially whatever it can to get our attention. Once we learn to finally listen to this internal language, we begin to complete a powerful circuit of personal communication and connection to Source. It is through our subconscious minds that we begin to interpret the language of our energy fields.

Personal Journeys—Night Vision

WHEN I WAS in the thick of my martial arts training, my teacher would have us go into the mountains at night during a new moon. We would spend a short time meditating and then go for a walk along the trails. The lesson was to soften the eyes and learn to see the energy fields of the plants around us. At first, the whole thing sounded crazy. It was dark and I was stumbling around wondering if I'd ever grasp this pseudo-Jedi nonsense. I kept trying to see with my eyes and was frustrated.

The lesson was to soften the eyes, because seeing with *shen*, or spirit, requires a more passive form of vision. Slowly, I began to relax into it and started to see "fuzzy stuff" on the tops of the plants. Of course, I thought that my eyes were playing tricks on me and I was just seeing reflections of city lights off them. After a while though, I started to see fluctuations in the patterns of this energy. It was almost like the fields shifted as we approached in an acknowledgement of approaching life forms.

I conducted this training for many moons until the vision of energy fields off of living things became commonplace. I could then start to see the energy easier in the daytime as well. It is incredible to see how powerful an energy field looks in undisturbed nature as opposed to a city setting. I started to see that forests and mountains had distinct energy fields themselves, while a particular valley would be alight with its own, "vibe," and I would watch the energy shift throughout.

Then I started seeing the same phenomenon in people. When they came in contact with certain people or groups of people, their fields would grow and get stronger. It was as if a group had its own characteristic field. I also saw the opposite. Some people's fields would quickly shrink around certain individuals or when speaking about a sensitive topic.

Night walking began to take on more and more meaning. I was getting so good that I started trail running during the new moon. This was intense because I couldn't afford the luxury of a single thought or I'd turn an ankle or fly into the bushes. It became a powerful meditation tool and forced me to be aware and awake because my life actually depended on it much of the time.

I share this story because talking about energy fields is nothing but talk until you experience them yourself. I was way too head-centered until I actually learned to see energy fields for myself. It became an experience instead of a belief.

The Big Picture

Essentially we are beautiful light beings who are part of an ever-growing fractal called Life. A fractal is generally "a rough or fragmented geometric shape that can be split into parts, each of which is a reduced-size copy of the whole." [Mandelbrot, 1982, p. 5] Apparently, any small piece of the Universe has encoded within it the image or signature of the entirety—just like a hologram. Thus everything that we do helps create and further all of creation. It is all beautiful as it is ever revealing itself to us. It grows around us and mirrors our internal state and mental images back to us. There is no outside versus inside as we are all one—we are all part of the same fractal with each part being a smaller exact replica of the larger whole.

So, shouldn't we be feeling better, you ask? Well, yes, but not in the way you may be thinking. Feeling better requires us to exist in a state of letting go, and not in a state of feeling desperately bad and trapped and longing to feel bliss. It is also not a state of poverty praying for wealth. It is a state of letting go and observing, of natural unfolding and healing. A governing principle of this Universe, as discussed, is Chaos, which is always chipping away at the sanctity and integrity of our energy fields driving us towards death and annihilation. Chaos drives our thoughts to density and allows us to slowly sink into sleep and oblivion—only to be reborn to try the lesson again. It becomes a sort of gravity pulling us down and into sleep. It is what feeds off the energies trapped in our shadows and it is what supports the internal "demons" we have created.

As Leonard Orr so aptly puts it, many of us are living with a pre-programmed "death urge" which drives our belief systems to take on aging and disease when we believe it is time. This death urge is personal and societal and at this point as it sometimes seems that we are in a race to the bottom on the international stage. [Orr, 1998]

Sounds terrible? Is this my awful fate you ask?

Only with ignorance and a lot of effort towards sustained ignorance would it be.

But before you might think sustained ignorance is a foregone conclusion, remember this, the energy of life is moving towards more life and the enhancement of itself. Life is an ordered system and the enhancement of that energy leads to awakening and liberation. The key is to enter your natural state and allow life to work through you. Life is moving towards evolution. It is driving living systems to grow and become more and more self-aware, away from ignorance. The balance point of gravity I like to call levity—the upward cleansing movement of integration and transformation. To "Rise and Shine" we are to take the "lead" of our daily experience and integrate it back into our lives and make "gold." This is the true secret of alchemy. It is the reconciliation of past memories and emotions back into the free flow of our energy fields. It is a release and there is no effort required in releasing. As a matter of fact, all of our effort and energy is constantly going into holding on. So we release and come whole. As we do so, we forgive our past and heal our wounds. We allow our energy to flow and allow ourselves to evolve and literally "turn on" our energy fields.

In reality, the energy of all creation is surging through us at all times, but we are the ones that put energy into trying to stop this flow because we are not okay with how we feel. Once the Light Body is activated, then the self-perpetuating light from within eternally sustains our energy field and we are complete—never to collapse under the weight of chaos again.

As the ancient Egyptian mystery schools say, we are born a "star" and have completed our task in the earth school. We become a source of Light unto ourselves and once "ignited," become a beacon for the further transformation and evolution of our species. Once we attain this enlightened point, we no longer need external sources of energy or information as we have become One with Source and are actually an emanating focal point for that One Energy.

There is something that stands between us and our natural state of divinely-guided consciousness though. And that is the nature of our suffering and the way we leak our energy into the shadows of our unconscious behavior. We need to examine and understand this mechanism in order to learn how to unravel our problems. Once we understand the mechanics of this system, we are fully empowered to change the way we operate and with this, we become free. The next chapter is devoted to this understanding.

*

CHAPTER TWO

THE NaTURE OF SUFfERING

*Now when you turn the light around to shine inward,
the mind is not aroused by things; negative energy then
stops, and the flower of light radiates a concentrated glow,
which is pure positive energy.*

—*Lu Tung Pin,* The Secret of the Golden Flower

he only way to understand a given solution is to fully examine the fundamental problem and address it. If our pure, undifferentiated state is one of infinite energy and connection with the Divine Universe (call it what you may—I will use various conventions throughout this work because there is only One), then our essential nature is perfect as it is.

Therefore, there is something that we are doing to cause these problems.

This is where the contribution of the Buddha comes in. Gautama Siddhartha Buddha lived from circa 563 BCE to 483 BCE. He was born into an aristocratic family and knew nothing of poverty and distress until one day he looked upon his subjects and observed things that shattered his paradigm. He could not reconcile in his mind the pain and suffering he saw in those people of the kingdom with the comfortable life he had been led to believe was the norm. This forced him to leave his princely life and to travel throughout the countryside looking for the answers to the meaning of life and the nature of suffering. As the story goes, after years of inquiry he became frustrated and sat under a Boddhi tree and decided not to get up until he had discovered the truth…which finally came to him. He woke up.

When people around him saw the transformation this awakening had visited upon the young man, they pleaded with him for an explanation—a way out of their own suffering. They could see that they were asleep and that this man was awake; they languished in night and he lived fully in day. He was glowing and carried an air of absolute peace. The Buddha explained it as follows:

The Four Noble Truths

1. Suffering is an inherent part of existence.
2. The origin of suffering is ignorance and the main symptoms of that ignorance are attachment and craving (or aversions and craving).
3. That attachment and craving can be ceased.
4. That following the Noble Eightfold Path will lead to the cessation of attachment and craving and therefore suffering.

And what is the Eightfold Path?

1. Right understanding or perspective (looking at things as they really are).

2. Right thought or intention (do the right thing morally and do not attach to worldly things).

3. Right speech (speak the truth and do what you say).

4. Right action (not acting in ways that would be corrupt or bring harm to yourself or others).

5. Right livelihood (don't make money doing things that harm people or the planet).

6. Right effort (make a constant effort to abandon all the harmful thoughts, words, and deeds).

7. Right mindfulness (constantly keep your mind alert to phenomena as they are affecting the body and mind).

8. Right concentration or meditation (mindful breathing and observation of the transient nature of all phenomena).

I will not go into a full study of the nature of Buddhism here—as there have been many wonderful books written on the subject—but I would like to circle in on the major points we are going to be examining here in this chapter. Namely, that life is filled with suffering and this is caused by our ignorance. This ignorance is what separates the sleeping from the awakened. It is the ignorance of the essential nature of our minds and how things come to pass.

At this moment of the first step of our journey, I must digress to say I can't tell you how many times I have had beginning students inform me that they tried meditating but they just couldn't...so they gave up. Oddly enough, difficulty with meditation seems to be universal. I remember sitting in audience with H.H. The Dalai Lama back in Dharmsala, India at his compound when a senior student asked: "Holiness, I have been meditating my whole life and I can't seem to be able to stop my mind". I looked back and nodded because I, like most of the others in that room could certainly relate. The answer from His Holiness was not what I expected, though. It went something like this:

I am the Dalai Lama and I have been meditating my whole entire life and I can't stop my mind either...you see my friend, you have to understand that it is not about stopping the mind. Increase the depth of the water below the tumultuous mind—deepen the entire ocean so that the whole body of water does not react to it. With little spacing between your mind and the surface, all you experience is choppy waters and chaos.

What this boils down to is that we need to create some distance between our essential selves and the noise that is constantly running in our minds. We tend to either identify with the chaos and go about our hectic lives or try to annihilate it through incorrect meditation techniques. The Dalai Lama was teaching us to develop our inner self and create some distance from the noise. The more we can identify with our true Identity, the less we are "knocked off of our perch" by the reckless noise of our minds.

This impacted me greatly because, like most of the other westerners in the room, I was trying to surgically remove the problem that I thought to be my loud mind. You mean embrace the noise? No, not exactly, but you must allow things to be what they are and stop jumping into the ring. Let's get into this…

One of the central tenets of Buddhist meditation is the principle that everything in the Universe is constantly changing. In fact, the only constant in this entire Universe is change. Therefore, as things come up in the mind, if we were to stay disconnected and simply observe them, within a few seconds they will pass. One thought simply replaces another in a seemingly endless stream of thoughts that are running and changing infinitely.

The problem is when we jump in:

The core teaching of the Buddha is that when we become attached to the thoughts that are running through our minds, we create attachments in the form of either aversions (I don't like that please make it go away!) or cravings (oooh, that's wonderful give me more, more, more!) Once we bite, we've created a cycle of suffering. This is what one of my meditation instructors calls "The Bermuda Triangle". [Hoon, 2008]

For example, Judy at work makes a comment I don't like and in my mind I think, "Wow, that Judy really is a piece of work! I wish she'd get out of here…she's ruining my lunch break." Now, I have created an aversion to Judy and her presence. Actually, I have an aversion to the whole idea of her. So instead of just letting it pass, now every second she's there I can't help but focus on what's wrong with her. Why is she still talking? Maybe

I should comment on those ridiculous shoes she's wearing...does anybody else think so? I mean, really—look at how she used three napkins... And so on and so on. Next thing you know—poof!—there went your entire lunch break. You spent it in your head being pissed at a lady who was just having a rough day and had no intention of upsetting you. Or maybe she did— who cares? But the next time you see her at lunch, all of the same thought trains pull right back into the station of your mind and this time you're convinced that she's worthless and make sure she notices you putting your stuff in the spot next to you so she can't sit there. That'll show her!

Maybe her dad died that day. Maybe she's coming down with a cold. Maybe she's bitter at the world for no good reason at all. It doesn't matter. You are responsible for your own reaction to an event because...

It is not the circumstance that causes the suffering but our reaction to it.

Here's the Bermuda Triangle: You (the one actually suffering), Judy (the current perpetrator), and your strong desire to not have her around (the polarity switch). This is a vicious cycle.

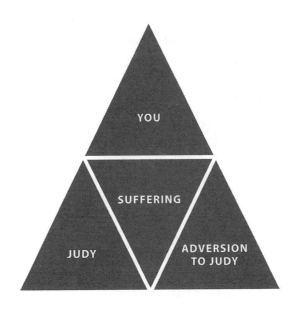

Aversion Triangle

Let's look at another example.

This time Judy is someone deemed likeable in your mind's eye. She always says the sweetest things and makes you feel better about yourself. Today, you've had a rough sales meeting because something you forgot to do caused a huge problem over in the fulfillment department. You need a hug and Judy is usually your gal. Unfortunately, unbeknownst to you, her stomach is aching and she can't see past her own pain to be showering anybody with anything today. You nestle up next to her, make some pleasantries, and wait for your Judy fix. It doesn't come.

You can't believe this! Even Judy thinks you stink. The one person who has always been in your corner is now ignoring you. How could she? So you keep fishing and fishing; trying to get Judy to renew her love for you. You want her to make you feel the way she always does.

TRAP #2

This time the triangle looks like this: You—notice how you're always involved in all of your problems; Judy's love—which you crave; and more of Judy's love, which she just hasn't released yet. Again, you've jumped outside of yourself and are hopelessly peddling to change the outer Universe to serve your inner needs.

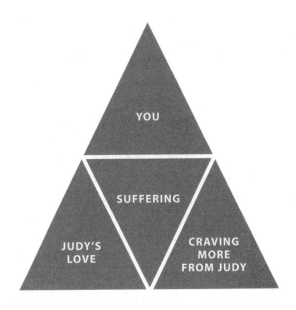

Cravings Triangle

This is where our energy goes all day every day. This is the nature of suffering. We incessantly try to bend reality to our will because we are not okay with how it presents itself to us.

Whatever happened to revelation? You know, when God reveals Himself to us in every given moment and we are to walk forward with an open heart (without judgment) like a hot knife through butter?

This, my dear friends, is the birth of impedance—the blockage of vital force in our energy fields. We misdirect all of our energy into trying to "fix" reality to fit our demands of it, and when it refuses to bend to our will, we then feel things we don't want and must force ourselves to "move" to the opposite feeling in an attempt to run away from failure. This warrants an example because it is an important concept that we will deal with again in this book.

Let's say you got dumped by your girlfriend in high school and the experience was terrible. You, at the wise age of 17 were sure that you had it all figured out and that you were going to marry this girl. She decides differently and you are crushed. You feel abandoned, detested, unworthy, weak, insignificant, and hopeless. Sound about right? So how long do you stay with those feelings?

The truthful (usual) answer is: as little as possible! You do whatever you can to get your mind off of that pain and move on. You drink, you play hours of basketball, you shave your head, you go out with the girl from your history class. You do everything short of cutting off your head to avoid feeling so miserable. Right? Or maybe you do the opposite. You start to identify with the misery and crave more the attention it brings you. Maybe mom feels sorry for you and lets you stay in your room and mope with no more chores for a while…

So here's the problem: Those feelings and emotions get stored in a databank that never goes away. Nothing ever goes away. The intense charge around it though; that's the problem. We tie ourselves down every day when we put away emotions that go unobserved and unresolved. Every time we have an aversion or a craving for a particular subject and keep putting energy into it, we create a charge that doesn't go away until we release it. We enslave ourselves with little power cells of emotional baggage that eventually wither away our energy field and our ability to live fully in the present.

Think about it this way. You were dumped by the high school girlfriend and what happened? Because you didn't like the way you felt, you put a tremendous amount of energy into the opposite feelings of joy, happiness, and feeling desirable, which, at the time, made you feel like you were pulling out of that mess. Instead, you created a monster. See, there's the energy of the traumatic event and then the opposite energy you created and infused into that emotional field every time it came up. As you averted it, you created polarity. You now have a positive and negative pole for this issue. You have effectively given it a life or energy field of its own and, because the same lesson comes up repeatedly in different flavors throughout life (the next girl, your business partner…), you continue to charge the original aversion with more and more energy. Now it is part of you. It lives in the shadow of your energy field (because it is unconscious) and feeds off of your vitality. It has actually begun to restructure your personality. Maybe you're now bipolar or maybe you hate women deep down inside but fancy yourself as a playboy who just hasn't found one that is loyal yet.

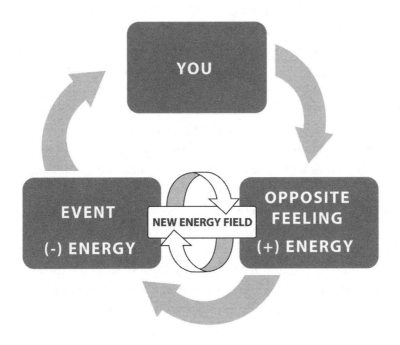

How Suffering Creates Trapped Energy

All of this stems from aversions and craving. We move to the opposite of what we feel and create a cycle of suffering. For those of you who are wondering how that works with cravings, that's simple, for there is what you have…and then there is more. What you have is here and what you want is there. You put energy into the future of more and create a gap between what you have now, which is unacceptable because you may lose it, to what you must have in the future to make you feel safe. Like money; what if it runs out? I need to stockpile all I can because I remember being broke and that really sucked so I can't have that. Therefore we need to sell more cars this month…we need higher quotas, more clients…

Don't get me wrong here. There's nothing wrong with making a living—a really good living at that—but be mindful of the underlying energy driving your action. Is it Right Livelihood? Are you running from your past or are you positively contributing to society? Are you spreading light and love into the fractal of the Universe?

It's all a game of ping pong in a way. We feel a certain way and say to ourselves, "wow that really feels terrible" so we volley. We run out to a movie or call that friend that always comforts us. That starts to create the spin—the other pole for a negative emotional energy field to be created. Then another event in life happens that triggers the same issue (volley), so we run back to our safe ground on the other side again (volley with some Margaritas at the beach this time). It happens again and again until we have supercharged an energy field around this sucker that can power three city blocks. It all lives under the radar of our awareness and thus, silently drains us of our vital life energy- leaving holes in our field for chaos and entropy to set in. It is making us suffer and age while all the while thinking we're doing everything we can to "live a better life and be happy."

Is this starting to make sense? I hope so, because you're going to have to understand this mechanism first before being able to rectify the situation. I can't do it for you but I can keep explaining the nuts and bolts so that once you get it, it's the only game in town. You can start cleaning your way to freedom and clarity.

Personal Journeys—Perspective is Everything

I WAS IN LIMA, Peru. It was 1998 and I had taken a couple of months off to travel in the ancient Inca lands. I was always fascinated by Machu Picchu and was determined to spend some quality time there.

I had decided to see the countryside and travel from Lima to Cusco by bus. I wanted to travel as the locals did and have some exposure to the culture. It was a 30 hour bus ride in the most uncomfortable seat I had ever been in. We had a number of mechanical problems with the bus and were delayed for several hours. The driver made occasional restroom stops right off of the road. I remember waking up from a nap to the squirting sound of diarrhea just outside the bus. One of the passengers was squatting just ten feet away from my window and relieving himself in a nonchalant public display. Nobody else seemed to care. Wow.

After taking care of my own business, we got back onto the dirt road and kept driving into the night. The windows were down and cold air mixed with dust from the road kept blowing in. I sat between two rather chubby native women who had both fallen asleep. Each had their head on either of my two shoulders. The bus was loud, cold, and the rattling seat was jamming into my tailbone.

We had another ten hours or so to go and it was only 2 am which meant it wasn't going to warm up any time soon. I was *miserable*. I was sitting there and tumbling down chains of negative thoughts when I was shocked back into the moment. Someone's chicken, which was clucking around the bus, had jumped up onto my head and just sat there!

That's when it happened. I snapped out of it. I was finally able to step outside of my story line and get a look at how incredibly funny the whole thing really was. Both my arms were pinned by the sleeping Peruvian ladies and there was a chicken hanging out on my head! The thought of how ridiculous I must have looked took over and I started to laugh to myself. In that moment, all of my self-pity and mental noise just went away simply by developing a new angle on the story. It was not miserable anymore—just incredibly funny. If only my friends could see me now! Sometimes the power of perspective has to jump right up onto our heads for us to wake up I guess.

The Cup

Here's an example that may better help you wrap your mind around this concept. Imagine being a teacup. You are the ceramic cup that is designed to hold whatever liquid comes your way. Inside, you are filled one day with tea, another with coffee, and another with lemonade. Maybe some wine or some cod liver oil comes through the next day. Whatever it is, you get rinsed, dried, and are ready to bear whatever comes along the next day. No problem right?

Our problem as humans is that one day tea comes in and we say, "Tea? Why would they give me tea? They know I like coffee!"—or "I love this particular coffee. I hope they use it again tomorrow. Oh, God, please make it be coffee again tomorrow!" On and on we worry about the contents of the cup not realizing that they are transient. We are the cup and can hold whatever comes our way, and when the liquid is gone, we are still the same cup. Without the rollercoaster ride of anticipation, worry, and grief over the contents, we can simply be a cup and embrace whatever passes through us knowing that what may come will eventually move through. There is no need to hang on, no need to struggle and wish for better days and absolutely no reason to budge reality. The mind works exactly in this way. One thought will come in and literally "bump" the previous thought out…on and on and on eternally. If we don't bite and jump in with our emotional reactions, the mind can be left to its own devices and we can passively observe.

Some would say: "Well that sounds pretty boring. What you're saying would mean we all sit around like useless blobs all day and do nothing". That's not the case at all.

Imagine that we have all been born as little holographic offshoots of the one flame and, the energy of life is moving through us and naturally driving us to the fulfillment of our personal dreams and destinies. There is plenty of inspired movement that comes from being present and tranquil. In our modern society, we have somehow equated the lack of chaotic strife and incessant noise with a lack of drive and initiative. Get out of your own way and see what drive really is. It comes from within and it is effortless. If you are sitting upon your chaotic perch and arguing with me, I challenge you to try sitting still and observing your mind for a ten day Vipassana meditation retreat and then talk to me about it. It's really easy to make excuses for yourself on this side of reconciliation, but before you do, please ask yourself, what emotions am I avoiding feeling and why am I so resistant to this? What trance am I under? Let's see if we can't discover that answer…

The Law of Karma

Karma is action and action is karma. We hear this word used all the time nowadays (often incorrectly) and many people associate it only with past deeds and some kind of good deeds score to be constantly tallied up throughout life. Well, all action is karma. It is either in harmony with the flow of the universe or not. It either perpetuates order or feeds chaos and the mechanism by now should be becoming clear. If you are struggling against feeling a certain way and bolster your intent into an opposite energy, you are creating polarity, imbalance and negative karma. What this means is that you are creating more work to do at a later date. This is work that needs to be worked off, or karma that needs to be cleared. You were not living in the present moment and, therefore, socked away a lesson for later by encapsulating it in time. You created a polar charge around a particular issue, thought, or memory and said at the time, "I can't deal with this right now so I'm going to put it away for later when I am stronger, richer, better looking, have more energy..." You see, tomorrow brings its own set of "crap" we can't handle so we will never have time to deal with it. We keep putting things away every day, charging them and filing them for a later date. It's no wonder that most people complain about fatigue by the time they hit their 30s. They are filled to the gills with yesterday's refuse and they keep shoveling it on. There is no amount of running or pushups I know of that can make this go away. It simply sedates us by raising endorphins and allowing us to feel okay for now. "I just need to get through this year or this quarter... "

The law of karma is not some esoteric principle outside of ourselves. We are intimately involved with it daily. All that we do creates it.

I have just spoken briefly of the chaotic side, but what about positive karma? How do we create that? Simple. First and foremost is to learn to be. Sit in your heart and be the cup. Most of us think we're making a great contribution to the world by performing loving, charitable acts as often as we can, and there is nothing wrong with this. It's a wonderful thing, and much needed, but ask yourself this: why are you doing it? Is it because God asks you to? Does it make you feel better about yourself? Maybe you're doing it because you cheated all of those investors out of their retirement by making a bad deal and feel guilty? Maybe you grew up poor and now want to give back?

The point is, come from a place of balance. Get out of the cycle of aversions and cravings. Don't make the charity one side of another ping pong match. Relax into your natural state and let the Tao work through you. Then all acts are charitable as the Grace of the Divine does the work and you don't get in the way.

The law of karma holds us accountable for our actions. Release your incessant struggle with the noise of your mind and allow things to come and go naturally. Once you get the hang of this, you'll learn quickly that most of our energy and effort has gone into this wasteful chaos. Most of our action or karma has come from this noisy mess. Welcome to the human experience of suffering. The more we can step out of these vicious cycles, the more our action is inspired and the more the Universal Force works through us and we become an agent of grace and love.

The Lucifer Experiment

One of my teachers speaks of a story that may or may not be true but I feel has important significance here. He speaks of the Lucifer Experiment [Melchizedek, 2000, pp. 411-419]. In this, Lucifer, being the brightest and most talented angel of God decides that he can do it better. He can create a reality within God's Creation that is more interesting. He has free will and God isn't going to stop him. According to this story, we, as humans, are all inside of this experiment. We have the choice—to see reality as it is and let it be perfect in and of itself, or to think that we can do it better than God and go it alone. There is an interesting resonance with this and the suffering we spoke of earlier. It seems that creating our "monsters" or "demons" (fields inside of the shadow of our energy field) is very much like this same process. The shadow, by default, is unconscious—where the light of consciousness is not shining. It is where we hide that which we cannot bear to see and inadvertently give it charge. We give it our energy until it contains more power than our conscious field. This is how I believe people are driven to rape children and participate in atrocities that make us cringe. They unknowingly feed energy into their shadows until the shadow takes on a life of its own and commands their actions. Much like Lucifer was given the right to do as he would within the Creation, we step out of the free flow of the All and isolate ourselves in the dark corners of our shadow wherein we charge unobserved emotions and thoughts we avert until they get the best of us.

The Buddha woke up from his slumber and those around him took note. The first step towards correcting this folly is awareness. This stops the downward flow of suffering and chaos and opens the channels of healing and reintegration. It opens us up to freedom and transcendence.

Trance Mentality

Milton Erickson, the psychiatrist who was the father of modern hypnotherapy, was once asked what it was like to put people into trances all the time and his response was: "I do not think you understand what it is that I do at all. I spend all of my time working to pull people out of their trances." We are a culture of zombies, walking around in our sleep, going through behaviors that do not serve us. Because they are unconscious, we remain unaware of them. They lie in the blind spot of our conscious minds and are always running. Being in the present moment creates an honesty with ourselves. Because we have avoided this for so many years, we have pumped vast amounts of energy into the opposing poles of these feelings and emotions. This acts to power up their charge, making them seem like impenetrable bubbles that we don't want to pierce. As more of our personal power gets siphoned away into the unconsciousness of the shadow, we become less aware of the current moment. After years of this, the empowered energy fields in our shadows start to run the show, and each of them take on a particular behavior, habit, or rationalization that serves as a defense mechanism.

Essentially, when the light of our awareness shines in the direction of a charged memory/emotion, we do one or a combination of the following:

1. Feel the feeling or recall the traumatic event for an instant and quickly channel energy into the polar opposite feeling (further charging the field in our shadow)
• One example of this would be faking the feeling of happiness when we are sad or blue.

• Another is spending more money than we can afford in order to feel or look rich.

2. Feel the charged memory/emotion and go into a story line that helps rationalize this energy—thereby empowering a false story and doing this long enough for us to believe it is true (creating an energy field around a lie we've created which acts as a buffer between us and the traumatic event).
• An example of this would be being afraid to go talk to an attractive woman and rationalize it by saying that you're too busy or that her hair is the wrong color.
• Another example is enslaving native Americans or African slaves and justifying the guilt by convincing yourself that you are saving them masking your guilt). Or maybe talking down to a server at a restaurant because they don't come from your "elevated" class in society (masks insecurity or social anxiety).

3. Feeling it and reacting into an activity or behavior that distracts us from the original pain
• This happens with people who are addicted to running or emotional eaters—both poles of the same refractory behavior. The people who are addicted to the "positive" behaviors here are oftentimes even more entrenched because they are convinced that they are fine (so long as they run 20 miles today) whereas a person who is morbidly obese usually understands that they have a problem but doesn't have the right tools to resolve it.

4. We feel it, we forgive it, and allow it to heal—dissipating the charge built up around it and bringing it back into the light of awareness.
• Absorbing this energy back into our fields is what makes us whole.

Trance is the way of our culture. TV induces trance by dropping ideas under our radar. Politicians use it all the time by repeating slogans and mottos that call upon our fears and then channel this energy into their agendas. In fact, society at large seems to operate around this unspoken language of the shepherd leading the weak. The weak are leveraged by their shadows. They are unconsciously trapped, and tapping into these energies draws their will-power and resources as they sleepwalk into someone else's vision for reality.

Again, the Buddha woke up. That is the necessary first step and also the step that needs to continue in perpetuity. We need to keep waking up to the current moment as our tendency right now is to quickly fall back asleep. Yesterday's awakening means little if we're back asleep right now. To finally snap out of our trance means to understand the mechanism that puts us there and to stop participating in it. We are the only ones that can create it for ourselves and we are the only ones that can fix ourselves, period. If anyone says they can do it for you, run!

Now that we understand how this is happening, we come to the harsh realization that we are the ones doing it. We are the ones that keep channeling power into this system and we are the ones feeding our shadows. Once we take responsibility for the core delusion that the "outside" world is what's holding us back and causing all of our problems, then we can finally sit back in the driver's seat (which we never left but were simply asleep at the wheel while our shadow was driving) and take control.

When we are in trance we can be leveraged, controlled, influenced, disempowered and manipulated by anyone who sees what's going on. The language of the subconscious mind is incredibly powerful and has been the subject of much popular "New Age" literature. On this subject I'd like to make an important point. Learning to control this system and understanding the nature of how it is programmed helps effect outcomes in the material world but to what end? Be very careful about teachings that stop short of the full liberation of your consciousness when evoking this knowledge. This is just a higher level of a trance mentality. Big boats and huge mansions are great toys to enjoy on the planet but, if that's your focus in your spiritual work, then welcome to being a rich zombie. The dangling of material possessions without greater understanding of reality and your central role in all of it is a huge distraction and many people in the West have fallen for this language of spiritualized materialism. The trance just simply continues.

The way out is in. Suffering happens because of our ignorance of how things work. We spend hours every day wrestling between the poles of aversions and cravings…falling asleep and waking up disappointed with ourselves that we just "did it again". Whether that "it" happens to be eating a whole box of donuts, goofing off on the internet when you're supposed to be writing a paper, cheating on your spouse, or conducting some atrocity, it's all a product of the same elemental mechanism—losing awareness and being driven by shadow behavior. The same mechanism that generates this cycle of suffering is what drains away our life force and slowly drags us down into ill health and broken dreams. Like the story of Dr. Jeckyl and Mr. Hyde, it is our energized shadow that does all the mischief and lands us into trouble. The sooner we stop feeding our energy into the darkness, the sooner we start to wake up and snap out of it. The sooner we snap out of it, the more power we can muster to go in and release more trapped energy and vitality. Then we can start living our lives for real. It is then that we are playing what my teacher calls, "the only game in town." This becomes the game of Alchemy— turning the "lead" of our personal experience stored in our shadows into the "gold" of liberation, understanding and true empowerment.

With a healthy understanding of where suffering comes from, then we are poised to do something about it. In the next couple of chapters, we are going to explore basic Taoist theory so that we can lay the groundwork for the practices taught in Part Two of this book. It is extremely important to understand what it is we are doing and why, because we need to command our entire attention on this subject matter. It is very easy to be overly dismissive in our modern culture because of the plethora of information we have access to. It is also extremely easy to fall into one of the classic pitfalls of trance mentality: namely, we read dozens of books and attend various lectures by well-intentioned people who are sharing information that can be helpful, and then we only take in what we think is useful to us intellectually. The defense mechanisms that we have created to "protect us" from deep-seated traumas from our past create dismissive rationalizations for why we are going to take a few quotes from this teacher and a couple from the next, and avoid their teachings that begin to probe what we've unknowingly shifted to our shadows. We don't need to follow through with the lessons they are suggesting that will actually challenge our stuff. Again, the solution is somehow out there and eventually someone is going to write a book that is going to save me...

No.

You are going to save yourself and it starts right now. Be hyper-vigilant throughout your reading of this book (and everything else in life for that matter). Remember that it all begins and ends inside of you. All of the trapped potential and freedom waiting to burst from within simply relies on changing your understanding of reality and how truly central you are to every one of the "random" events happening all around you.

We are going to get into the specifics of the ancient Taoist practices that were specifically designed to correct this imbalance as taught to me by my masters. In order to do this correctly though, it is important to engage in a quick primer on Taoist thinking and philosophy. We need to have a set of rules and language through which to practice and the next couple of chapters will serve this purpose.

※

CHAPTER THREE

A LIFESTYLE IN BALANCE

*The Way of Heaven is to reduce the excessive
and increase the insufficient.*

—Lao Tzu, Tao Te Ching, *Chapter 77*

he wisdom of the ancients came from something we often take for granted—Mother Nature. The Taoist way is founded on the premise that we are all One with nature and that the careful observation of nature and Her rhythmic cycles will give us clues about ourselves. In fact, we are the embodiment of the elements of nature, so harmonizing these forces inside of ourselves is a profound act of union with all creation. The basic Taoist principles of Yin and Yang speak of a Universal system of complimentary opposites that mutually enhance and reinforce each other. What is up without down or left without right? These concepts need each other in order to make sense. The premise of the work that we will be learning in this book is based on the nature of this polarity and the way these opposite poles interact with each other.

The Symbol of Balance

We often take simple things for granted. It's a hallmark of our crazy civilization to relate simplicity with stupidity and rest with laziness. We want more, we want it faster, and we want it now. But as soon as we get it we're over it and we want the next thing.

In the non-stop hectic world we have created for ourselves, there is no time or place for rest, tranquility, relaxation, and quality time with loved ones. Whatever happened to lazy Sundays or simple, good healthy living?

In the excellent book, The Power of Full Engagement, authors Jim

Loehr and Tony Schwartz outline the need for rest and recovery as balance points for our stressful daily lives. Essentially, people are far more productive when they have allowed themselves to "power down" and have filled up their batteries again. A great deal of research has been done recently which has shown this to be essential for elite athletes, but now, the same thing has also been proven true for everyone else. [Loehr, 2003]

YOU MUST REST

Getting proper amounts of rest should be an obvious first part of this equation, but the second part is also worthy of note and it has to do with stress. When Han Selye first coined the term in 1956, he called negative stress distress and positive stress eustress. The term we use so often in our daily lexicon always seems to have a negative connotation, whereas the concept of eustress (like euphoria which is a positive feeling) is actually a good thing for our bodies and minds. [Selye, 1975) In fact, stress is the reason we are here. Stress on biological systems has driven life towards adaptation and evolution for billions of years. We would be blobs of protozoa without stress.

SO WHY IS STRESS GETTING THE BEST OF US NOW?

The answer is simple (says the Taoist)—lack of balance. We have allowed our distress, and our perceptions of events in our lives to have the best of us. Mental stress and physical stress are different, however, and in fact, there's also spiritual stress, and it's important to tease these out here, one by one.

Physical Stress

This comes from overtaxing our bodies while not allowing them to rest and recover adequately. This may be overexertion at the gym after 30 weeks of inactivity or it could be pulling an all-nighter and expecting to perform well the following day at work without any repercussions. These are obvious examples. How about hunching in your office chair for eight hours a day, five days per week, and 50 weeks per year for the last 16 years? There's some real physical stress on the lower back and shoulders.

Most of us can relate to physical stress because we've all been tired or injured in some way in our lives but what about the opposite tendency- the LACK of physical stress in our lives? This is actually reaching epidemic proportions in our country right now.

IT'S CALLED EXERCISE AND IT IS GOOD FOR YOU.
Again, remember that everything in our lives needs balance—there is the yin and the yang of all things. Too little physical stress makes the body flaccid, weak, and unresponsive. In fact, studies show that increased weight-bearing activity helps increase the production of Growth Hormone in the brain and helps increase and better regulate sex hormones and immune function. [Mastorakos, 2005]

THE BODY LIKES EUSTRESS WITH RECOVERY.
It likes to be pushed just hard enough and then be given the tools to repair itself so that it can push just a little harder next time. This is called growth and evolution.

What are these tools then? Sleep is a key. Most of the body's growth hormone is produced in deep Stage 4 sleep. [Kalus, 2009] This is the kind of sleep you get once your mind and body have settled down through your daily thoughts and worries. It is the depth to which we retreat for our systems to shut down and repair. Dead tissue is shuttled away and new healthy tissue takes its place. The body literally renews itself at night when our conscious minds (that insist on perpetually creating recklessly) go offline and our subconscious minds can take over and handle physiological processes.

Think of Disneyland. Thousands of happy tourists parade through there everyday, making a mess and leaving it in disarray. Even with the small army of employees they have scavenging the park all day for trash and sorting out problems, there is a lot that goes on when the park shuts down. This is when the night crew comes out and fixes the mess left behind from the previous day. No stone is unturned because tomorrow, thousands of people will be coming in again looking forward to the "perfect" experience that is Disneyland.

Now imagine if the Disney night crew didn't do their job one night. You show up in the morning fresh off your flight from the Midwest and notice a half eaten cotton candy on the chair next to the entrance. You go in and see a smashed caramel apple on the pavement. There is trash everywhere and all the employees look tired and agitated. What happened? Well, the night crew slacked off last night and things are a little messy. What if the night crew decided to not come back at all? Then the day crew works double time to clean up the morning after and is beat by day's end. Now, how about if management decided that the park would "get more done" or "make more money" if they simply didn't close and kept the day crew working 18-22 hour shifts? Well, Disneyland wouldn't be such a happy place after a week or so would it?

That's how we treat our bodies. We beat them up incessantly all day with heavy food full of preservatives. We don't take time to rest throughout the day, and then we expect them to hang in there when we meet the guys for drinks or maybe see a movie with Betsey knowing the alarm goes off at 6 am the next morning. Exercise works the same way.

We cannot do hundreds of reps of bench press or wear out the pedals on a stationary bike and then expect results without letting the body recover. The growth of muscle tissue comes from provoking it and slightly tearing it during activity. The body then mends these tears when we are resting by laying stronger and denser muscle tissue in the region of the tear because, obviously, that muscle is now being expected to perform more. The body allocates resources where they are needed but needs the cues (exercising specific muscle groups) and the rest in order to stay in harmony. Providing raw substrate in the form of food (protein) is also a critical component of this dynamic that we will discuss in a bit.

If we continue to challenge and provoke our bodies in a healthy way, we continue to develop more lean body muscle mass and we continue to improve the pumping capability of our hearts. This provides us with healthy blood flow, healthy brain function, good lymphatic drainage, and good-looking skin. In fact, the steady progression of our fitness to being more and more adaptable becomes a cue for our brains to continue to produce natural Growth Hormone, which is a powerful chemical that literally helps reverse the aging process. [Mastorakos, 2005] It makes us strong, fit, clear, and healthier all through a natural means of continued training.

Clinical Encounters—The Shadow of the Ultra-Fit

BEING IN SOUTHERN California, I see a good number of elite athletes in the clinic. There are a number of triathletes, Iron Men, professional athletes, and weekend warriors I see every week. Everybody is really absorbed in pushing themselves and conquering their weakness and inhibitions. I oftentimes see a strong parallel between the way many of these people treat their bodies and the way our Western culture treats the Earth. We will push it and it will comply!

Looking at the lab results on many of these individuals is shocking. They may be climbing mountains now but their adrenals look like they are 40 years older than they are. Many of the men complain of erectile dysfunction and the women complain of insomnia and anxiety attacks. It's almost as if they are willing to go to any heights to silence the noise coming from their shadows. Most of them are going about it the wrong way. Some listen and we get them better with lifestyle modification, acupuncture, and herbs. Many of the others go on until they collapse or replace too many joints. I even see yoga injuries. People are so busy pushing themselves that they forget to feel where to stop, breathe, and relax.

Moderation is the key here. Keeping the body healthy is much easier than trying to fix it after the fact.

There has been a great deal of progress made in the past years in the realm of exercise physiology and I have included a number of resources in the appendix for your review. You might also visit taoistpath.com where I have pooled together the best information I've found that will help you become the best you can be in physical fitness.

The obvious other contributor to physical stress is diet. We literally are what we eat and, unlike a couple generations before us, many of us are eating fast, processed foods that have been deprived of their nutrients and pumped full of hormones and preservatives. Here's an interesting concept: food comes from the ground.

We have reached such a level of sophistication in our ultra-modern society that many of the children I meet have only seen shrink-wrapped fruit and food that comes in boxes. Actually, most of the people I went to college with were the same way. People in big cities have very little access to the earth and have a terrible connection with where our food truly comes from.

Most of us in America overeat. The portion sizes are huge and our culture is one of abundance. Present day agribusiness has modernized farming practices with genetically-modified organisms and dangerous pesticides, and helped reap abundant harvests that have provided crop yields that were not even dreamt of two generations ago. The problem with such overproduction is that, apart from the consequences of using pesticides and GMO's, these methods degrade the topsoil and rob it, and the vegetables that grow from it, of vital nutrients. We keep eating more and more volume (and calorically dense food) and getting less and less nutritive value with each meal. Or, we are told that our food has been supplemented and bolstered with ingredients that have been chemically isolated and inserted into our produce. This results in manufacturers having the opportunity to proudly brag about the health values of Lycopene…in ketchup! Somehow, we have ceased to consider the value of whole foods eaten in their natural forms which is the only way to ensure we get the full spectrum of ingredients together which nature intended-or at least how our bodies have evolved to absorb them. There are chemicals inside of whole foods that have naturally evolved to work together to aid in digestion, absorption, and neutralization of toxins; none of which have been matched by the sophistication of modern science to date.

Our lives have become calorically dense and nutritionally poor, as we must shove more down our throats to get the same nutritional benefits, with expanding waistlines and higher rates of cancer and disease as the end result. Worse, in order to get these foods to last on shelves, they have been chemically enhanced and pumped full of hormones and growth factors. Our bodies have developed over several million years of evolution and have adapted around one thing: nature.

Proper physical rest and recovery revolves around healthy eating habits. It is important to find your resting metabolic rate (RMR) which can be estimated using some standardized equations or through metabolic testing, which can determine an exact value. From here, you can accurately establish what your current caloric expenditures and needs are and then modify your diet based on your goals. Again, there is balance in everything. If you under eat, your metabolism slows down (and goes into emergency mode) telling your body to store fat and if you overeat, your body cannot burn the extra calories fast enough and stores them as fat. The key for most people is to eat every three hours to keep the blood sugar stable and to have enough protein with each meal/snack. There are a number of basic recommendations on diet in Part Two of this book.

This is in no way a book intended to solve the weight loss crisis in this country but I have listed some excellent resources in the appendix on this subject. The key is to stay balanced and avoid spikes in your blood sugar. A golden rule for this is to never eat carbohydrates by themselves. Always have them with a protein and a fat source. Also, eating a mostly vegetarian diet with lots of leafy green vegetables is essential for overall health of the heart. Fruits and vegetables give us abundant amounts of antioxidants which help scavenge through the body for harmful free radical and help prevent heart disease and cancer.

Our bodies are the most precious things we have. They are the chariots for our souls and spirits. They are the alchemical agent that we will later learn to transmute and refine. Learning to manage physical stress and strike the perfect balance between positive stress and adequate recovery is the key here.

IN THE TRADITIONAL method of training for Chinese Kung Fu, there were no belts to be awarded. When a student first arrived at a school or a monastery, they were given a white sash to help hold up their pants. Over time, these sashes became dirtier and dirtier with training so the more senior students could be distinguished by the dark color of their sash. A black belt or sash simply meant that you had been there quite some time. When the fabric started to fray, that indicated even more seniority. The traditional Grand Master's sash is actually white. This came from a student who was there so long that their black sash had completely frayed and was now white again. This symbolized a homecoming—a full circle journey of the master back to the beginner's mind.

In my school, students did not even begin with a sash. We had a system that ultimately used different colors, however, as an adaptation to the environment here in America. I trained diligently for six months before I was even qualified to test for my white sash (even after having high ranking belts in other traditions).

The initial hour of my first Kung Fu test was nothing but deep stances. The predominant one is called Square Horse, which is a very low, wide stance that puts a tremendous amount of pressure on the leg muscles. This was one of my first lessons in learning to relax *with exertion*. The only way to sustain a deep stance like that is to breathe into it and sink. The pain in the legs is simply a sensation and it is my reaction to that sensation that causes my suffering.

Talk about a rough way to learn a lesson! After a solid hour of stances, the test began and lasted another three hours or so. The level of physical exertion was enormous but I learned something that day. I learned to rest and recover while simultaneously moving and exerting. I always thought that you had to do one and then the other. That was my polarity consciousness talking. The balance of the Tao must be found in everything and then everything becomes effortless.

Mental Stress

This too has reached epidemic proportions in the West. Although it takes the same amount of time for the earth to turn around the sun, this time seems to be quickening every year. We are all slammed with our commitments. According to the 2005 US Census Bureau, most Americans have a commute to work that averages a hundred hours every year.

We come from a species that would typically walk several miles per day and take rest in the shade when it was too hot or we were too tired. We would eat when hungry and have a high level of physical exertion daily which kept our hearts pumping and endorphins kicking. Stress came when a Saber-toothed tiger popped into the cave, and we had to scramble and hide for dear life.

So how has it changed? Something happened along the way when the monkey finally stood up and we began to develop the pre-frontal cortex in the human brain. As we became self-aware, we began to develop a complex psyche that our animal counterparts don't seem to exhibit. With awareness of the self came the mental dialogue and the neuronal relays through the thalamus that associate past memories with emotions. These clusters of memories/emotions loop through and generate thoughts or reactions along these lines over and over. [Pert, 1997, pp. 131-145]

Sound familiar?

Back to the chapter in the nature of suffering here, we can recall that the Buddha had something to say about this subject. We have an event, and then we have our reaction to that event. We tend to either go towards the given subject (cravings) or move away from it (aversions) and in both cases create a cycle of suffering. As Dr. Alfred Korzybski says, we create levels of abstraction from the original event, which pulls us and our mental energy farther and farther from the present moment. [Korzybski, 1948] All our power is here, now. As we allow ourselves to go barreling down our careless thought trains, we move further away from the power of the present moment and circle into a cycle of suffering and mental stress.

Again, there is positive stress and negative stress. We always refer to the negative variety because we are all held in such captivity by it but what about positive mental stress? The Buddha would assert that one is to maintain a level of mental equanimity. This means staying in the space of non-judgmental presence and simply observing phenomena as they wax and wane through our perception.

Positive mental stress comes in the form of healthy problem solving. In our schools we are given a number of math problems to solve for homework. These are designed to get us to apply principles we have learned to a specific area and deduce an answer based on a certain set of rules or theorems. Once we figure out a math problem, then other similar problems become easier to solve as we have gained familiarity with that type of problem. We are then promoted to higher levels with new problems and more complicated solution sets. We continue to refine our problem-solving skills and become more efficient at things. What happens when we grow up though? We are all complaining about the problems we have in our lives! Positive mental stress is to learn how to take a particular circumstance and look at it rationally. This means being honest about all of the factors and variables involved. Every aspect of a problem gets factored into its solution. Once we learn to challenge our brains and work through our life's problems, the game of life becomes fun.

The issue with most people is that they have, over the years, attached emotional shadow aspects to their life's problems. The solution set is clouded by an array of aversions and cravings, which have picked up a great deal of charge. This is why getting outside help is often useful. Sometimes it takes another person to rationally look at what we are struggling with in order to see it clearly. We are still the ones that have to fix it, but that outside view inwards can often help us see through our blind spots in relation to the problems that seem to linger in our lives.

Puzzles, math games, Sudoku, memory games, chess, and thought-provoking books are all forms of positive mental stress—as long as you remember to take these on with an attitude of leisure. Creating a healthy ritual of challenging the mind routinely helps the brain lay new neuronal connections and keeps us healthy. In fact, these types of activities are what I recommend to my patients with Alzheimer's and other degenerative diseases of the brain. Exciting the brain with information and challenges leads to neuroplasticity (associated with youth and high functioning) and the opposite leads to neurodegeneration (associated with aging and loss of physical/mental function). [Kukolja, 2009]

Yes, this is all wonderful to be made aware of, but what about my goals and aspirations? What about the joys of human experience that give us meaning and focus?

I would argue that those fall under the realm of Spirit and will discuss them momentarily. As far as the mind goes, it is important to remember that the mind is our tool. We oftentimes identify with the tool and get confused by thinking that we are our minds. Think of it this way: your mind is a product of the billions of calculations and perceptions going on in your brain which acts as a receiver or antenna for cosmic energy from the Universe. All Source energy is here now and our brains are the organic antennae that tune us into this. Our minds are the self-conscious reflection to this endless activity streaming in and out with millions of bits of information. Like the guys sitting at the console watching all the funny green symbols streaming down in the Matrix movies, it is our challenge to separate and watch the rumblings of the machine—not think we are the machine.

So that is the first step: stop identifying with our minds and learn to observe the perpetual motion and noise without reacting to it. Only through this mechanism can we be freed from negative mental stress and regain the bandwidth to perform the functions we really want. It is only through this method that we may find ourselves and lead a purpose-driven life.

Spiritual Stress

Spiritual stress is something that many people in our day and age suffer from. Life is a beautiful thing when it carries meaning and purpose. We are all here to learn, love, and grow. Each heart has an earnest desire and it is to be fulfilled. I'm not talking about getting that new Porsche your neighbor has but more like, going on safari and seeing the pyramids. How about learning Spanish and starting a winery in Chile? Or maybe having a small flower shop and reading Shakespeare at your local café? How about getting on board and helping us save the earth so our grandchildren could have a planet to live on? The need to survive drove early man to innovate and invent all sorts of revolutionary tools and technologies. In modern society, we have not been forced to deal with threat of the survival of our species for thousands of years…until now. We have finally come full circle and, because of our technological advancements, we are again at a point where we may face extinction. Survival teaches meaning and it is time for us all to wake up and get involved.

The truth is that each of us has likes and wants things that make us happy. The problem is that many of us have strayed from here and are "stuck" doing jobs that we don't like and "stuck" in a life situation that is not allowing us the time, space, energy, or money to follow through with those dreams. So what happens? We show up at a crappy job and can't wait until the next break and make comments like "It's only Tuesday!" as the week crawls on. We then become the breeding ground for mental noise and this stagnation that takes over the system. "We" don't exist so we assume that our minds must be it.

Let's look at it another way. Assume your body is a computer and your mind is your operating system and software. First of all, how many windows do you have open at any given point? What about mental viruses (belief systems that are self-sabotaging)? When's the last time you optimized your disk? Do you have enough power or cooling fans on your hardware? How about updates to your software? This might make sense to you, but still, something is missing…

What are we working on?

You could have the fastest supercomputer in the world with all the best software and can sit there playing Minesweeper until enough time passes by and you get outdated and sluggish in performance. Aimlessly browse the internet for a while and you'll pick up some nasty viruses and maybe go nuts reading too many conspiracy theories…and all for what?

Exactly. We need to have something to work on. Do you build houses or count galaxies with your computer? Do you manage money for households or create websites for newlyweds? The point is, unless there is a job or task at hand; a purpose in life, then you could have the best system in the world and, over time, it'll just rot away.

Now that's assuming we've all got supercomputers too. Most of us have been treating our bodies pretty horribly and are running on low mental efficiency. We have hundreds of applications running subconsciously and, when it comes time to focus, we have limited resources available for our conscious minds…we get tired and frustrated as our minds are less sharp and fatigue quicker.

It is usually easy to recognize when our performance is starting to slack. We get tired at our desk and want to go sneak a nap in the car or maybe we read the same line over three times on an email and still feel confused about the author's meaning. Most of us are at least aware of the fact that our mental computers are running inefficiently and have taken it upon ourselves to enroll in a number of self help courses or read a handful of books to fix this problem. The real question again is: why? Once purpose is found in life, then we can easily set our bearings while optimizing our systems becomes a small bump on the road. We have set off on a journey, and changing the oil filter is just another task to handle as we excitedly hurry to get going.

Many of you may be thinking, "Great—that sounds good if I had a purpose!" Ok, touché. It is true that a great number of people are struggling daily with this notion of purpose. Remember this: nobody can tell you what your purpose in life is. You already know it and if it seems like it is fuzzy or unclear, learn to calm your mind and follow the principles in this book and you will find that the answer has been under your nose the whole time.

Two Types of Immortality —Balancing Death with the Life Urge

Since the beginning of time, humans have been faced with two basic trajectories for the continuation of their "light." The first one is the one practiced by over 99% of the population right now and it is a relatively simple formula:

I realize that I am mortal and will someday pass. Therefore, if I have children, my blood or my light can pass forward into the future and I will, if not be immortalized, at least extend my legacy into the future.

This path presupposes that we pass a part of ourselves into our progeny and that they will, in turn, carry on the tradition and sustain the life of the family or blood line for years to come. This is the obvious choice of most people on the planet for good reason; it is certainly the easiest. No matter how insignificant or unaccomplished we may feel on our deathbeds, there is some comfort in knowing that our children will do better or achieve more. Unfortunately, there is no level of spiritual sophistication required for this process and we see countless children being born into terrible situations with parents who can neither support them financially nor emotionally. Instead of being the cherished co-creations of lovers who work together to bring a life form into this world, and who are cared for, loved, and taught so that they can benefit from the wisdom and advance our species, these children have parents who have severe mental or spiritual disharmonies who in turn thrust these states upon their children.

In short, people who don't have their acts together are bringing children into this world following an unconscious "spell" or formula that has been burned in biologically. Carrying the species towards further advancement means more than just diversity, it means loving our children into existence. The most evolutionarily advanced circuitry in the human brain is in the frontal cortex, which helped us develop higher moral reasoning and evolution. Children who are loved and cared for show a greater proliferation of cortical neurons in this region and develop more balanced and evolved brains. [Bellis, 2005]

Too many people have children because they regret that they were not able to be the person they wanted to in this life and hope that they can somehow mold their child into the perfect form they could never attain themselves. Their quest for immortality ends with conceiving children and putting all their desperate hopes into them.

Here's some good news: it's never too late to start working on ourselves at the same time. In fact, we owe this to our children. Yes, it is important to support and nourish your children and love them unconditionally, but what about yourselves? Later in this book we are going to illustrate techniques for personal development and spiritual enhancement that bridge the gap between the first and the second type of immortality, which is personal immortality.

Personal Immortality is a concept that has been saved exclusively for the great saints and holy men and women of our species, it seems. Apparently, people are able to accept the immortality of Jesus of Nazareth and his re-birth but are unwilling to accept the notion that, they too, are capable of it. There are, in fact, dozens (if not hundreds) of accounts of human beings who have purportedly attained immortality throughout our history. However, it's easy to dismiss these as ancient linguistic conventions and go back to burying our heads in the sandy comfort of our "only" human mantra by refocusing on getting each other pregnant. Or we can stop for a minute and look at what this implies. Leonard Orr, the father of Rebirthing, wrote a provocative book called Breaking the Death Habit—The Science of Everlasting Life, wherein he described his adventures through India searching for (and meeting) several yogis who taught him the secrets of immortality. His main teacher became the famous Babaji, who is known as the father of all yogis in the East [Orr, 1998]. My personal lineage comes from an unbroken line taught by the famous Lu Tung Pin, the most famous of the great Taoist 8 Immortals. [Wong, 1990, pp. 123-124]

So let's get into that question that might be in your mind right now—do I mean actually physical immortality?

Physical immortality means nothing. It suggests that our current physical structure is in some way locked in and that this appearance actually represents who we truly are which is simply not true. It is the ego trying to grasp at the only thing it can identify with. Many of the famed immortals in human history have allegedly taken on previous physical forms at times when appearing to their disciples. Babaji supposedly likes to take on the form of a young man when he appears to his students. However, he has reportedly taken on thousands of other forms when appearing to other seekers, as needed. The physical vehicle is a shell, a mask used by our consciousness to play at a particular game on this planet. On the other hand, our spirits are immortal, but most people assume real access to something so intangible is impossible. It's as if people believe that our spirits come into physical bodies, hover around while we do the physical thing for 80 years or so, and then go back to the pearly gates and hang out with God again. So where does all of the work come in?

It has to do with Awareness. When we become aware of our internal dynamics, we begin to make contact with the Infinite Source from which we all come. In my Taoist lineage, the ultimate work is to turn the light of awareness around and perceive the purity and enormity of our being. It is to shine through the veil of the ignorant trance we are in and wake up to our Eternal selves. My experience in the cave at the age of eight was an abrupt break in the mindless trance I was in. A sudden event triggered a set of memories of the Infinite that pierced through this veil of ignorance and showed me a glimpse of the vast Universe beyond my perceived mortality.

If our goal is to learn about our essential nature and wake up to our true selves, once we become fully aware of who we truly are and learn to control the vital energies of our mind/body/spirit axis, we are then capable of creating what is called the "Light Body" in many spiritual traditions. When we realize that we are truly Light and Consciousness, we stop identifying with our physical appearance. Every atom in our body is borrowed from the Earth and will return to the Earth. The more we realize this and evolve, the more activated our light body becomes and the more we are "a light unto ourselves," rendering this cycle complete. At this point we can choose to be reborn or not but our conscious awareness comes with us and the veil of darkness (and more appropriately ignorance) is lifted.

Things vs. Experiences

What if our goal was to collect experiences on this planet, not things, or to share wonderful stories and have great laughs. What if we are here to discover ourselves all over again and find the majestic beauty in being and not doing all of the time. We can spend our lives hoarding a bunch of useless crap or traveling the world and hiking through the mountains. The problem is that most people have given up on fixing the world so they have resolved to live a life of mediocrity whether they know it or not. Either you decide the direction of your life or your TV will do it for you.

WAKE UP AND LIVE.
In the last 200 years, we have drained the world's resources and polluted the planet at an unprecedented rate. The writing is on the wall. This cannot last. Life is driving us to evolve to higher states of consciousness and to reward positive traits. Stopping the insanity starts with each one of us.

Buy local organic produce and enjoy meals with your family and friends. Spend more time in nature and see how it affects your state of mind. Things literally wake up in people once they have been out in nature for a while. We essentially start to harmonize with the vibrations of the plants and minerals. Our chaotic energy begins to calm down and our mind starts to settle. With a calmer nervous system, the circulatory system becomes more efficient and our general health begins to improve. We want less things and are happy with the experience of life- living it to its fullest.

Here's a simple little exercise:

Go out into nature and find yourself a river or a stream. Make sure there is running water you can hear. Simply sit and listen to the water flowing until your thoughts begin to silence. When all you can hear is the river, then it is time get up. Practice this a number of times and allow the beauty and majesty of nature to cleanse and calm your energy field. What a wonderful start to this journey…

※

CHAPTER FOUR

BASIC TAOIST THEORY MADE SIMPLE

The Way gave birth to the One.
The One gave birth to the Two.
The Two gave birth to the Three.
And the Three gave birth to the ten thousand things...
—*Lao Tzu.* Tao Te Ching, *Chapter 42*

aoism is the philosophy of syncing up with nature and doing that which comes naturally. It is very similar to the traditions of Naturism and Shamanism with a fundamental distinction—it bases its primary understanding of reality on the principle of balance. This balance is between the forces of Yin and Yang. These complementary opposites exist in an ever-changing and flowing dynamic state that constantly self-corrects and harmonizes. The ancient philosophers of China used the term "Tao" for the Supreme Ultimate or the Universe as we know it. It is the All. In the beginning, there was Wu Wei or the Great Emptiness and from this came Yin and Yang.

Yin / Yang Symbol

YIN AND YANG

Everything in the Universe has a Yin and Yang component to it and all things have a balance point. For example, there is no meaning to the word "up" if the concept of "down" didn't exist. There is no "hot" without "cold." This primordial distinction not only relates to everything around us, it is also what fundamentally drives the motion within us. We, being an active functional aspect of nature, exemplify the same polar balancing and, with sustained attention to this subject matter, can find the Tao, or the balance point in all things.

Essentially, there was the original state of the Universe wherein all things were One. There was Unity consciousness and Eternal togetherness of all things and then, BOOM—Polarization. All things all at once are imbued with this elementary concept and perception of separation. This is the mark of polarity. Now, it is critical to remember that these poles are the seemingly opposite characteristics of the same objects or things. This is the polarity that gives us a Dualistic view of the same phenomena. Yin and Yang are constituent parts or mirror reflections of the same One which is simply split into two, the same way a beam of light splits when hitting a prism. This is a concept that will become very important in the ensuing chapters and, suffice it to say, bears mentioning here. In the beginning and in the end, it is all Tao. Polarity is just the game we are playing.

Let's go through some basic examples of yin and yang so that we can better illustrate this concept.

YIN	YANG
Earth	Sun
Cold	Hot
Down	Up
Matter	Energy
Female	Male
Passive	Active
Soft	Hard
Body	Spirit
Materialism	Spiritualism
Science	Religion

Yin and Yang Examples

These are obvious examples but will help further illustrate a point in our understanding of human nature. Namely, the distinctions we make in our approach to self-growth and enlightenment. We are either on one end or another in our culture. Either you work for Wall Street and drive the big cars or you wear patchouli and tour with the band. Either you are a Democrat or Republican, for Abortion or against it, patriotic or unpatriotic, with us or against us...

The mark of our society is one that is stained with the rigidity of dualistic thinking and we suffer from its intolerance daily in our public discourse.

GRAY IS WHERE THE GOOD STUFF HAPPENS

Gray is the fusion of Black and White/Yin and Yang. It is the understanding that there is balance, communication, and interaction with all things at all times. We, in the United States live in a culture that was started by a group of religious fundamentalists (Puritans). Sex was evil and women were witches. Everything was Black or White and there was judgment all around. It was neither fun nor tolerant. We are still living in the shadow of that polarized ideology, and the national discourse echoes that imbalance. The insanity of the Red Team/Blue Team mentality has allowed us to stray from our humanity and has watered down the quality of human intellectual interaction, the meeting of ideas, and peaceful disagreement. Fundamentalism (in all religions and creeds) is a child of this imbalance, a reflection of our collective ignorance.

As Above, So Below
> —Alchemical Axiom Attributed to Hermes Trismegistus

To attain balance in our lives and the world around us, it is important to realize that we must first establish that state within ourselves. The external is an emanation of the internal. We are the holographic projectors and the "reality" we see beyond our flesh and blood is simply the reflection of our internal state.

Yin and Yang represent the totality of creation from opposite sides of each other. Together, they are whole, and together, there is balance. One cannot exist without the other and we cannot examine anything without a balanced frame of reference, which is looking at both sides and finding the middle. The polarity created by Yin and Yang can be compared to the "Breath of Life" in biblical texts. At first, there is only Tao in this differentiation. Then, movement begins and the energy of life starts to stir and revolve around itself, swirling myriad things in the Universe into being. It is as if a centrifugal and centripetal force erupted simultaneously both creating and destroying…rising and falling…growing and decaying. In balance, the Universe sustains itself and grows slowly in sentience and capacity. We can compare it to an oak tree. It grows a bit every year and then sheds weak branches in the autumn, which then become mulched as compost for its own growth the following season. The early Taoists learned everything from observing nature, deep introspection, inner energy cultivation, and developing gnosis. Gnosis is defined as the inner knowing of truth by a mystically enlightened human being. They discovered the principle of Yin and Yang to be the driving force of all life and this concept is inextricably linked to everything else we will discuss in this chapter.

If we look at Yin and Yang as two inverted waves that are flowing along a central axis, we get an image like this:

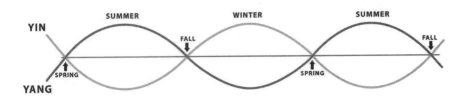

Yin and Yang Seasonal Interplay

In this depiction, we see the interplay of the seasons and how they relate to the rising and falling tides of Yin and Yang. The Equinox points are when the forces come together on the axis and the Solstices are at the extremes of one or the other. If we take this interplay and add an element of torsion, or twisting, into a three dimensional model, we end up with something that looks like this:

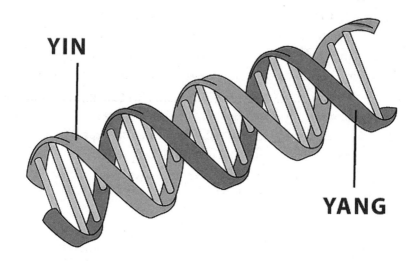

YIN

YANG

The Double Helix of DNA resembles the Interplay of Yin and Yang

This double helix model of DNA serves as the information storehouse for all life on this planet, and the interplay of these stands dictates which proteins are synthesized and how we express physiologically in nature. This remarkable dance between the polar forces directs the language of internal energetic communication and becomes the basis of much of our transformational work down the line.

THE THREE TREASURES

Once the Universe is split into the polarized binary system of Yin and Yang, then there arises a distinction between the different levels of material manifestation. If Spirit and Matter, which at the level of the Tao are one and the same, are separated with the birth of Yin and Yang, then we start to see a scale of densification versus illumination. Remember, Yin and Yang are relative to each other always. There is no Absolute Yin to speak of...things are only Yin compared to something else. One can say "hot" when it's 100 degrees out and one could say that is very "yang" but that's assuming there's an understanding that an average day is say 72 degrees. Then, a 100-degree day would certainly be more yang in this instance but what if we compared that to a 350-degree oven or the surface of the sun? Then the 100-degree day is suddenly more Yin compared to these.

In regards the "gradient" from Spirit to Matter, we can illustrate it like so:

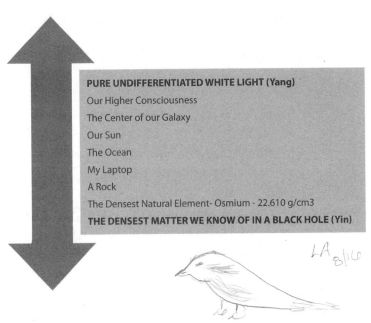

PURE UNDIFFERENTIATED WHITE LIGHT (Yang)
Our Higher Consciousness
The Center of our Galaxy
Our Sun
The Ocean
My Laptop
A Rock
The Densest Natural Element- Osmium - 22.610 g/cm3
THE DENSEST MATTER WE KNOW OF IN A BLACK HOLE (Yin)

Density gradient From Spirit to Matter

Now if we are to take this gradient as an example, then we can hold it as a frame of reference for the Taoist understanding of the "Three Treasures"— Jing, Qi, and Shen. Using a similar spectral differentiation as above, we can illustrate the relationship of these as such:

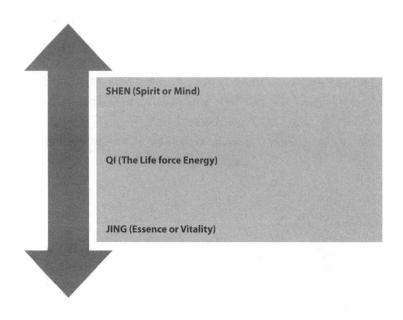

The Three Treasures gradient

In this depiction, we see that the polarization of Spirit and Essence creates the currency of life (the Qi energy). It is the medium or language of communication of All That Is. This is why it is so powerful to work with Qi. When we understand the dynamics of Qi flow in our bodies, we can then begin the Alchemical process of bringing the poles of Spirit and Essence back to a balanced equilibrium. In the duality-free stillness, we have direct access to the Zero Point Energy Field and are capable rewriting the code of how we manifest in 3D via our DNA. A common example used that is quite useful is to compare these to a candle wherein the wax is the Essence, the flame is the Energy, and the aura around the flame is the Spirit.

The Candle as a Metaphor

The goal is to preserve the Essence (wax) and sustain a healthy flow of Energy (flame) so that the Spirit (aura) can soar. This is a simplistic example and much will be said about this in Part Three but before we go there, let's look at each of these "Treasures" individually.

Personal Journeys—Putting Out the Flame

MY KUNG FU teacher sat us down one day to teach us how to put out a candle from a distance. He turned off the lights and set up a candle about three feet away from him. He then gave us specific instruction on how to breathe and move our *qi* energy in order to put out the flame. He then demonstrated and knocked the flame out from a distance.

We were amazed but quickly postulated that he was moving the air with his fast moving hand. We figured that he was fanning out the flame. So he took a couple steps back and did it again. We were still thinking of the physics when he smiled and took another *few* steps back and did it again.

He then began to walk out of the room with a smirk on his face. Just before he was out he turned and said, "You need to connect the energy of your heart with the flame and become one with it. Feel the element of fire within you and *know* it. Then you can extinguish it with your mind and intention."

It took several months of trying to punch the flame out before we started to understand what he was talking about…

Jing—Essence

Jing is the essential vitality that is stored in our bodies. Remember, the Taoist understanding of reality is intimately tied with the internal understanding of our bodies and the movement of the life force through us. Jing is the most Yin of the Three Treasures and it represents the core of our material existence. It is a most precious substance that is to be cherished and guarded.

Very similar to the way that polarity created the spectrum of energy to matter, the Essence is differentiated as well. We have our "Pre-Heaven" Essence, our "Post-Heaven" Essence and our "Day-to-Day" Essence. They can be illustrated like this:

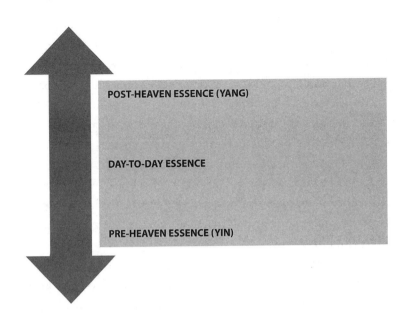

Essence gradient

PRE-HEAVEN ESSENCE

This is the essence that comes from the blending of the sexual energies of our mother and father. This is the energy that nourishes the embryo and the fetus during pregnancy and essentially comes downstream from our ancestral DNA. It determines our individual, constitutional make-up, strength and vitality and is what makes us each unique. [Maciocia, 1989] It's the hand we've been dealt through mom and dad. There is a tremendous amount of history, information, and karma that comes through our bloodlines via the DNA that gets registered at this level of our Essence. Some people are blessed and many others have come in with a number of challenges in regards to this. Now, this is the aspect of the Essence that's the most challenging to increase, and much of the information in Part Two of this book will unlock the secrets of how we can do just that through the practice of Qi Gong. Suffice it to say, this is an integral piece of the puzzle and must be addressed in our energetic cultivation.

What we come in with

POST-HEAVEN ESSENCE

This form of Essence is attributed to our lifestyles and is quite changeable. The Post-Heaven Essence is what we derive from foods and fluids after birth. It's what we do with ourselves once we've come into the world. It has a lot to do with early-stage development and the quality of our nourishment from our birth onwards. There is a great deal to say about this topic in regards to healthy bacterial colonies in the gut, breast feeding, quality of foods, and the loving environment a child is brought into, and there's a whole chapter devoted to this in Part Two of this book. We can't really help what happened before conception or during our infantile development (of course we can do so for our children), but we certainly can help what we do with it from here.

This aspect of the Essence really can be cultivated and positively affected by lifestyle and practice as well. In fact, it is a critical aspect of our practice to continually refine our Essence and increase the amount of condensed Jing to work with.

DAY-TO-DAY ESSENCE

If we were to use money as a metaphor, the Pre-Heaven Essence would be a locked away Family Trust account that we know is there, yet is relatively inaccessible in our day-to-day dealings. Our Post-Heaven Essence would be our money market saving account; we can tap into it, but at a price. And then our Day-to-Day Essence would be our checking account—being deposited to and drawn upon daily for our various needs.

Being derived from the other two types of Essence, this variety is stored in the kidneys, but "having a fluid nature it also circulates all over the body, particularly in the 8 Extraordinary Vessels" [Maciocia, 1989]. It can tap into both the Pre- and Post-Heaven reserves and replenish itself and it serves as the body's primary backup system. In other words, when the Qi (or energy) of a given system starts to become diminished, the Kidney Essence is able to reinforce it by flowing through the eight extraordinary meridians into the primary channel that is deficient. It acts as the reinforcement for all of the body's energies like a backup battery that supports our systems when there is an outage. You can also think of it as the overdraft protection account on your checking. Now that being said, it is critical to keep this system healthy for day-to-day functioning in order to maintain health, but if we want to enhance our health and state of being, then that is where the practice of Qi Gong serves its purpose. We shouldn't barely be making ends meet every day, but instead, must be in a state of relative overflow and abundance. This will then give us the energy we need to cultivate strong Light Bodies and open up our perception.

So although this form of Essence is the easiest to access and can be more readily restored, it is still considered Jing in our scale of density. It is the baseline backup system for the Qi or energy flow of the body. Going back to our money metaphor, in relation to the other aspects of Essence, our day-to-day is more liquid but in relation to our Qi or Energy flow, it is like a fixed savings account. Again, notice how Yin and Yang are always relative and how they create a spectrum for comparison. Essence is denser than Energy and is therefore less "liquid" in cash flow terms. Our Essence is our equity. Yes, we can borrow against it … but at a cost. The point is to store it up and create an endowment that propels us into eternity.

Qi Energy

Moving up in refinement from the denser Essence, we have our second "treasure," which is our Energy. This can be likened to all of the metabolic and physiological processes in the body that are constantly running. This Qi Energy is the currency of life. It is always moving and in flux. It is traveling through an energetic matrix or network of channels throughout the body we call the meridians. These pathways of energy flow have been known for thousands of years by the Taoist masters and are the basis for the practice of acupuncture, which has become increasingly popular in the West mostly due to the excellent results people see with it.

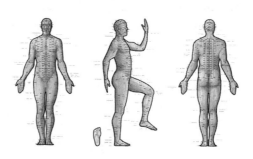

Acupuncture Meridian Pathways

Taking the example of the candle, the Energy is the flame. It is what sets things in motion. An unlit candle can be considered potential energy but it takes that spark of life to get things moving and really make a candle fulfill its purpose, which in this case would be to light up a room. Our energy works in very much the same way. It is the life force that comes into a fertilized embryo (once spirit is imbued with matter) that really gets the show on the road and it's that same Energy that carries us through our adult lives helping to fulfill our purpose.

Now, the ancient Taoist masters spent countless hours meditating, cultivating, and studying these phenomena and we have come to understand that there are several types or qualities of this Energy to speak of.

ORIGINAL QI

This form of Energy is essentially the energetic equivalent of Essence. It is Essence transformed into Energy. Being a dynamic and rarified form of Pre-Heaven Essence it is essentially the foundation of all the Yin and Yang energies of the body. The Original Qi serves many purposes in the body being almost like a firestarter. When other forms of energy are incorporated into the system, it is this Original Qi that "activates" them and sets things in motion. In turn, it is constantly nourished and replenished by the other "Post-Heaven" sources of energy, which we are about to discuss. It is housed in the "Gate of Vitality" between the two kidneys and becomes a very important and active agent in our practice of Qi Gong.

FOOD QI

As the name suggests, this is the energy we derive from the food that we eat. This is the essential first step to having healthy energy flow in the body and it stresses the importance of having a clean and healthy diet. This is where the Stomach receives and the Spleen and the Pancreas transform our food into a usable form of energy, which then travels up to the lungs to mix with air.

GATHERING QI

This is the form of energy that, housed in the chest, is derived from the Food Qi mixing with air. Once the raw ingredients from ingested food are assimilated, they need to mix with air to form this type of energy. This stands as a testament to the genius of the ancient Taoists. In modern bio-chemistry, we know that in part of the digestive process there is a remarkable relationship with a symbiotic cell type called the mitochondria, which creates what we call the Electron Transport Chain. [Shier, 1996, pp. 107-111] Essentially, this is an energy accelerator that allows us to use oxygen in a very dynamic process to help extract large amounts of energy out of simple sugars. Prior to this system, all life on this planet worked anaerobically (without the use of oxygen) and the evolution of this cycle enabled eukaryotic cells (of which we mainly consist) to develop efficient energy extraction systems. This was the beginning of the evolutionary pathway to more elaborate and complicated multi-cellular structures of which we are the end result. The ancient Taoists did not speak in this language but they could literally see how these energetic currents moved through the human body and developed a complicated and accurate model to describe it.

This Gathering Qi serves to nourish the heart and lungs as well as flowing downwards to aid the kidneys. It is just as important as the energy we derive from food and this becomes the emphasis of much of our Qi Gong, or energy work in Part Two. The cultivation of energy and healthy oxygenation of the system are intricately tied to one another.

TRUE QI

This is the form of energy that is the end product of the above-mentioned processes. When the Gathering Qi is formed, it is activated by the Origi-

93

nal Qi (which we called the firestarter) and from this interaction True Qi results. This is the undifferentiated form of energy in the body, which then branches off to perform the various functions required by the system. This True Qi takes on two forms in the body: the Nutritive Qi, and the Defensive Qi.

NUTRITIVE QI

This is the type of energy that circulates internally and nourishes all of the internal organs. It is closely related with the blood and, in fact, flows with the blood to bring energy to all the systems of the body. There is nothing in the body that does not interface with this form of energy, as it is the main "currency" of internal nourishment. Think of the True Qi as the total revenues a country gets from taxes (food, air, water, and Essence). In this example, Nutritive Qi would be the domestic spending on cities, bridges, infrastructure, hospitals, etc. It is designated to nourish the interior.

DEFENSIVE QI

If the Nutritive Qi is the domestic spending, then this form of energy is the armed forces and border patrol. It protects the exterior from pathogenic invasion and regulates the body temperature by controlling the opening and closing of pores on the skin. It is the gatekeeper to the body and needs to remain charged and healthy in order to keep us protected. At any given time, we are surrounded by billions of hostile microorganisms that would quickly invade and devastate our systems if it were not for this form of energy. It regulates immunity through the skin and mucous membranes, and is itself regulated by the Lungs, while being supported by the Essence and Original Qi.

Sounds like a complicated picture but it really isn't too bad. Let's look at an illustration that will help us better understand this system:

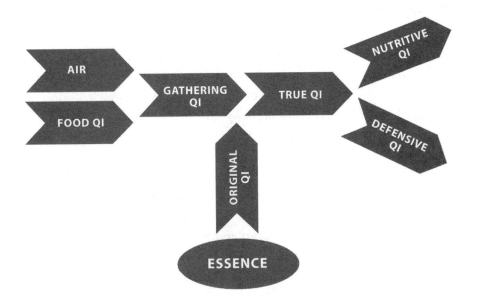

The Creation of Qi in the Body

This basic system very adequately explains the flow of how the body's energies develop and are maintained. It also paints a picture of the complexity of the process. It is almost impossible to routinely eat terrible foods and successfully practice energy cultivation because the Food Qi sits at the foundation of this entire process. It is also important to note that this system of inter-related energies is very much like an ecosystem that needs to be maintained. A weak Defensive Qi will either come from a weak True Qi level, or if it has simply weakened through continual assault, will eventually drain the True Qi, which backs it up at the expense of the Nutritive Qi. Taking this example on the macro scale, we have a whole host of problems in a country that can no longer pay for domestic programs (Nutritive Qi) because of a long expensive war (Defensive Qi) that is draining resources (True Qi). Combine that with a faltering economy (Low Gathering Qi) with a smaller tax base, we suddenly get hit by both sides and have a crises on our hands. Sound familiar? As Above, So Below…

Shen (Spirit)

The last of the "Three Treasures" is the one the West is enamored by: the realm of Spirit. It is the paradise to which we run in the West. So it is really important to broach this subject correctly because we're walking into very polarized territory. What do I mean by this?

Well, we live in a culture (Western Judeo-Christian-Islamic) thinking that humankind lives in a paradigm outside of the garden. Again, we were ejected somehow (or so says our creation myth) and we have to behave and do as told (even kill in the name of our God) in order to earn the rights to be allowed back into Heaven—"Heaven" being this off-planet realm where God and all of His Angels hang out and watch us from "above." We have bought into a storyline that pegs us as pathetic, materialistic sinners who are essentially wretches that need salvation. We have to petition for Divinity to intervene and "save" us from our evil human nature, which is obviously despicable. [Lash, 2006]

So let's carefully tiptoe through this mess because that is not how we Taoists see it. Actually, there are billions of other people on this planet who see it differently and, having traveled the world a fair amount, they seem happier than us. And no, they're not sacrificing human babies and chucking virgins into the local volcano, they are earning their daily bread and hanging out with family and loved ones. They are happy to see each other and are kind to guests. That is the world we were born into. Somehow things have gotten messy in the West where we feel justified in killing each other over interpretations of the same book.

The Taoist concept of Spirit does not exist within some far-off realm where we'll go for some kind of afterlife reward if we behave here on earth. On the contrary, it is right here and now. Remember, Tao differentiated into Yin and Yang—Spirit and Matter—therefore, Matter is nothing without Spirit. They are complementary opposite views of the same life. When we cultivate Shen (which is also translated as Mind) in our Taoist practice, we only do so by holding the critical anchor of Jing and the smooth flow of Qi intact. Stated another way, we cultivate the Essence in the body and make it robust with life and vitality, then we use this efficiency and excess of energy to refine Spirit further and further. This does not mean venturing into magical realms and talking to spirits (which is certainly possible in astral travel). It means developing a deeper understanding of reality here and now. The more we potentiate our Essence and condense it in our kidneys, the more we can see the Universe for what it really is. Like a mighty oak tree that sends its tap roots deeper and deeper into the ground, we can use these incredible bioelectric "generators" of energy we call our bodies to literally "turn on the light" and wake up.

When you realize how perfect everything is, you will tilt your head back and laugh at the sky.
—The Buddha

When the Buddha was asked what Enlightenment felt like he simply stated that he "woke up." Chances are that you've already had a number of moments where you too "woke up." Sometimes it is even sustained for a longer period, but the sleepy state of ignorance keeps creeping back in…like a spiritual gravity sinking us back to the lull of a sleepy zombie. In this practice, we carefully cultivate the Essence and refine the Spirit to stay awake and live in that state perpetually. This comes with an activated Light Body, which we will discuss in detail later on. Our practice of taking the lead of our personal experience and transmuting it into the gold of spiritual awakening is the key to this process. This metaphor applies to the Great Work in two ways here:

1. It implies that we are to take our dense and powerful stores of Essence and refine them into pure undifferentiated Shen. This does not mean using it like a tank of gas and burning it away, but instead connotes fusing it with Spirit by bringing Yin and Yang together. We must wake up our Eternal Nature in every atom of our body and impregnate our material base with its spiritual counterpart, so we may unlock incredible reserves of energy to wake up and shine. *BALANCE*

2. The lead to gold metaphor is also applied to taking the lead of the unresolved energies in our shadow and releasing it. It involves bringing the skeletons out of our closets and making things right in our lives. Once

Shadow/PAST INT - holds onto E that we could be using positively.

97

we release these hidden things, we'll have opened up room for the Source energy to flow freely through us again. This is the other side of the practice where we must, with our newfound energy released from our Qi Gong, apply the light of conscious awareness to the blind spots in our shadow.

The refinement of Essence into Spirit unleashes a tremendous amount of energy, which will eventually be fed into our shadow if we remain mindless. This will then rapidly highlight and magnify all of the problems we are having in our lives because they will now have so much more to feed upon. Therefore, it is critical to practice both sides of this equation. The energy work gives us more power to apply to waking up, but only if we stay focused on doing so!

In the next section, we are going to study the concept of the Five Elements in Taoist thinking. These are the flavors through which reality emanates once movement begins with Yin and Yang. But it is important to relay another fine point about the concept of Shen before we do so. The Five Elements differentiate the Shen into five aspects—remembering that all material manifestations will naturally mirror a spiritual quality. The five aspects of Spirit are:

1. FIRE (Shen)—The central notion of what we would consider Spirit here in the West. Fire is the house of the attention where the Mind/Spirit focuses its gaze. It is also the seat of compassion and love, which are the energies that intimately connect us with all Life. Housed in the heart.

2. EARTH (Yi)—The concept of the Intellect—the mind and its powerful facility for concentration. Also our ability to digest concepts and ideas. Housed in the Spleen.

3. WATER (Zhi)—The Will or Intention—the driving force of our manifestation of inner wishes and our ability to transform these desires into tangible reality. Housed in the Kidneys.

4. WOOD (Hun)—The house of the "Ethereal Soul," which is the aspect of our consciousness that helps reconcile the interface between the Heart's desires and the physical reality that surrounds us. This is largely the aspect of us that is involved in astral travel and it does a good deal of problem solving while we are asleep. It is housed in the Liver.

5. METAL (Po)—The house of the "Corporeal Soul" which connects us more to the body and its lessons. Metal represents the energy of decline— the fall is when things return to the earth and get mulched. This aspect of the soul deals with grief and letting go. It is housed in the Lungs.

So the Shen or Spirit, like all other things in this practice, is differentiated along the spectrum of the Five Elements.

THE FIVE ELEMENTS

Once the Tao splits into Yin and Yang, it also manifests in five distinct flavors of emanation, which we call the Five Elements. The early Taoists were insightful observers of their natural environment and understood that there was no separation between man and the natural world. They made keen observations about the cycles and patterns of nature, and this led to a profound understanding of medicine, agriculture, astronomy, astrology, martial arts, and philosophy. Nature lies at the very core of the Taoist understanding of the Universe.

The exceptional shamanic teacher Alberto Villoldo has noted that the indigenous peoples of this planet never saw themselves as being ejected outside of the garden, but as stewards of the natural world. [Villoldo, 2000]

Through a personal connection with nature and detailed observation of the seasons and the movement of the stars through the sky, the ancient Taoists understood all reality to be represented by Five Elements. These elements related to material, emotional, and spiritual matters in that they represented the entirety of our experience on our planet. But it is always important to remember that they are all aspects of the One—that pure realm of consciousness that exists in an un-polarized, wholly integrated state. Through differential emanation, the Five Elements represent the flavor and richness of life and how it moves and expresses itself. Remember, before the separation into Yin and Yang, there was the formless and unified whole, the Tao. The split into Yin and Yang created movement. With Yin and Yang, there are two complementary and opposing forces that dynamically flux into one another. They create the dance of life. All things move and exist through this dance, as it is the very agent of the life force itself. Now, Yin and Yang have further differentiated into the Five Elements, which give life its flavor and richness. They give a broader array of qualities and characteristics to the Universe and increase the depth of our physical experience. The following table gives us a basic impression of these elements, the broad range of their correspondence with the world, and how they map our experience of nature and ourselves.

Element	Fire	Metal	Water	Wood	Earth
Color	Red	White	Blue/Black	Green	Yellow
Flavor	Bitter	Spicy	Salty	Sour	Sweet
Season	Summer	Fall	Winter	Spring	None
Internal Organs	Heart/Small Intestine	Lungs, Large Intestine	Kidneys Bladder	Liver, Gallbladder	Stomach, Spleen
Directions	South	West	North	East	Center
Emotions	Joy	Sadness	Fear	Anger	Pensiveness
Stage of Development	Growth	Harvest	Storage	Birth	Transformation
Virtues	Righteousness	Propriety	Courage	Benevolence	Faith
Planets	Mars	Venus	Mercury	Jupiter	Saturn
Sense Organs	Tongue	Nose	Ears	Eyes	Mouth
Tissues	Vessals	Skin	Bones	Sinews/Tendons	Muscles
Sounds	Laughing	Crying	Groaning	Shouting	Singing

Five Element Correspondences

We will actually be using much of this information later when we discuss how to troubleshoot problems with this framework, and more importantly, how to correct energetic imbalances using this system.

The Five Elements provide us with a greater degree of distinction on where any given thing, subject, or thought will be within its balance point of Yin and Yang. They show where the flow of energy is and how it is expressing at any given time. Allow me to illustrate this with a number of diagrams here.

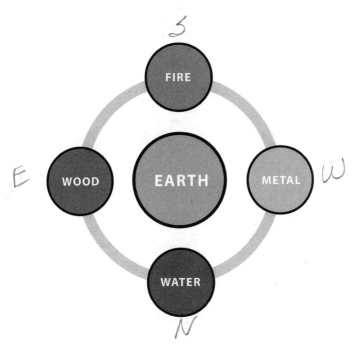

Basic Five Elements Diagram

This is a basic diagram of the Five Elements and their relationship with each other. It is important to note that in the Qi Gong system we will be studying shortly, it is recommended that we stand facing the south for our practice. This explains why we diagrammatically place the Fire element on top and Water below. Assuming we are standing in the Earth position, facing South would put Fire in front of us with Metal to our right, Water behind, and Wood to our left. Again, we will use this information in the next couple of chapters when we learn how to cultivate these energies and balance them within us.

This particular representation shows the essential alignment of the elements but does not show the movement of these energies until we introduce the principles of Yin and Yang to the equation. Once there is movement (through polarity), we begin to see the cycles of nature manifest and we then have the Four Seasons.

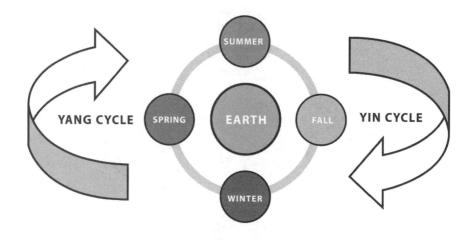

The Five Elements with Yin & Yang ——> Movement

So in this diagram, the Earth element represents the center around which all of the other elements revolve. Notice how the seasonal elemental correspondences are closely tied to the increase and decline of energy in the annual cycle. The Yang energy rises out of the winter, comes to a balance point in the spring and is at its full expression in the summer before if begins to decline back through the fall and eventually to the cold, quiet, stillness of winter. Similarly, the Yin energy picks up at the Summer Solstice and gains momentum through the fall. It is at its height in the winter and then slowly fades through the spring as the Yang energy comes up. Notice that this entire system is simply a circular spectral representation of the movement of Yin and Yang in nature. It is all the same phenomena, as there is ultimately only one reality.

Now this system is remarkably similar to many Native American spiritual and medicinal traditions, and, in fact, with proper understanding, they can be used interchangeably. Nature is nature—period. Different cultures have evolved to understand and interpret its movement in a slightly different way but we all understand what winter is no matter where we are from. Of course there is less fluctuation of these seasons at the equator (where the forces of yin and yang are more balanced) and there is more abrupt change at the poles.

The preceding diagrams give us a relatively simple framework for understanding the Five Elements and their interactions with each other, according to the Taoist system. They give us a reference point for our energetic practice, and they ground the entire system into something we can all relate to—nature. Taking the cardinal directions out of the equation, we then have an overlay of this elemental system on the human body, which the Taoists consider to be a microcosm of the entire Universe. The following cycle is what we call the Generating Cycle. It comes from the observation and understanding that the energy of nature flows through this particular sequence.

The Generating or Nourishing Cycle

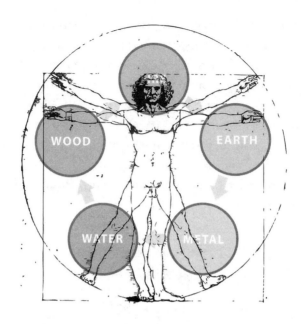

The Five Elements Overlay the Human Body

Wood catches Fire or decomposes and turns to Earth, which over time settles to Metal (minerals), which then returns to Water (aquifer or rivers), and finally nourishes Wood (plants and biomass). The cycle repeats endlessly. In this system, we call Wood the "child" of Water and simultaneously Wood is the "mother" of Fire. This system allows us to understand the proper sequence of our current situation and how that relates to the overall cycle of things. For example, say we are having digestive problems (Earth) due to a weak system. We can obviously help bring energy to the Earth element—which is the primary afflicted element—but we can also put energy "upstream" into the Fire element, which will then naturally flow into the Earth element as well. Along the same lines, maybe the Metal element is what is really weak and it's draining energy out of the earth element "downstream." In this case, we address the issue with the Metal element and the Earth energy should fill back up naturally. It is important to note that in a cycle of life, a disharmony along any point in the circle has repercussions throughout the entire system. This applies to our minds, our bodies, our families, and our planet. The point is that everything applies to everything in the cycle of the elements and that is why we must constantly strive to maintain balance and harmony in everything that we do.

The Generating Cycle (also called the Nourishing Cycle) helps us see the correct flow of energy through the five elements and to understand how that energy pertains to us and our circumstances. This brings us back to the concept of basic awareness in all things. To properly perceive what's going on around us, we need to look at the bigger picture and see the larger cycles of energetic movement that all things are related to. Only with this sort of "bird's eye view" can we understand the nature of our circumstances and help bring harmony to energetic cycles that are oftentimes larger than us.

Using the same basic framework, there is one more important relationship among the Five Elements: the Controlling Cycle. This cycle shows the checking or controlling functions of the elements and how they relate to each other.

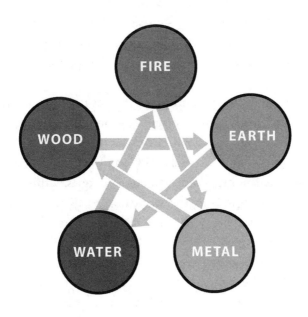

The Controlling Cycle

In this sequence, Wood controls Earth, which in turn controls Water and so forth. What this means is that we can use a checking element to control another element that has excessive energy and is out of balance. For example, someone who is very stressed out has an overactive Wood element (liver or gall bladder), which can be controlled by the Metal element (lungs and large intestine). So introducing energy into the Metal organs can help control the overactive Wood which can easily exert a negative influence on the Earth element (stomach and spleen). We see this all too often in the modern world where people who are chronically stressed out end up having digestive problems. In chronic conditions, the Metal element gets drained because it's constantly trying to exert control over the overactive Wood element. Because of this, we will also see a decline in the Metal element, which oftentimes manifests as colds/flus (lungs) or constipation/diarrhea (large intestines).

This cycle is also very helpful in understanding the interplay of emotions and our mental health. For example, if a given person is overcome by the emotion of fear (Water element), then it is overcontrolling the Fire element (joy) and draining that system as well. We can come in then with some Earth energy to pacify the fear and breathe energy into the corresponding organs and see a radical change in that person. That is the basis of Taoist magic.

The only way to learn this and to get it right is to assume this mystery person is you. All healing must originate from within. One of my great Masters, Sifu Carl Totton, often tells us: "First help yourself, then help the people." Much of our internal Nei Gong (or inner alchemy) involves learning how to harmonize these elemental energies within ourselves and use our bodies and minds as the workshop to figure it out and get it right. Once you learn this (and you will by the end of this book), then the ability to help another person is the natural extension of this skill. First we allow the flow of radiant light to return inside ourselves and then we shine it out to help others. Many people will try to save the world without addressing their own energy first. In my experience, this is where most seekers fail in our modern culture. Even in our charity and benevolence, we use the "outside" world as our frame of reference and point the inner eye outwards for information and salvation. The central tenet of Taoist alchemy is to turn the light of awareness inward and to explore the universe within you. From this infinity within, we are then able to unlock all the secrets of the outer world and understand our true nature. From within we find Heaven.

THE TEN THOUSAND THINGS

From the emanation of the Tao we have Yin and Yang, the Three Treasures, and then the processes of the Five Elements. These lead to the fundamental spiritual, energetic, and material framework of all that exists in the Universe. It is the code, so to speak, of Creation and co-creation through which all things come in and out of existence. In our day-to-day lives, most of us live in the world of the "ten thousand things." We are drowning in the minutia of the reflections of creation and we are sliding further and further from the natural world from whence we came. Our Western creation myths teach us to dominate nature and fear our sexuality. Our polarized minds show us struggle and discord everywhere we look and this becomes the basis of our hologram. This becomes the foundation for the thing we call the "world" in which we live. That world, much of which is mutually agreed upon by cultural beliefs and religious norms, becomes the essence of our understanding of reality. We see the reflection and lose the Source. The Source, in Taoist thinking, is not some "extraterrestrial off planet god" (coined by John Lamb), but the Spirit of Nature Herself. [Lash, 2006] Taoists don't proclaim that there is a Creator or a Diety that kicked down a bunch of rules, but very much like the Buddha, ask us to observe and see for ourselves. Watch nature. Focus on your internal energy within your body and trace that back to the Source within you. All the answers lie waiting…all the peace comes from within. When the Buddha was asked if there was a God, he simply showed them how to meditate and observe their own minds. His stance was to let them find God themselves or they would never truly know Him.

Returning to nature means returning to balance. Built into the natural world are a series of ingenious safeguards and control mechanisms. The elements feed each other and help control overgrowth or overexpression by checking one-another. Nature finds its own balance and we would be wise to follow suit.

There is an axiom in my tradition which states: "Taoist Way Not Forced." In other words, smile and float downstream with things as they naturally unfold. Being alive is effortless, but we encounter a number of problems in our modern world, many because of our separation from the land. Eat when you're hungry and drink when you're thirsty. Think of it this way; 15,000 years ago, our ancestors lived off the land in small tribal villages located strategically around natural resources or they migrated around following herds of animals throughout the different seasons. Most of life's aspects are pretty predictable, really. Chances are you are going to get hungry at some point in the next three to five hours and you'll probably be thirsty as well. Food and water mean survival (they always have) and the acquisition of these resources was and is the most vital task at hand. Sure, there was competition for resources and the danger of predators in the wild and that surely kept them on their toes (and awake), but the lives of primitive people were pretty much centered around food, water, and survival.

Now, in a given 24-hour period, how many of those hours do you suppose our ancestors had to work for life's necessities? Well apparently, our pre-Neolithic forefathers had it pretty good. Anthropologist Marshall Sahlins called these so-called primitives "the original affluent society." Apparently with a labor of a mere 15 hours a week, hunters and gatherers can provide for all their needs. According to William Irwin Thompson:

> *They have far more leisure time then an agrarian community, caught up as it is in what Marx called "the idiocy of rural life," and they certainly have more leisure time than the harassed factory and office workers of the industrial era. With their population adjusted to carrying capacity of the environment, hunters and gatherers rarely starve, for they are not dependent on the fortunes of a single crop. With their needs so easily provided for, primitive humanity devoted most of its spare time to matters of ritual and art. [Thompson, 1996, p. 120]*

Now with the advent of agriculture, people started to band together in small villages, and resources began to get pooled and traded. The mainstay of all ancient cultures was grains and domesticated animals. It was the cultivation of these grains that led to the marks of what we call "civilization."

As a society, it made us more efficient at extracting food from our environment and allowed us to stay put and call a single place home. According to Jared Diamond, geographic good luck was what led to the technological advance of Middle Eastern cultures and, subsequently, Europe. Diamond argues that the existence of super grains like wheat and barley, and domesticated animals such as cows, ox, pigs, and horses allowed Europeans to get ahead of the technology game and develop specialists like blacksmiths and a dedicated warrior caste. These were the warriors that took the world by storm after years of plagues and crusades. They were innovative and battle-hardened. They took the New World with relative ease and vastly increased the riches of their European nations. Their innovations have pulled us off the land and have created a whole society of "specialists"—buzzing around rendering service to each other in an abstract world filled with complicated interdependencies. It has been said that we can thank the vegetables for bringing us to this point and now, in turn, we have become vegetables ourselves…separated from nature and immobilized in artificial settings staring at two dimensional computer screens with flashing images of the natural scenery we were once a part of. Now nature is a screen saver…

Our advancement in technology has allowed our population to grow, and it has propelled us into a much more stagnant physical existence, and one that is detached from our natural environment. This disconnect from the Source (Nature) has allowed us to become more deluded and confused about our place in the world. It has slowly severed our connection with the gold of our origins and pulled us down into the lead of our confusion.

Transforming our lead to gold means waking up from the delusion that the "ten thousand things" are actually Reality. What we see is a reflection of our best interpretation of Reality based on our limited senses and our limited understanding of how Yin/Yang and the Five Elements work. We wake up to this by examining these forces in our own bodies and seeing how they reflect back to us as the world around us. Our bodies are our quickest path back to the force of all Creation.

The Taoist Way is to stay tuned into your inner voice and the musings of your body. Love your body and take good care of it. Give it water when you're thirsty and eat when you're hungry. Sleep when you're tired and yell when you're mad. It means living life in the moment and not repressing emotions and natural impulses when they express themselves. How many times have you noticed yourself getting nervous because you've had to go to the bathroom for 30 minutes and are still holding it in because you're on the phone? How many times have you witnessed an injustice and not spoken up because you thought that it was not your place? The energy field records these and stores these memories as vibrations that stay in our fields and wreak havoc.

In my experience, many people share a story like this: a guy yells at his girlfriend, a clerk, or his kid in a public setting where you and a number of other people bear witness. You think of speaking up but bite your lip or come up with some excuse in your head about why you should not. The event is over and you've driven off but the story in your head has just begun. You see yourself stepping in and standing up for justice (maybe a pretty girl was there to witness the event). You possibly play out some combat scenario in your head, people notice your bravery... What could have been a simple statement in the present moment became a 40-minute dialogue in your head all the way home. Your shoulders have risen and you have a mild headache by the time you get home...all thanks to the imaginary story in your head that released real stress hormones into your blood stream.

What would have been the Taoist response to this? Say your peace in the moment and move on. What if he punches you or it turns into a crazy scene? Did you stand on the side of justice or not? What's right is right—always. Call him out and then call the cops. Here's a better one though—how about you heal the anger inside yourself and clean the energy around the whole scenario? The Buddhist view of Right Action asks us to abandon harmful thoughts but our actual practice of nonviolence can start altering the world around us. Once we start viewing the world as a wizard, the rules change. All of the petty conflicts and struggles we see in the world around us are merely reflections of US—yes all of us. They are in the collective unconsciousness of our species and as Dr Hew Lin boldly states, if you witness it, then you are responsible for it. [Vitale, 2007] The job of the alchemist is to turn lead to gold. When you see a wound or an imbalance, heal it right then. Don't wait! Clean it up and move on. If it has presented itself to you, then it is your job to heal it. Conversely, if it is not on your radar right now, look back at your own two feet and see what path you're walking on.

I WAS IN THE *pampas*, or swamp lands of Bolivia with a small group of people. We had taken a jungle boat through miles of rivers and tributaries to get to a particularly beautiful area where there was a good deal of wildlife. There were three guides assigned to the group and I had made friends with them quickly. I was trying to practice my Spanish and get to know the locals instead of chattering away with some of the tourists on the boat. I dislike traditional tourism but this was the only way to see what I wanted to see with the amount of time I had left.

There was a sloth in a tree nearby and a group of American girls wanted to get closer for a photo. One of the guides was quite the show-off and he was certainly on stage trying to impress the girls. He suggested that he could climb up the tree and bring the sloth down for a photo. The other guides and I voiced our opinions and told him not to. A sloth a slow-moving monkey-like creature that is indigenous to that area.

He went for it despite our strong dissent. The guy climbed up the tree and started to pull on the sloth's leg. He kept tugging and tugging but the sloth wouldn't budge. This slow-moving creature was so at peace and so harmless, we felt horribly. We kept yelling for him to stop and I got up to go get him and pull him away. I didn't need to travel very far though. It seemed that sloth had had enough and, in an instant, it went from cute slow-moving creature to an animal in the wild with real survival instincts.

BOOM! It was the quickest punch I had ever seen and it nailed the guide right in the nose. He fell about ten feet from the tree and was flat on his back with blood all over his face. The tourists were screaming, the sloth simply went back to his business, and I was doubled over with the other guides, roaring with laughter. We'd told him to let up and leave Nature be. We had to console him and tend to his wounds—wounded face and wounded ego.

The Taoist Way is one of peace, harmony, and honesty. It entails being aware of the cycles and currents of nature and living by those precepts. It demands that we bring balance within ourselves to everything we encounter and act spontaneously out of the living, breathing moment. This serves as the basic framework for our understanding of Taoism. We'll need this for the next few chapters where we are going to roll our sleeves up and start tapping into our vital energy. First we'll need awareness of our energy fields and then we'll correct the imbalances. Once clean, then we get a clear look at our true nature, which is our birthright, and the path in front of us becomes quite easy, actually. Let's take the next step…

※

PART TWO
The Practice

CHAPTER FIVE

TENDING To THE PHYSICAL VEHICLE

To keep the body in good health is a duty...
otherwise we shall not be able to keep our mind strong
and clear.

—Buddha

ur bodies are the temples within which we work to illuminate our understanding of reality. They are the space and time reference points we reside in within the fractal patterning of the Universe at large. Because of the holographic nature of our Universe, any part contains within it the whole—from infinity up to infinity down—it's all the same, it is all the Great Tao.

Caring for our bodies must become the foundation of all holy practice, for our consciousness experiences reality from our physical bodies in the form of visual, auditory, and sensory information. The polarized chasm of Western thought has created an imbalanced view of spiritually that distrusts the body. From a Taoist perspective, this cannot be farther from the Truth. It is vitally important to understand that the fall from the Garden of Eden of Western creation myth is not an idea shared by the naturalistic religions and philosophies of the world. We are the caretakers of the Garden and our bodies serve as the focal point for our practice and understanding of all things.

To reclaim the body's position as the lynchpin of our practice, it is important to address a number a vital aspects of how the body works and what it needs to thrive. In the previous section we discussed the Five Elements and their correspondences with the organ systems of the body. This knowledge is very useful in our understanding how to care for the body. In Chinese medicine, it is said that one is to not administer any acupuncture or herbs unless the basics of diet and lifestyle are addressed. [Dong-Yuan, 2002]

That means no medicine will work if you aren't living right! This is a statement that runs headlong into the beliefs we have in the Western allopathic medicinal model. These basic principles have been perpetuated and reinforced by market interests in the medical field that promise us that we can live how we want, and for as long as we want, junk food and all. We are led to believe that drugs will cure us of anything. The doctor is your emissary to good health (which in this pathological model equates to a lack of disease) and he will save you. This has led an entire nation into a healthcare crisis that is crippling our economy. Diabetes and heart disease are mostly diseases of lifestyle and are huge moneymakers for the medical industry.

The whole system is screwed up because doctors only get paid when people are sick, and drug and insurance companies have voracious appetites for profits. A lifetime patient who subsists on various drugs is worth a bundle to these pharmaceutical firms. The root of the word doctor is from the Latin word docere, meaning "to teach." Most of the doctors I know are too busy dealing with people who are too sick to teach and despite good intentions, are trapped in a bad system. In contrast, the ancient Chinese model emphasizes that you should pay your doctor to keep you healthy.

This approach speaks volumes for the benefits of diet, exercise, stress management, stretching, and any other act of conscious self-care. Remember, it is the separation of Yin and Yang in our perception that has us discussing the body as being separate from our Spirit. They are all one and we are simply speaking of them separately because of semantics.

The Four Wheels

We can essentially break down the concept of a conscious lifestyle into four categories: Diet, Exercise, Sleep, and Mindset.

DIET

We are what we eat, and there is nothing more profound and sacred as our communing with the Earth when we thankfully ingest its bounty into our bodies. Food is the fuel that feeds the energy of the body, and as discussed before, it is Food Qi that is our Post-Heaven foundation of energy. We must eat a healthy diet filled with essential nutrients in order to have a fit and strong body. According to Ling Shu, a foundational book on Chinese medicine, it is when nourishment enters the stomach after birth that sets the initial flow of the energy in the meridians. The food that we eat determines the quality and quantity of energy in our fields and our body's capacity for growth and development.

We should note that food also holds a powerful place in people's blind spots. Food is where many people fall into a trance-like sleep allowing the action to simply fall under the radar. And while it can be difficult to bring unconscious eating habits to light, I have come to understand while working with thousands of patients that people who are able to wake up and actively engage in changing their eating habits are the ones that get better. It is so incredibly easy to fall into an old trance with food that almost everyone does it. To illustrate, I have been to several spiritual events where people are fully engaged in groundbreaking work, but revert back to mindless zombieism during the lunch break. It often takes hours for the instructor to bring them back into the room. That is why most monasteries have built rituals around eating in order to keep the light of awareness on it as much as possible.

Clinical Encounters—A Wake Up Call

A BUSY LAWYER patient of mine had come in to me for severe back pain. He had gained 70 pounds since his father's death and had buried himself in work. I repeatedly spoke with him about diet and exercise but wasn't getting through. One day he came back to my office and told me that he had enrolled in a weight loss program and was taking it very seriously. Happy to hear it and curious about what had finally snapped him out of his trance, I asked him about its trigger.

He replied that he had been going to the same Mexican fast food chain for dinner for years. At one point, he had become so busy that he actually stopped entering the restaurant and switched to the drive-through so he could continue working the phones in his car. This went on for months until for some reason he went in this past time and walked up to the counter and ordered his usual. This girl at the front looked at him in shock. She remembered him from before and hadn't seen the gradual increase in weight. In horror she replied, *"Dios mio! No! No mas! You go home...no mas!"*

My patient was shocked out of his trance. His father had died of a heart attack and here he was putting career in front of his health. The girl at the taco place saved his life!

Here are a few common bad habits with food:

1. MINDLESS EATING

Going into trance or simply talking through a whole meal without any attention on the meal in front of you...We need to cease hypnotically scarfing down meals without stopping to give thanks and think of where this food came from.

2. OVEREATING

It is advisable to stop eating when just over half full. We often consume huge portions with "finish your plate" mentalities. Don't waste food. Simply order less or eat less per sitting and save the rest for a snack later on.

3. BAD CHOICES

Processed foods are out. Frozen dinners are a no-no. Eat live, organic, locally-grown fruits and vegetables in season and never eat conventionally raised meats. Grass-fed and free roaming animals makes for healthier meat choices. The quality of our foods is very important and our overall health depends on it.

4. WAITING TOO LONG

If you're starving by mealtime it means you've waited too long. We make bad food choices when our blood sugar has already crashed so that physiologically, we're in panic mode. We should be eating something every two to four hours depending on our individual constitutions. This way our blood sugar stays stable and the brain doesn't put us into stress mode.

As a general rule, carbohydrates should never be eaten on their own. Essentially, we want to keep our blood sugar stable and provide good quality carbohydrates to our bodies. This means eating foods that are low in the Glycemic Index.

Good Carbohydrates (those low on the Glycemic Index)

Apples	Celery	Peppers
Asparagus	Cucumber	Plums
Beans	Honeydew melon	Snow Peas
Broccoli	Kiwi fruit	Spinach
Blueberries	Leafy greens	Tomatoes
Cabbage	Peaches	Young Summer Squash
Cantaloupe	Peanuts	Zucchini
Citrus Fruits	Pears	*Most non-starchy vegetables*

Eat More of These Foods

Bad Carbohydrates (those high on the Glycemic Index)

Bananas	French Fries	Parsnips
Breads	Fruit juices (eat whole fruit)	Pasta
Carrots	Honey	Potatoes
Cereal with added sugar	Mangoes	Pretzels
Corn	Mashed Potatoes-instant	Raisins
Corn Chips	Oatmeal- instant	Rice- instant
Dates	Pancakes	Sugar
Doughnuts	Papaya	Waffles

Try to Avoid These Foods

It is frustrating to hear one study contradict the next in the wild world of nutrition. Most of these studies generalize what the "average person" should be doing. My recommendation is to apply your personal consciousness and mindfulness to your diet. If you believe a particular food or food group may be bothering you, go off of it completely for three weeks and see how you feel. This is called an "Elimination/Provocation Diet" and we use it for patients who are experiencing forms of food intolerance. With the advent of modern farming practices, more and more people are showing intolerances to gluten (wheat, barley, and rye), dairy, soy, nuts, and other foods. The key is to avoid suspect foods and see how you feel three weeks after you reintroduce them. If your body shows a reaction (fatigue, foul mood, gas, bloating, headaches, nausea, or depression), then you should avoid those foods and let your body thrive without them.

It is important to note that in the Chinese medical system, the digestion is regulated by the Yang, or active aspect of the spleen, which warms and transforms the food. Therefore, it is advised not to eat too many raw uncooked foods, as this creates an additional burden on digestion. Soups, broths, and congees are highly recommended for anyone who is having any signs of digestive insufficiency (gas, bloating, fatigue after meals, mal-absorption).

Water intake is another important consideration. It is recommended that we consume 2.5—3 liters of water per day as a minimum. Spring water is preferable. Green Tea is a wonderful antioxidant and has great health benefits but it is important to not replace water consumption with tea, as this will dehydrate us by stimulating urination. Coffee is too acidic and dehydrating. Water heals by helping to maintain a healthy histamine response, enabling digestive juices to be properly secreted, detoxifying the system, and many more reasons. [Batmanghelidj, 2003] Drinking enough water is critical to all body functions of the body. Many of us run around in a chronically dehydrated state. As far as cultivating energy goes, things will simply not flow correctly without adequate hydration in the system.

If you have digestive problems, there is a chance you have what's called "Leaky Gut Syndrome," which is a condition that arises when the good bacteria in the gut have been compromised. These bacteria are responsible for the regulation of pH (acid/base balance) in the digestive tract and many of their byproducts aid digestion and assimilation. When these colonies get compromised (usually through use of antibiotics and drugs), then the digestive wall gets damaged and larger molecules begin to permeate or slip through the cracks. The body then mounts an immune defense and there's a huge fight in the gut that leads to bloating, swelling, indigestion, and fatigue. [Campbell, 2008] This subsequently leads to whole-body inflammation and a cascade of other diseases if left untreated.

A leaky gut calls to halt the consumption of grains and starchy foods and the ingestion of high dose pre- and probiotics. This will give the system a break while the body heals itself. In my clinical experience, people who suffer from this malady (of which there are many) don't even have the ability to digest the expensive vitamins and minerals they keep buying, and always wonder why they're so tired. They are losing the war going on in their guts! What's worse, undigested proteins from dairy and wheat (casein and gluten) don't get broken down properly and are then leaked into the body as casomorphins and glutomorphins, which are essentially morphine-like molecules that create very real food addictions for us. [Campbell, 2008]

Getting a handle on food isn't just important, it is critical! Follow the basic guidelines in this section and you will see things begin to change almost immediately. This does not take the place of qualified, individualized help though. I've included resources in the Appendix of this book to help you take control of your diet. It is a lifelong study and the good news is that we get several chances to get it right every day. The take-home message for this section is one you've heard before: wake up! Be mindful of your eating habits, pay attention to what you are eating and how you are eating it.

Personal Journeys —Adjust Your Diet to Your Lifestyle

BEFORE I FOUND the Chinese martial arts systems, I practiced some of the Korean arts for a number of years. High kicks and aggressive stretching started to bother my right hip, but I was young and invincible in my deluded mind. Years later, I started to have persistent achy pain after all those thousands of roundhouse kicks.

Busy with school and work, I decided to give my training a break for a number of months and allow my hip to heal. I went from 30 hours or more of aggressive training per week to almost nothing except for some mild yoga. Prior to this, I simply could not eat enough to keep the weight on and probably had the ability to digest a car tire. I was on fire and could eat anything.

Four months later, it occurred to me that I had forgotten to turn down the dial on my food intake as my appetite and subconscious eating patterns were dialed into the exertion level of a serious martial artist, yet my lifestyle had shifted to that of a mellow yogi. I put on a good 15 pounds! I had fallen asleep to my shifted caloric requirements and was piling too much fuel into a much less active machine.

I quickly adjusted my diet down and tuned up my cardio exercise. It didn't take too long to turn around, but it certainly wasn't as easy. I fell asleep to the basic math that determined my body's growth and woke up out of balance. Whoops. They say youth is wasted on the young....

EXERCISE

Traveling through India and Asia while on sabbatical, I ran into a number of spiritual aspirants who did nothing but sit and meditate all day. Such daily devotional work was commendable but their bodies were falling apart as they suffered from many of the same problems I encountered with patients in California. Neither population really moved. Poor immunity, low energy, achy muscles, weak joints, and low morale were just a few of the health problems.

Moderate-intensity exercise is essential to maintaining fitness. Breaking a sweat daily for at least half an hour is the minimum exercise requirement recommended by the Surgeon General in 1995. That's to stay healthy. Living in Southern California, I'm surrounded by a number of fitness enthusiasts who are religious about exercise and many of them are able to train up to an hour a day but most will encounter hiccups in their plans at least a couple of nights a week. It is difficult to stay active and fit in modern life with traffic jams and kids to pick up, let alone if you live somewhere in the middle of the country where almost nobody is exercising.

Over the years, I have had extensive training in the Chinese martial arts with an emphasis on the Shaolin tradition. A quick story about the Shaolin temple:

In the early 5th century, an Indian monk by the name of Bodhidharma traveled to the Shaolin temple in China and took up residence outside the grounds, where he sat in silent meditation for a long period of time until the monks took notice of him. When invited to come into the temple he immediately took notice of how the monks were weak and sickly. He then proceeded to teach them a series of mind-body exercises and introduced a more rigorous labor regimen for their day-to-day activities. With the introduction of his powerful yoga techniques (the Qi Gong which we will study soon) and physical exertion, the monks began to gain strength. This heralded the start of the golden age of the Shaolin temple wherein the monks were transformed into the famous "Warrior Monks". With superior skills in the martial arts, they became the defenders of good and justice in ancient China. Bodhidharma is known as the first patron saint of the Chan Buddhist tradition, which is called Zen in Japanese. [Ch'an, 2004]

The Shaolin kung fu philosophy of daily hard work mixed with rigorous training, created a superhuman which is nothing more than your birthright. We all have the capacity, and I would argue the need, to develop our bodies to become strong and resilient. It strengthens our bones, aids our circulation, boosts our immunity, clears our toxins, raises our metabolic rate, helps us burn fat, supports our joints, and lifts our mood.

If you're not already taking a morning walk, start ASAP! It increases your metabolic rate for the rest of the day and cues your body to start burning fat instead of sugars preferentially. A brisk morning walk for 20-60 minutes followed by a healthy breakfast will set the energetic tone for the day and boost mood and circulation very quickly. Just build this into your daily routine. Yes, the first few days will be rough with the earlier alarm clock but, within a week, most people are off to the races and are happy they are doing it.

You also need weight-bearing exercise. This is critical for the development of muscles and bones. Basic squats, lunges, curls, dips, pushups, pullups, and rows are a good way to get started. What we want to do is stress (remember eustress?) the muscles into activity, which signals the brain to release more growth hormone (increasing Post-Heaven Jing) and further develop the system. Either we are busy growing or deteriorating. We need weight-bearing exercise to support our lean muscle mass and nervous system. There is no quicker formula for aging and rapid decline than a sedentary lifestyle. Muscle development is a key factor in keeping the body-brain connection active.

Stretching is your friend. I would say that 90% of the musculo-skeletal injuries I encounter in the clinic are a direct result of inadequate stretching. People are just too busy nowadays for stretching and they pay the price. Maybe it isn't active enough for some. Maybe there's no time because you just arrived and your friend is ready to start the tennis game so you pick up your racquet and strain your elbow ten minutes in. Consider it the Yin activity for the Yang aspect of your routine. They need each other.

Cardiovascular exercise is key. Cardiologists consider the legs your second heart, and we need to break into a sweat daily in order to expel toxins, drain, lymph, and keep the heart muscle healthy. Again, this is where a lot of people injure themselves so it is important to stretch before and after exercising. It is also important to train the leg muscles and strengthen the lateral stabilizers of the hips in order to avoid injury when running. I'm a big fan of long hikes with added weight in a backpack to keep the heart rate up. Running is rough on the joints and most people hurt themselves trying to get into it and then are put off from exercise all together. Time outdoors is always good, especially with fresh air and sunshine. If you have a history of heart problems or suffer from shortness of breath or dizziness, please consult your physician before jumping into a cardio program. It is always important to be safe in what we do.

Finally, as mentioned in Part One, recovery is a critical aspect to all that we do. The body needs rest in order to rebuild tissues and recover from exercise. A majority of the elite athletes I have worked with exhibit signs of adrenal fatigue and their lab work confirms this. They are burning up their Essence by pushing too hard and not allowing the Yin aspect of their activity to match their drive.

Again, balance is key in everything that we do. The body needs stress in order to continually evolve and grow in a healthy light. Too much stress damages the system and not enough stress is the result of sitting on the couch and watching the tube. Balance is the operating ideology of all Taoism and we need to attain this in all aspects of our lives.

SLEEP

Speaking of recovery, there is no better solution for fatigue found than sleep. It is a critical process that we often take for granted. It is our chance to rest our conscious mind that has been working diligently all day. We have millions of bits of information going through our minds every given second. Our conscious mind can only handle a very small fraction of them because it has to reconcile what it sees outside of ourselves with the artificial identity we've created (called our ego). The ego routinely faces catastrophic collapse daily as new information challenges its definition of itself and forces reconciliation. With all of the energy we store subconsciously into the shadow, we also have millions of reactions to emotions we don't want to feel and memories we'd rather forget. These load up defensive arguments and rationalizations that challenge our consciousness all day. Whatever is brought into the light of conscious awareness must be either absorbed into our greater self-identity or stuffed away into the shadow to deal with another day. Sleep is where much of this gets cleaned up and the brain is allowed to process and make sense of the day's happenings.

Personal Journeys—Hibernation Saves the Day

TAOIST MASTERS APPLIED the philosophy of rest and recovery to their daily lives. It was an extremely busy time in my life and I had gone more than a year and a half without any real down time, constantly overcommitting time and energy.

I'd been teaching a classroom full of students in Los Angeles about eating seasonally and was working on the next lesson's curriculum (which was about modulating our energy output to match the seasons), and that's when it finally dawned on me. I was totally exhausted and had run myself into the ground. I had been so motivated to help people that I had forgotten my teacher's primary axiom: "First help yourself, then help the people." I was being a terrible Taoist.

It was late fall at the time and winter was already showing in the trees. I had just been hit with the reality that "go with the flow" had not been part of my life for a couple of years. The flow should have landed me in a hammock long ago. I went about clearing my schedule in the winter and pulling my energy out of all noncritical tasks. I kept my practice and a modified exercise program.

Committed to rejuvenation that winter. I gave my body sleep as often as I could. At first I slept 12-13 hours per night and most of the weekends. Laziness was my commitment, my way. I learned to say no to friends when the phone rang. In this hibernating "staycation" I spent a lot of down time thinking and catching up on little projects in the house. The operating motto was "rest when you're tired." That was pretty much all the time.

It took about three months before I noticed that the dark circles were gone from under my eyes. My achy low back was no longer bothering me and the low-grade anxiety that seemed to always be there was gone. Some of the mental noise is purely physiological, our bodies trying to tell us what they need. In my case I needed sleep. Eventually, I felt like doing things again and had a renewed enthusiasm that came from deep within. I was restored and felt healthy again. Lesson learned. Now I needed to find that balance in my everyday life. Sure, you could crash in the winter after a crazy year but those are big swings of the pendulum. Was I going to be able to find that balance in an average day? That turned out to be the real Taoist training because it required mindfulness.

Aside from the profound mental reorganization, sleep repairs tissues throughout the body and expels toxins. The modern world exposes us to toxins at an unprecedented rate and we need our body's detox pathways to help clear these poisons at night. Inadequate levels of sleep severely compromise this system and force us to carry these toxins into the following day.

Sleep is a critical place for tissue recovery and growth. During Stage Four sleep, the body releases growth hormone (Vital Essence) into the bloodstream, which helps trigger the muscles and tissue to stay young and to proliferate. This ultimate Yin activity becomes the basis of our regrouping and repair at night. This is why a minimum of six to nine hours of sleep are necessary for most people. [Kalus, 2009]

As we develop our energy bodies further, many students find that they require less and less sleep. This is possible because they are doing a number of things that work cumulatively:

1. They are refining their Essence through the practice of Qi Gong.

2. They are learning to stop storing charge on thoughts and emotions, thereby keeping more vital energy in their energy fields.

3. They have an expanded self-image and need less ego reconciliation at night.

4. They are healthier through adjusted diet and exercise, so they have more efficient bodies and a healthier metabolism.

5. They are not stressed out over minutia, which impacts their brains less.

6. They are connected with their purpose in life and are being driven by a force from deep within that is actually doing all the work.

7. They smile and enjoy the ride.

Yes, we can look forward to needing less sleep with sustained practice but that should not be a goal of yours. Sleep is wonderful and counterbalances the yang nature of our society. Relaxing and dreaming are healthy. Later on, as we cultivate the Hun or the Ethereal Soul of the liver, then we can lay our bodies to rest and stay consciously awake through our astral travels. This becomes our Dream Yoga and is an integral part of waking up fully. When ready, it carries our consciousness into the astral world while the body is resting.

Until we get to our lofty training goals, however, let's go over some basic sleep hygiene rules to help you get better sleep now:

1. No caffeine after 2 pm. The stimulating effects can stay with you for several hours.

2. No TV in the bedroom. It sends pulses of light to our pineal glands (third eye) that signal the brain to stay awake and alert and kills your sex life/intimacy.

3. No bills or stressful business in bed. The bedroom is for sleep and making love. Keep everything else out.

4. Keep the temperature cool and a window cracked for fresh air if you can (68-72 degrees is the average for most people that induces the best sleep).

5. No big meals three hours before bed (unless you suffer from insomnia wherein you want a small snack of fat/protein to stabilize your blood sugar before bedtime).

6. Write down what's on your mind so you can deal with it the next day.

It's a healthy practice is to know in the morning what you need to accomplish on any given day and make sure you do it before going to sleep. Don't take unfinished business to bed with you as it'll keep your mind unsettled throughout the night. If you consistently have unfinished items on your daily schedule every evening then it is time to examine your goals and better manage your expectations of yourself. Are you being unreasonable with what you expect of yourself or are you chatting with people at the Starbucks for too long and neglecting what you need to do? In any case, it is never time management but event management that is key. It is the number of events we commit ourselves to that crunches our time and get us stressed out.

Part of the process we're learning about here is the process of becoming honest with ourselves and bringing to conscious light all of the side deals. These deals are the unspoken agreements we have running in the background that cause us grief and stress. Essentially, either drop it or handle it. Whatever it is, stop dragging it around with you.

MINDSET

The way we see our bodies and the way we live our lives are a direct reflection of our internal state. The levels of stress we experience have a profound effect on our bodies and, although we have an entire chapter devoted to Taoist mental practices, I feel it's important to speak of this subject in relation to our bodies here.

In my clinical experience, most people in the West have compromised adrenal glands because of long-term stress. This is directly a result of lifestyle practices. For example, a person who has a hard time eating on time routinely calls upon their adrenal glands to secrete Cortisol as a blood sugar stabilizer. It helps pull stored sugar out of our reserves because the brain cannot go without food. As the primary organ in the body, the brain will sacrifice other systems to get what it needs. We go through a few years of this and the person has developed hormonal problems, insomnia, long-term exhaustion, anxiety, and low back pain. The extra Cortisol in their system told their bodies to store fat (which it does when it is in emergency mode) so they can't lose weight...no matter how hard they exercise. Then, the adrenals finally exhaust their reserves and the Cortisol just isn't being produced, so the body uses the next system in line to get sugar; epinephrine and norepinephrine. They are jolted out of bed with a racing heart and they have a low-grade level of anxiety that doesn't seem to go away no matter how many trips to the Bahamas they take. Now they are in trouble.

This is why I am including this discussion in the physical body chapter because basic lifestyle habits that we take for granted can damage the body and put us far back on our heels. I have a number of students who come in with great intentions but we have to slow down their training because they have simply drained their Essence to such a degree that they need to spend a year or more restoring them before moving on to more advanced training. Of course, they feel great once they are restored but, I'm trying to save you that hassle.

We need to develop a mindset of reverence and good will towards our physical bodies. We must treat them like long-abused children who now, finally, need the extra attention and love they deserve. We need to listen to them and ask them what they need and then give it to them. This becomes a practice of honoring the needs of our physical vehicle and raising it to its rightful place as the very altar of our spiritual practice. Remember, balance is the key.

THE FIVE ELEMENTS AND MINDSET

Let's pull the grid from Part One of this book back to see the elemental correspondences in the body:

Element	Fire	Earth	Metal	Water	Wood
Yin Organ(s)	Heart, Pericardium	Spleen	Lungs	Kidneys	Liver
Yang Organ(s)	Small Intestine, Triple Burner	Stomach	Large Intestine	Bladder	Gallbladder
Emotions	Mania	Worry	Grief	Fear	Anger

Five Element Organs and Emotions

Each of these elements is not only associated with the internal organs listed above but also with the associated emotions. Mania, Worry, Grief, Fear, and Anger are manifestations of imbalanced energy in the Five Elements but they are simultaneously expressing as pathology in their corresponding organs. Heart palpitations, indigestion, shortness of breath, chronic exhaustion, and vertex headaches are also respectively brewing within those emotions and vice-versa. As Above, So Below… Everything is associated with everything else in Taoist thinking so physical lifestyle habits can influence mental patterns, while emotional disturbances can show up as physical ailments.

This obviously speaks volumes about the importance of caring for the body, inside and out. The good news is that the body has an amazing ability to self-regulate so good diet, balanced exercise, and adequate sleep go a long way in healing many illnesses. This includes problems with the internal organs. The point to take home here is that in order to wake up, we need to do so on all levels and it starts with the body. Cleaning up the temple is the necessary first step in the alchemical process.

✳

CHAPTER SIX

THE ANCIENT PRACTICE OF QI GONG

The breath is one's own mind; one's own mind does the breathing. Once mind stirs, then there is energy. Energy is basically an emanation of mind.
—Lu Tung Pin, The Secret of the Golden Flower, *Chapter IV*

he literal translation of Qi Gong is "energy work." It is an Asian form of yoga that has been around for thousands of years. Much of it is performed while standing but there are a number of seated sets as well. There are hundreds of systems that have come down from various lineages and many of them focus on different fields. Many are health-oriented, while a separate group come to us through the martial arts lineages. These sets act to harness willpower, focus, and help the practitioner channel their energy through their palms. There are also a number of sets that have come down from the temples and monasteries that are more focused on spiritual cultivation and depth of meditation. Some involve moving and others are visualization based. Almost all of them involve specialized breathing, which is coordinated with the activity at hand. The guiding principle of all these practices, however, is the coordination of the eyes, with the body movements, focus of the mind, and the breath (for the moving practices in particular). For the more passive, non-movement exercises, we focus the vision inwards and explore the inner realms as we guide the breath to various inner chambers.

Let's take a moment to look at this formula again and see if we can dissect it a bit further. We are looking for the coordination of all—not just a couple—of the following to take place in order for our Qi Gong to be effective:

1. EYES
Considered the gateway to the soul in the West and believed to guide the Shen or the Spirit in Taoist theory. It is said that the Qi/Energy follows the Shen/Spirit and the blood and body fluids, then in turn, follow the Qi. Therefore, the eyes become the "command center" if you will for the Spirit to control and guide the movement of the energy in the body. Later on, we use the same system to direct energies outside of our bodies to effectuate healing and exert our influence on the environment around us.

2. BODY MOVEMENTS
These are the actual sequenced movements of the Qi Gong exercises. Many of these follow the pathways of the energy meridians that run through the

body. They also often trace the outer edges of our energy fields, smoothing and caressing the potency of the energy flow in our Light Bodies. These movements often involve various degrees of exertion, and depending on the system you are training in, can actually be quite rigorous. Recall the story of Bodhidarma and the Shaolin temple. He actually created a routine (the Famous Tamo's 18 Hands of the Lohan) that fully mixed Kung Fu with Qi Gong with high levels of exertion. This aspect is very much like the physical yoga systems we see in the Indian traditions. Some hold static postures while others emphasize more dynamic flow and continuity of motion.

3. MENTAL FOCUS

This is a critical aspect of the practice and is the one that is most often overlooked by students who learn the exercises, but then quickly fall back into the sleepy trances of their days; thinking about bills or the next set they'd like to learn. Paying attention is a critical component to any energy work as it engages the Fire energy of the Heart and ties the Spirit in with the actions at hand. The ancients say that it is the linking of Attention and Intention that creates mastery in life. Here, we are asked to focus in on the action at hand and to stay engaged in the body movements and tracking them with the eyes. It demands our mental focus and presence and the reward is immense. This aspect also draws on the Yi, or shen of the Earth element.

4. THE BREATH

It is the vital breath that is said to circulate through the various meridians and it is the energy from the air, if you recall, that mixes with the Food Qi to create the functional energy of our bodies. The coordination of breath with body movements and attention drives energy through the designated pathways and opens up blockages. We use breath to open up these pathways, but also to gather and store the breath/energy in specific reservoirs (called dantiens) in the body. An adept learns to extract vital energy from the air through breathwork.

As simple as it seems, it is this framework that sets the precedent for all of the magic to occur in Qi Gong. Now, there is much to be said about the specific movements and the deep understanding of the energy pathways and how they affect us, but if we were to take this level of focus and coordinated thought/breathing into our day-to-day lives, we'd be far ahead of the game. The good news is that we are about to learn about these pathways as well and we are going to unlock and understand the mechanisms of action here. We will be engaging the intellect (Yi) and the focus (Shen) with the will (Zhi). Once this "vertical axis" of Fire-Earth-Water has been activated, we'll have finally unlocked the first hints of our tremendous potential and a number of powerful changes start to happen.

The Vertical Axis of Spirit linking Attention and Intention with Intellect.

This axis gives us the mental and spiritual alignment we need in order to connect all aspects of our being into our bodies while in our practice. It connects all the various aspects of ourselves through the practice that snaps us out of our trances. Once we correct the flow of energy and divert it away from all of the wasteful patterns of our past, then we can start to gather and accumulate power in our reservoirs and use this as a buffer against disease, fatigue, or simply falling back into a sleepy trance. That being said, I want to emphasize a critical point in understanding Qi Gong (or life, for that matter). When we speak of storing energy we are speaking of creating places where we condense and refine the quality of the energy moving through us. We condense it to nourish our essence and refine it to illuminate our Spirit but we want to be careful to not think of it in capitalistic terms.

There is no need for more energy at all because there is an infinite amount of energy available to us here and now. In fact, all the power that ever was or will be is here and now. So it is important to not get into the acquisition game of energy and realize where it comes from. There is no outside source from which we draw energy like water from a well. The entire force of the Universe is flowing through you at all times and in all places. Therefore, it is the impedance, or the blockages we create that makes us feel a sense of lack. We channel much of it subconsciously to our shadow and we simply close our minds to the limitless flow of it because it would simply break our ego's definition of ourselves. We keep our foot on the brake pad and wonder why we're exhausted all of the time.

The goal of Qi Gong isn't an addition process but it is more a subtraction process.

The more we can get out of our own way, the more we can let the universal flow of energy to move through us. We become an agent of its good will and we take our rightful place in eternity. This is not in some far-off heaven but here and now. Qi Gong helps us wake up to the living, breathing moment in which we can finally take part. An important aspect in "getting out of the way" is reconciling the stuck energies in the Horizontal Axis of grief and anger/frustration.

The Horizontal Soul Axis of Human Emotions

This axis is intimately involved in the rising and falling trends of our mental and emotional upheavals, while it is simultaneously tied with the cycle of life and all of the trials and tribulations of the soul. It is important to not be deferential about this and to be engaged in the process of reconciling imbalances on this axis. It is at this point where most people get stuck because this is where they store the majority of the repressed charge in their shadows. Our desires for addition (Wood) and our reluctance to let go (Metal), lead to a great deal of clinging and suffering. In playing this game, we get out of balance and unconsciously pour more and more energy into creating monsters here.

In Chinese medicine, the lungs represent the Metal element, which descends energy naturally, while the liver represents the Wood energy, which naturally rises. The lungs sit above the liver in our bodies and it is the dynamic tension of trying to maintain this inverted energetic flow that is the essence of life. One pushes up from underneath as the other pushes down. Upon death, the Shen of the liver, the Hun, ascends to Heaven and the Shen of the lungs, the Po, descends into the earth. We need them to check each other in dynamic tension or they will separate and we will perish. Bringing harmony to the proper flow of the horizontal axis is what keeps our lives running smoothly and plugs us into the power of the vertical axis. The proper alignment of attention and intention requires a healthy understanding of the human condition and, far from running from it, we are to be engaged, aware, and awake moment by moment.

The Dantiens

Much like the Indian system of chakras that represent different aspects of the Light as it expresses through our physical bodies, the Taoist system uses three main energy reservoirs called the dantiens. There is a lower dantien, located approximately three inches below your navel between the front of your torso and your spine; the middle dantien which is centered in the sternum (at the center of the chest and level with the heart), and the upper dantien that is housed slightly above the eye level in the forehead (the third eye). The lower and middle dantiens range in size but can be approximately the size of a small bowling ball, whereas the size of the upper depends on the level of attainment of the individual...usually anywhere from a golf ball to tennis ball in most people.

The lower dantien is the area where we first learn to direct our breath. It is the foundation of the energy body system. The Taoists believe that it is important to start with the heaviest and densest forms of energy in our cultivation and work up from there. Again, Yin and Yang have differentiated and the heavier and more Yin aspects are located lower in the body. In fact, Hui Yin, which is the first point of the conception vessel (energy meridian), is located in the perineum and is considered the most Yin aspect of our anatomy. It is the base of our torso's energy field and is the point from which the lower dantien energy emerges and returns to. Anchoring the breath and the Shen (which is more Yang in nature) down to this region brings the first level of balance to our systems. Think of it like a construction job; a solid foundation below, gives us a steady structure above. As above...

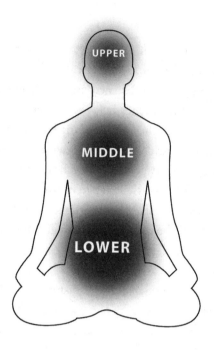

The Dantiens

Our goal is to systematically balance the energies of our bodies from base to crown and only move forward once we have done so successfully. We want to concentrate our energy into the lower dantien and then draw upon this core region for every movement. All of the body's energy currents need to run through the lower dantien so that the Original Qi and Post-Heaven Essence are nourished. The more energy we can release to these systems, the more efficiently we can metabolize foods and run our day-to-day processes. The more we do this, the more we'll be able to free trapped or blocked energies.

As we optimize the flow of clean energy through our energy fields, we are then faced with blockages, which carry with them mental and emotional content that is deemed undesirable—things we've stuffed into our shadow. The more light and awareness we bring, the more our shadows become illuminated, which leaves less space and power available to hidden subconscious processes. This can be a bit unsettling to face, but we now have increased energy and awareness to deal with what's there. This is when the middle dantien comes into play. We use the energy of the heart to forgive these events and memories. We learn to disengage from our typical response of empowering them by running and pumping energy into a polarized solution. We use the lower dantien to bring up the power (almost like activating a battery and plugging into it) and then the middle dantien to transform what's been trapped in our shadows, which we now finally have the strength and ability to deal with. From here, the new energy is released and refined in the upper dantien and becomes pure, undifferentiated light of awareness. The more self-aware we become, the easier this process gets. Alchemy is actually quite fun once the engine gets going. There's always something to clean…always energy to access and things to unlock. Once you get this, there is never a dull moment in life. Once all three dantiens are healthy and fully activated, we then get into some interesting practices that are beyond the scope of this book but will not be kept secret.

Personal Journeys—Falling Up a Hill

I WAS SCHEDULED to climb a mountain in Bolivia with a couple of hard-core Swiss guys. The massive peak wasn't K2 but difficult nonetheless. Mind you, we had just flown in from the jungle, which was 200 feet below sea level, and were on our way up to base of Wayna Potosi Mountain, which was at 15,000 feet, the following day! We were to summit at over 20,000 feet.

We hurriedly got our affairs in order and got as far as the car would take us by evening time. We had to hike for a number of hours to the glacier, which was at 18,000 feet. This was where we were to practice using our ropes and ice picks for the following day. It was hard to breathe, and we spent a couple of hours practicing climbing up and down tall ice walls. We set up tents and camped on the glacier that night.

I had a hard time getting enough air and could not get warm for the life of me. I basically shook all night in my crappy rental sleeping bag until the guide summoned us at 1 am. We were to hike with headlamps and summit just after sunrise. I was happy to get going—anything to warm me up! We had some tea and some eggs and were on our way up the glacier.

Our guide was in front and the three of us in tow behind, each a safe distance apart on a rope. It was slow going to begin with and it just got harder. I remember being able to take a number of steps per breath at first. As we got closer to the top, I was taking one breath per step. One of my Swiss counterparts was vomiting while the other became delusional and was talking to himself. I had a mild headache and recalled reading that we were supposed to descend with signs of altitude sickness.

No way! The machismo spirit won out and we decided to pummel on. I got to the point where I was taking multiple breaths per step and was basically pulling one of the guys up to the top. It was miserable and I had a decision to make. I had to commit here. Either make it to the top or die trying.

It wasn't until another half hour of suffering when something dawned on me. Why was I being so stupid? I remembered the story of the Taoist Master who linked the energy of his dantien to his disciples and pulled them across a raging river. This was the story that got me into this mess! If this Taoist magic stuff really worked, then I would be able to use it now!

I figured that if a Master could link his dantien to others' and create a connection, then he was doing so by anchoring the connection with his mind or Shen. I figured I'd do it a little differently. I assigned my lower dantien to the top of that mountain and created a strong connection with it. I then breathed down to my lower dantien and focused my energy there. Once the connection was in place, I simply created gravity between the two points. I allowed myself to "fall up the hill" as my lower dantien was being tugged by a strong connection with the top of the mountain.

Next thing I knew, my rope was getting tight as I found that I was pulling away from the Swiss guys behind me. The guide (who must have been part mountain goat) was quite surprised by my sudden burst of energy. Realizing that I was linked by ropes to the other two behind me, I then attempted to do what the Master in the story did. Whether I actually did it, or they were being encouraged by my tugging of the rope, I don't know. All I know is that I was suddenly leading the charge up the mountain and, once at the top, I felt an incredible sense of heat in my lower dantien as I literally walked straight into an ice-covered rock with my dantien leading. I had to release the gravity consciously before it would let go.

We sat for a while and reveled at our accomplishment. More importantly, we reveled at how the world looked from that high. We could see the curvature of the atmosphere. We stayed for a short while and then quickly got down to base camp…each step getting lighter and easier all of the way down. Getting up there was nice but the real lesson for me was finding the power and magnitude of my lower dantien. Something very real happened there.

The Different Types of Qi Gong Practice

There is a Yin and a Yang aspect to everything, which includes the actual energetic practice as well. We studied the various types of energy in a previous section and this is where some of that information comes to light. The Nutritive Qi and the Defensive Qi are the main types of energy running through our bodies. They service our cells and our myriad physiological needs. There are practices designed to emphasize one or the other. There are also practices designed to enhance Shen or Spirit as well as internal practices designed to cultivate and refine Essence and awaken the Spirit within. Here are the designations of the various Qi Gong practices:

1. WEI GONG
This practice concentrates on the exterior energy responsible for health, immunity, and the defense of the system against pathogens and disease. It is designed to route energy to these external "force fields" (The Defensive Qi as illustrated in Part One) and create an energetic barrier that protects the internal organs from outside invasion.

2. QI GONG

General term for the practices that bolster the Nutritive Qi and also support the Defense Qi. It increases flow to the different systems and provides the body with the necessary boost it needs to nourish and heal itself. Qi Gong is the most balanced approach but needs to be modified depending on the circumstances of the individual or for progressing into deeper work.

3. NEI GONG

Considered the higher alchemical practice that is taught in the temples and involves a great deal of dedication. Nei Gong emphasizes the cultivation and preservation of Essence (sexual abstinence mixed with specific practices) so that it can be further condensed and refined to Qi and Shen. Nei Gong leads to the formation of the Light Body and is what has been passed down by the famous Taoist Immortals. It takes many months of Qi Gong practice with mental and emotional reconciliation before Nei Gong is considered safe.

4. SHEN GONG

This practice applies to the cultivation of focused attention and, specifically, the cultivation of the psychic senses that help us perceive energetic rhythms. This aids in clairvoyance, clairaudience, long distance healing, astral travel, and psionic warfare/mind control. This is obviously high-level stuff, but should not be considered the most important. As far as I'm concerned, the real gold is in the Nei Gong which effectuates personal transformation. Shen Gong is often taught to priests who need to intervene in crises, heal ailments, and perform exorcisms. It is an important part of the knowledge of the Tao, but the danger in the West is when glorify the "powers" as an end in themselves, and it can then serve as a dangerous ego trap.

In the previous chapter we emphasized getting the physical body healthy and fit. It is vital to start with the foundations of Qi Gong and work our way up. This means diligent work on our stance work, which will help ground our energy down and give us roots. Stances develop the lower dantien and strengthen the Wei Qi. Once we build a strong foundation, we can really begin to reap the powerful benefits of this practice. From here, we learn about the mysteries of the Tao and become more self-aware.

Words of Caution

We need wax for a candle to be a candle and serve its purpose. The practice begins with foundational work that will strengthen our muscles, bones, energy flow, and resolve. So please do not expect a magic carpet ride on day three. We are blessed to have these systems available to us, and it is truly fortunate that the air of secrecy that originally surrounded these arts has been surmounted in our Information Age. That being said, there is work to do and shortcuts are dangerous. One of my Chinese teachers did not realize that when he first arrived and taught this practice to a number of students in Los Angeles in the 1960s that drugs were rampant in American culture at this time, and a handful people in the room were tripping on LSD. He was perplexed by the odd mannerisms and the chaotic energy flow of these students. Many of them literally blew out their circuits by taking uppers, downers, acid, and weed while practicing. They thought more was better. They were wrong.

Taoism is about maintaining balance and harmonizing the polarity consciousness that has infected the minds of our culture. Sure, you can get away with shortcuts for a few days or weeks (with the help of stimulants and drugs), but you'll quickly burn out. This is not healthy behavior, and we are here to correct it. The Way is the training.

I have been practicing and teaching in Southern California for several years now and I have encountered a great many "hungry ghosts." These are spiritual shoppers who are looking for a quick fix and will do something that is convenient, but are not willing to put in any real work. This happens especially if the work challenges them to face the content in their shadows. Similar to the discussion we had in the previous chapter on eating habits, I find it very telling to see how a student engages in a practice and with what level of commitment. When someone is given a specific diet to avoid foods that they are allergic to, and they fail to comply because it is "too hard," then that is a telling characteristic of a zombie… powerlessness to face themselves. I see people who want the "fireworks" with the Qi Gong but are unwilling to do the foundation-building. They are impatient and will get nowhere. The great masters with whom I have studied had zero tolerance for this type of attitude and showed these characters the door. I'm a bit more accustomed to Western hand-holding, but I will tell you this: if you do not wake up and replace trance-induced bad habits with positive behaviors, you are going to live an insignificant life and die a zombie. I'm here to help, but I can't do the work for you.

So now take a deep breath with me and let's get into the training!

※

CHAPTER SEVEN

QI GONG EXERCISES

*If a man knows the method to nourish the breath,
he is able to become an immortal.*

—Tao Tsang Vol. VII

ooking at pictures of exercises in a book may not be the ideal way to learn in the modern age of web streaming. Actually, no media format is ideal, as these traditions have been passed down through direct transmission for thousands of years. Oral and personal transmission are the only means allowed. Moving and sequenced sets are harder to illustrate in a book than standing or seated static exercises, but the real key is to convey the work accurately so that the reader can learn it and practice correctly.

In light of this, I have developed a program that sets things up correctly for your energy practice. We will learn three traditional exercises in this section that will get you well on your way to better health, stamina, and energy flow. If this work feels right for you and you want to go further, I have produced three DVDs with several sets and exercises you can study that will segue you into the private instruction lessons of the advanced Nei Gong. In the past, we would all be studying at a central location (temple or monastery) where your progress could be monitored and corrections made. In light of the changes and the "flattening" of the world, I have created an internet-based platform through which you can monitor your progress, track your training, and upload video exams of each set for review, and it's available on taoistpath.com. Here, we can ensure proficiency and make corrections along the way. By the time you are ready for personal instruction, we will have already had a healthy working relationship.

We want nothing less than a complete transformation for you. Holding that transformation in mind, it is important to practice all of the exercises in this section of the book. This means the physical practice (diet, exercise, sleep, and basic lifestyle modification), the three exercise Qi Gong practice in this chapter, and the mental/emotional/and spiritual practices that follow. You do the work and you reap the rewards. The formula is that easy.

Exercise 1—The Standing Form (Qi Gong/Strength Building)

This set comes from the Shaolin tradition and is quite challenging at first for many people. Most people in the modern age have weak postural muscles and are not accustomed to deep lower abdominal breathing. These deep stances help us build resolve and also help us develop a powerful connection with our lower dantien. The hand postures help open up energy flow through our shoulders—where many of us have trapped energy—and also through our axillary arteries (in the armpits). Try to stay in these stances for a designated amount of time and try to maintain your stances consistently. This may be difficult at first but you will quickly find that you can do more and more with sustained practice. It is okay to feel challenged in your leg muscles but do not force your way through joint pain. You can turn your feet slightly outwards if your knees bother you. Occasionally, some people feel lightheaded during the early stages of this practice which is caused by massive energy reserves being released. Just have a seat and begin again when you've gained your composure. It is perfectly natural to feel a rush of energy rise to the head during this exercise. Keep the tip of the tongue lightly pressing the roof of the mouth and breathe in and out of your nose on this exercise. If you feel light headed or that it is too intense, then it is okay to exhale out of the mouth.

Being a static exercise, we will examine each posture individually here. Pick a designated amount of time to stay in each posture and then you can increase the time as your proficiency develops. Thirty seconds to a minute per posture is enough for most people when they start. Try to add 30 seconds per posture per week if you can, this will quickly propel you into a very strong practice and the energy that gets freed up in your system will feel great. It will serve as an encouragement to keep practicing.

OPENING STANCE—SQUARE HORSE

Even weight distribution between both legs. Head up straight with hands at waist level.

STANCE #1—PALMS UP / RESISTING UPWARD

Imagine very heavy weight on top of each palm—resist to keep them up.

STANCE #2—PALMS DOWN / RESISTING DOWNWARD

Imagine a force pushing up from the Earth against your palms—work to stay in position.

STANCE #3—FINGER TIPS UP / PRESSING OUTWARD

Now the imaginary force is coming in from the sides like elevator doors closing—hold outward.

STANCE #4—PALMS UP / PRESSING AGAINST SKY

Now an imaginary force is bearing down on you- use dynamic tension to resist against it

STANCE #5—PALMS DOWN / POURING ENERGY INTO THE HEAD

Let your palms rain energy back down onto your head and body.

STANCE #6—PALMS FACING CHEST / GATHERING ENERGY IN TORSO

Feel the energy swirl between your palms and your torso—gather energy into your heart.

STANCE #7—PALMS FLAT BEHIND BACK FINGERS POINT FORWARD / CONNECTING WITH THE GROUND

Round out the elbows and feel your kidneys fill up with energy. Inhale and move energy up your legs and arms all the way to your head. Exhale the energy out your palms and feet into the Earth.

STANCE #8—PALMS TOGETHER / GATHERING ENERGY IN THE HEART

Rest into prayer position and allow the energy to gather in your heart.

One final note; this exercise is from the Shaolin Kung Fu tradition and is hard work. As you progress in this practice, work to take your stances deeper and really activate the leg muscles. This is a wonderful thing. It creates a good habit of allowing us to push through certain blockages and trains us to deal with muscle pain (and burning!) with equanimity. Remember, Shaolin is the birthplace of the Zen tradition and when you put this art into actual practice, it is the physical body's reflection of the mental practice of non-reacting to aversions and cravings. The Shaolin system trains the "Bodymind" as a unified complex and, proficiency in this training leads to excellent meditation skills.

Exercise 2—The Triple Burner Exercise (Wei Gong/Qi Gong)

This exercise uses a series of dynamic standing postures with breath work just like the previous exercise, but it also incorporates another layer of sophistication which is the practice of guided visualization. The Triple Burner Exercise is an effective health set that teaches us to use our Shen to guide our energy to certain places within our body. With sustained focus, we learn how to heal ourselves and to bring the light of awareness to different body parts. It is our first venture in guiding Qi internally and the mastery of this principle allows us to move into higher principles of Nei Gong.

BASIC STANCE

Stand in your basic Wu Chi posture with feet shoulder-width apart. The hands are off to the sides with a bit of space under each armpit. This practice uses what we call "Four Point" balancing where we balance our weight on the balls and heels of each foot. Touch the tip of the tongue to the roof of your mouth and breathe in nose and out nose to the lower dantien. This is what the starting stance looks like:

FIRST POSTURE—UPPER BURNER

Hold your hands in the tree position in front of your chest.

- Keep breathing in nose and out nose to the lower dantien.
- Stay with your Four Point stance throughout this entire exercise.
- Start breathing to your palms and feel a white light emanating from the center of your palms into your upper chest.
- Simultaneously, reflect this light back from the upper chest to push against your palms.
- Feel the exchange of energy between the palms and the chest. Shift your attention to this area but keep breathing to the lower dantien.
- Stay here in this posture until you feel that all of the energy in this region is fully cleared before moving to the next posture. When you can sense only clean energy and white light, that is when you're done.
- Organs to clear: Heart, Lungs, Pericardium, Glands in the Throat.

SECOND POSTURE—MIDDLE BURNER

Move your hands slightly lower to the level of the lower sternum.

• Continue the same practice until you feel that this level is completely clear of any blockages.
• Remember to inundate the area with pure white light and really focus on the exchange between the palms and the torso.
• Organs to clear: Stomach, Spleen, Liver, Gall Bladder, Upper Intestines, Pancreas.

THIRD POSTURE—LOWER BURNER

Move your hands slightly lower to the level of the navel.

- Continue the same practice until you feel that this level is completely clear of any blockages.
- Really focus and clear as many energetic blockages are found in the gut region.
- Organs to clear: Kidneys (in the back), Bladder, Intestines, Sexual Organs

---

FOURTH POSTURE—KIDNEYS

Move your hands behind the back with palms flat facing the ground behind the kidneys.

- Connect the light coming from your palms with the Earth.
- On the inhale (in nose), visualize liquid white light coming up from your feet and your palms all the way to the crown of your head.
- On the exhale (out nose), push this energy back down into the earth through the palms and feet.
- Continue to draw energy up to the crown on the inhale and back down into the earth on the exhale for several breaths.
- When you feel like your body is free and clear of any blocked energies, take a long exhale out of the mouth and move to the closing sequence.

• Rub from the backs of your shoulders (one at a time) down the outside of the arm to the pinky with the opposite hand and then back up the thumb side into the chest.
• Circle and rub your heart region and then your lower dantien.
• Rub your kidneys with both palms.
• Rub down the backs of both legs while bending forward and up the front while standing upright again.
• Tap your lower dantien three times with both hands.

NOTE—This sequence is also available for you to view online at taoistpath.com.

With continued practice of this set, you will develop clarity of mind and a clean energy field. This is a critical skill for us to grow and understand our essential nature. When we stop identifying with the "noise" and we clean our energy fields, we become more and more aware of who we truly are and it is one of the most liberating things we can do for ourselves.

Exercise 3—The Silk Weaver's Exercise (Wei Gong/Qi Gong)

This particular sequence is a health set that helps open up and dilate the meridians. It is of Buddhist origins and has been taught for years as the quintessential health set of the Qi Gong tradition. It is to be done three times. Two moving repetitions and one with the eyes closed doing the entire thing through visualization. This set is a moving set, so, in order to preserve the integrity of the motions, I recommend, if you have Internet access, that you go to the following link: taoistpath.com

There, you have unlimited free access to view the exercise and make sure you are doing it correctly. All of the fundamentals are important for this exercise, which means the tip of the tongue touching the roof of the mouth and a feeling of heaviness in the lower body. Please spend some time learning this and burning it into your body's memory so that you can practice it anywhere you may be. Learning sequenced movements is an important practice that not only makes us more aware, it helps develop the brain and nervous system.

SEQUENCING

In an ideal situation, it would be best to practice exercises 1 and 3 in the morning (outdoors in fresh air if possible) at least 30-60 minutes before breakfast and after a short walk to get the blood moving. Yes, this means getting up earlier but the benefits are priceless. Exercise 2 can be done at any point throughout the day as well but preferably before 9 pm. Do not perform it too close to bedtime as it may stimulate you too much and cause insomnia. Play with it and see what works best for you.

Qi Gong Rule: Do not eat 60 minutes before training and at least 30 minutes after training.

This may be difficult in the mornings especially but it is important to observe. What I have done for years is I wake up, go for a run or brisk walk, do my practice for 30 minutes or so, then jump in the shower and go through my preparatory morning routine (bathroom, getting dressed...) By then, I'm ready to eat anyhow and things have settled. Eat a healthy breakfast and be on your way.

Exercise 2 is a great thing to do around 3-4 pm when your energy starts to fade. Again, just a few minutes in a short set is better than nothing and you'll feel great.

Make it a point to get all three exercises in every day and you will start to feel a profound difference very quickly. It is important to note that a great deal of stagnant and trapped energy will be released throughout this process. Occasionally people feel dizzy and/or lightheaded in the first couple of weeks (especially in Exercise 1). Take it slowly and work your way up to greater difficulty with it. More time and deeper stances are where you should aim to be but all within reason. Remember, Taoism is about balance. There's good stress and unhealthy stress. We want to walk that razor's edge and stay right in the middle—pushing ourselves to evolve and grow without overstepping our limits. When you commit to making it your daily practice, then the pressure is off and you can keep moving the marker forward every day.

A good example of this is kung fu high jumping training. When a young monk starts his training, he is given a baby stalk of corn to plant and care for. His assignment it to jump over this stalk ten times daily with both feet. He does this religiously for months on end until he realizes that he is clearing several feet with a vertical jump! This is how your practice will progress. Follow the instructions carefully and integrate the exercises from the rest of this chapter in order to make the training complete. Remember, picking and choosing what's most convenient for us implies that we are acting out of trance and avoiding what makes us uncomfortable.

The Way is the Training!

*

CHAPTER EIGHT

MENTAL PRACTICE

Whatever form your inquiry may take, you must finally come to the one "I," the Self. All these distinctions made between the "I" and "you," Master and disciple, etc., are merely a sign of one's ignorance. The "I" Supreme alone is. To think otherwise is to delude oneself.

—Ramanda Maharshi

etting the physical body healthy through lifestyle, and activating the proper flow of energy through Qi Gong, are essential steps to waking up and snapping out of our trance-like slumber. However, we have to maintain the correct mindset in our training or we'll be running around in circles for a long time. It is futile to bring up the amount of energy running through our systems while continuing to play the same games of our past. If we don't wake up and clearly recognize our habits and tendencies of old, then we may as well not even start. Simply put, there are a number of places and/ or circumstances where we tend to leak our energy. These holes need to be plugged up. In Part One of this book we spoke of polarity and the tendency of the human mind to channel energy into the opposite polarity of what we are feeling. Essentially, we channel our energy into situations that we are uncomfortable with and reinforce them through our ignorance of how our energy systems work. The point being that we really don't have anything to "do" per se, other than accepting Reality as it is in every moment. Our judgment (or our aversions and cravings) of any given item or situation is where we literally breathe Life into our lack of acceptance of these things and this is what births our monsters.

Because we have come to understand the nature of how we create such harmful mental karma, we are now poised to practice just the opposite. We are going to learn something that is at first very difficult to do for the human mind, but is an important step in our journey. This is to do nothing at all. In the silence, we come face-to-face with our essential Self—the true identity Ramana Maharshi refers to as the "I". As mentioned in Part One, Karma is simply the action that we take. This applies to the mental, emotional, spiritual, and physical. Anytime we move to do or create something, we are generating Karma. Every time we react to a given thought or statement, our mental waves reflect this reaction to the edge of the Universe and back. Instead of being listening stations for the symphony of the cosmic Tao, we are broadcasting stations for the reflections of our shadows—spewing chaos and noise into the universe.

The ancient Taoists spoke of the concept of the Yi, or the intellect, creating a disturbance in the heart. The disruptions of the mind manifest as an invading space that slowly grows and eventually nudges out the Shen of the heart. When the Shen doesn't have a house to settle in, it cannot reside in the body and we perish. Therefore, a big part of the Taoist Alchemical practice is the clearing of this disrupted Yi from the heart.

This is an exercise that will start to create an understanding for us of the overactive role our minds play in every instant of our lives. Practice it daily in silence, and then take it into your day to day. The goal is to be constantly practicing this at all times day and night. You may think to yourself—"how am I going to get anything done then?" The answer is simple: You'll get more done efficiently when you are not blowing away all of your energy into chaos. Trust. Practice.

Taoist Mental Practice

PREPARATORY STEPS
- Sit in a quiet place with your spine straight and body relaxed.
- Rest your hands on your knees with the thumb and index fingers touching.
- Take ten breaths to your lower dantien (three fingers below your navel)—
- In nose and out nose.
- Settle into your breath and relax your mind.
- If we are going to practice and cultivate inaction which is the opposite of doing, then what do we do?
- There is only one action allowed in this exercise and that is the last action that bridges us into the realm of inaction.

BEGIN THE PRACTICE
- Your only action item is to ask yourself, "What am I doing right now?"
- Whatever it is that you are mentally engaged in, simply stop doing that, and relax.
- Stay in this state of inaction but constantly pose the same question to yourself: "What am I doing right now?"
- You'll find that you tend to get pretty busy doing something all of the time. We get caught in past memories, future concerns, emotional pitfalls, and, oftentimes, nonsensical random thoughts. Don't get upset and think

of yourself as a failure—welcome to the nature of the monkey mind. We all have this noise and we are all constantly jumping into the mental ring with it and fighting it to exhaustion.

• Again: "What am I doing right now?"

[handwritten annotation: It's the focus on exactly what you're doing]

TAKING THE PRACTICE WITH YOU

• With continued practice, you will learn to become more aware of this tendency and how much effort you are putting into this chaos all of the time. The only reason we feel any lack of energy is that we spend most of our time leaking it through this freight train of nonsense that's constantly running through our heads.

• Once you get a sense of how this practice works, simply program your subconscious mind to continue to ask it of yourself throughout your day. True meditation is a state of being, and not what you do for 20 minutes on your cushion.

• Let it function as a self-diagnostic or correctional program that keeps pulling your awareness back to what it is you are actually doing in the present moment.

• You will find that, with time, it is tremendously liberating and you will learn to relax more and more into your intact energy field which will reveal the true "I" to you.

I often get questions about the principle of inaction by Western students. The general theme is, "if I were to relax and do nothing all day, then how can I perform my job and feed my family? How do I reconcile this paradox?" To them I often share the following story:

There is a famous tale of a Zen monastery in the mountains where an enormous boulder rolls down into the grounds after a storm. A number of monks were fretting about it when the Master came to inquire about the noise and fuss they were making. Without giving it another thought, the Master simply picked up the huge boulder and carried it off to the side of the plaza. Unable to believe their eyes the monks asked their Master how he was able to perform such an extraordinary feat, and his reply was:

"I simply relaxed as deeply as I exerted and lifted."

Don't worry about what you insist on getting done. If it needs to be done, it'll happen naturally at the right time. We spend most of our time and energy playing out scenarios or anticipating an action instead of relaxing and doing it naturally. We're so tired by then that most of us become unable to perform the action when the time is right. Practice these exercises and don't fall into a mental trance. You'll be better than fine.

✳

CHAPTER NINE

EMOTIONAL PRACTICE

If a person's mind is not excited with thoughts
there is no coming and no going
there is no exiting and no entering
then [the Spirit] constantly abides naturally [inside].
                                    —Tao Tsang Vol. IV

aving created a precedent for our understanding of Reality and the nature of our suffering, we can then bridge into the healing of the soul. The "Horizontal Axis" of the soul (Metal, Earth, and Wood) is where we have stored many lessons and energy that remains trapped and stagnant. It is this trapped energy that feeds our internal demons and feeds the insane behaviors that plague us so much. It doesn't have to be this way. With Qi Gong, we are now poised to delve into the darkness of the shadow and start the alchemical process in full force. To find the lead which you will later turn into gold is easy, you simply need to discover the things that bother you the most in any given day. It may be your reaction to your husband's dilly-dallying in the garage, or maybe the behavior of a certain co-worker. Whatever might be upsetting you, chances are you're no stranger to it. We are mostly plagued by issues and traumas of our past which linger in our consciousness for decades .

Energy fields are connected to our attachments. They fall into families of issues by topic and class. As Alfred Korzybski describes, we start with what he calls the Original Event and then we keep branching out from there into levels of "abstraction." [Korzybski, 1948] An example of this would be a person who is bullied in his early school years by the popular kids. He takes on an "anti-jock" stance in his consciousness which eventually becomes anti-establishment sentiment in his adult life. This person eventually gets violent with their supervisor and loses yet another job blaming the "system." He does not realize the behavior is stemming from the early event that created this whole faulty belief system. We get further away from the essential truth of the original event and begin to create storylines for ourselves to make it acceptable. The more energy we pump into this artificial field, the more impossible it seems to penetrate this mutated, powerful field and face the truth. We create monsters out of undesirable events and we feed them until they own us.

Here's the way out:

First and foremost, to stop the bleeding we need awareness of these patterns, and forgiveness in the moment. Using the mental practice taught in the last chapter, we should be constantly scanning to see what mess we're about to get involved in and stop it right there. You will invariably find that you're about to go down a very familiar road. This is where the Attention of the Shen (which is housed in the Heart) comes in. We have detected a given behavior or karmic action from an old theme and have recognized that we are about to go into some old trance behavior. What can we do? First, you must acknowledge this behavior, and then, focusing in on your heart, immediately go into forgiving whoever, whatever, and however anyone was involved. Far from the polarity consciousness of our reactive minds, the Heart holds our personal connection with the Primordial Tao. It is our true state of being prior to the separation of Yin and Yang. Once we tap into this with the energy of forgiveness, we can then hold it in our Heart and consciously reclaim our power back from this event/memory. We do this by understanding the fundamental split that took place in our minds, and then we pull back the energy we deposited into the opposite pole.

For instance, say our father was abusive to us as a child and we still harbor ill-will towards him even though he's now a broken-down old man. The typical behavior we automatically default to when he calls is to get very short and cool with him. You could be out at the pool with the family having the perfect day and then he calls. Your breath shortens, your pulse speeds up, and you are suddenly in a very different space. What's the first thing to do? Recognize what it is that you're doing right then. You are the one getting revved up. You are raising your blood pressure and you are the one lowering your voice and going from smile to frown over this. What then? Stop it. Recognize the unconscious behavior and then stop it in that instant. Yes, I understand that's easier said than done, and that's due to such a massive charge around your relationship with your father.

The stored energy is like a balloon about to burst. This is where we must change our typical behavior or else we'll feed even more negative energy into our chapter of "father". This is where we drop into our Heart. Forgive him for whatever he has done right there and then, and with the energy neutralized, begin to see the pattern for what it is. Every time he comes up in your thought field, a slew of emotions race in and fires you up. Instead of channeling daggers, channel forgiveness to the man himself. Forgive him, forgive his behavior, forgive yourself and forgive the situation. Thank him for the lessons he has given you and for the opportunity to be more loving. Understand that his behavior (whatever it was he did or still does) is a product of an imbalance. He was acting out on his demons and they, in turn, have infected you. Do not accept them! The only way we can get infected is if we buy in and then co-create that imbalanced energy ourselves.

A powerful thing to say in this instance is: "This is not my energy... these are not my demons...and I do not accept this into my field."

Having withdrawn our energy from our typical patterns, we may then focus on the original spilt which created the charge around this field and apply our knowledge to actively mend that schism. Remember, all movement and life begins with the split into Yin and Yang. Therefore, our polarization of the energy related to this given event charged it and brought it to life. Our recognition of this allows us to withdraw our attention from this polarity and reunite the energy as a whole again. Focus on the item in your mind's eye and simply feel where you've been misdirecting all of your energy. And remember, it's your power so it should be easy to find. Once you reclaim it, pull it back into your lower dantien and then seal it in there mentally. From here, watch the energy field of the original issue collapse, and then continue to forgive it until it is completely gone. You should be able to heal any particular issue after following this behavior several times, and the more focused you remain, the quicker it'll all be done. If you catch yourself leaking more energy into the shadow when you think about a subject, simply trace your way back to the root of it. Like the pull of gravity, follow the cord of energy back to the original event and confront it there. This is the quickest way to heal these attachments. They don't want to live in the shadow. All discordant energy wants to return to the Source...think of it like a homecoming. Pull all of your fragmented pieces back into yourself.

Clinical Encounters—Letting Go

EMILY CAME TO me for acupuncture after years of trying pretty much everything. She had seen MDs, DCs, psychotherapists, hypnotherapists, and faith healers. Nothing had worked for her panic attacks. I immediately got the sense that she was a "shopper,"- the type of patient that wants you to tell them what they want to hear. They'll accept help only on their terms. She had smut on everyone she'd seen before me but I was going to be her savior…I was the hero that was going to help her this time…

I had been here too many times and was not about to be another of a long string of failures for her. I kindly said that I wasn't going to be able to meet her expectations and that she shouldn't waste her time and money with me. This infuriated her. She begged and pleaded that I help her. I responded that the only way I could do anything was if she let me in. My terms were simple: we were going to find the original trauma and heal it by feeling it. Somehow I got through to her and, two hours later she walked out and never had another panic attack again.

The power of honesty cannot be underestimated. We traced her discordant energy back to its original event and it was a clean-up job from there. I taught her how to watch for emotional triggers in the future and she was elated to have found such helpful knowledge that she could apply herself. It was also a powerful moment for me because it reinforced two things: 1) this stuff really works and 2) nobody can do it for you…you must do it yourself. I helped Emily heal the wound and that made her whole. It really helped me understand my role as a physician: to teach is to heal.

The next step is not always necessary but is certainly helpful. If you fully understand the previous steps, you can heal emotional issues and absorb your power back from your shadow. The more practice you get, the easier and more enjoyable it will become. The next exercise is a tried-and-true practice of Taoist alchemists designed for internal healing of organs and emotions using the Five Elements. In order to properly understand this system, it is important to recall our earlier discussion of energy fields and vibration. Everything we see is at the same time a particle and a wave- energy and matter simultaneously. We have become so fixated on the material world in our current thinking that we fail to see the energetic basis of the same phenomena as they coexist. Color and sound are distinguished by their waveform. Slight variances in frequency will change the color or the pitch of something. The cells of our body respond to vibrational frequencies as surely as they respond to chemical messengers. [Lipton, 2005 p86] The ancient Taoists understood this and they developed a system of vibrational medicine based on color and sound therapy that has been effectively helping people for thousands of years. I use it in my clinic with patients frequently.

Let's go back to our charts of the correspondences of the Five Elements so that we can reinforce our understanding of this science.

Element	Fire	Earth	Metal	Water	Wood
Yin Organ(s)	Heart, Pericardium	Spleen	Lungs	Kidneys	Liver
Yang Organ(s)	Small Intestine, Triple Burner	Stomach	Large Intestine	Bladder	Gallbladder
Emotions	Mania/Lack of Joy in Life	Pensiveness, Worrying too much	Grief/Inability to let go of things	Fear/Lack of drive and initiative	Anger/Frustration Depression
Healing Colors	Rich Red	Sunshine Yellow	Pure White	Dark Blue	Vibrant Green
Yin Healing Sound	Haa	Huu	Shh	Fuu...u	Shh...u
Yang Healing Sound	Kee-D	Hoo-R	Hoo-D	Yaa-R	Jaa-R

Five Element Sounds

Taking this matrix and assessing which emotions are challenging us in a given situation, we can examine the color and sound of that organ and focus on them. Notice that the Yin and Yang organs have different sounds associated with them. The Yang sounds are depicted with a dash and a capital letter on the end which signifies a "hard" sound which is a sudden transition whereas the Yin sound with the ellipses is a softer sound. These are traditional Taoist healing sounds/techniques which I have been teaching patients for years. I've uploaded sound clips of these at taoistpath.com for you to be able to hear them. Search your field and determine which one you feel needs the attention and focus on it. Of course, you can do both simultaneously using color and sound. Let's go through an example for someone who is dealing with a lot of anger.

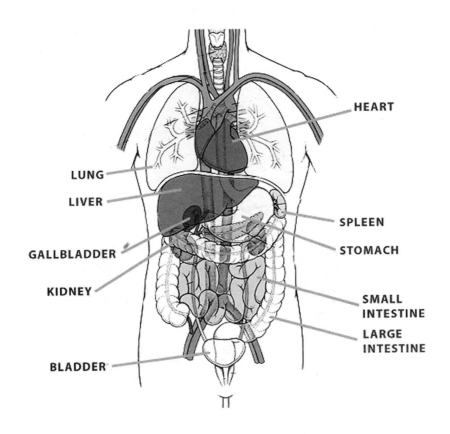

Internal Organs

In this case, this person would focus green light (the color of fresh grass growing in the spring) over their liver located along the right side of the rib cage—see figure above). Inhale the green light to the area and chant the organ sound Shh...u (the first sound drops into the second) on your exhale. Do this softly and repeat over and over until you feel the energy is cleansed. Imagine the light to be a puffy cloud surrounding the organ on the inhale; then condense it into the organ on the exhale while making the healing sound. If you'd like, you can also use the same green light over the gallbladder but now you will chant Jaa-R on the exhale.

You can cycle through all of the elements to conduct a maintenance round or simply focus on an afflicted element. This exercise is particularly effective for problems with the internal organs. Simply go through the same exercise and allow the pure color/sound of the element to cleanse and heal the organ. This is an example of what I call "harmonic tuning," and it allows us to hold pathological or imbalanced vibrations against their correct archetypal gold standards and give them the space to self-correct.

Once you feel proficient at this, you can also apply the same practice with the Generating and Controlling cycles we mentioned earlier.

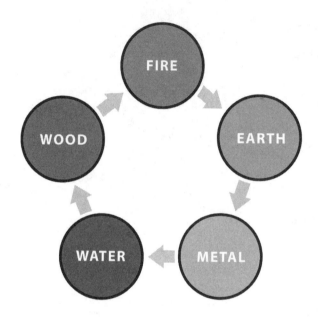

The Generating Cycle

USING THE GENERATING CYCLE:

In this Generating cycle, you can follow the arrows and heal the Elements up or downstream from your afflicted element in order to help bring balance to your system. In this scenario, Water is the "mother" of Wood and Wood is the "mother" of Fire and so on. Take the previous example of a disharmonious Wood element—say we have focused the healing there, but still feel edgy and frustrated. We can then feed the "mother" element of Water and focus dark blue light to the kidneys while chanting (Fuu…u) on the exhale. This may bring the necessary healing to the

Wood element (by bolstering its "mother") which has been drained over several years of emotional turmoil. Since everything is in a cycle, things upstream or downstream may be affecting what you are feeling right now. Use your intuition to scan internally and see where the attention needs to be focused.

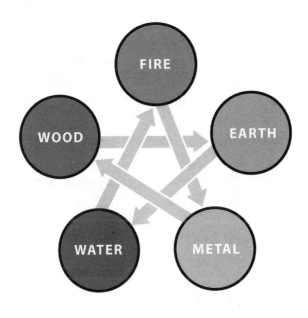

The Controlling Cycle

USING THE CONTROLLING CYCLE:

In the Controlling cycle, Metal controls Wood, which in turn, controls Earth which controls Water and so on. You can support the Metal Element to check or control the Wood element if you need further assistance. Focus white light on the lungs while chanting Shh on the exhale. When scanning your consciousness and uprooting old emotional trance content, you need to feel this energy and determine whether the energy is in excess (feels full or hot) or deficiency (feels empty or cold). If you don't feel you can feel energy well enough yet, practice exercise #2 in the Qi Gong section frequently and you will soon be able to sense the variations in energy current. Is there too much energy overflowing in this system, or not enough, making the system crave more?

You can nourish the "mother" of an element by using the Generating Cycle for a deficient case, or you can use the Controlling Cycle in a case of excess. If you do not feel comfortable with your determination of which way to balance, you can stay with the first exercise of bringing light to the afflicted element. Once you get the hang of that, you can work your way into the more advanced techniques but I encourage you not to worry about it. Bringing pure, undifferentiated light and a healing sound can only heal an imbalance. Worst case scenario: you have healed the wrong organ/element system. There is no downside for this and the organ will thank you for it.

Before we start this mental/emotional cleaning we need to orient ourselves in Time/Space. This is done very easily out of the Middle Dantien or Heart Center (middle of chest vs Heart organ which is shifted slightly to the left). Here is the process:

1. Sit or stand facing the South.
2. Close your eyes and center your awareness in your heart.
3. Focus a beam of light from your heart up through your crown of your head and to the center of the Universe.
4. Send another beam down through your perineum to the center of the Earth (all beams start at the heart center).
5. Now, send beams out in all four cardinal directions starting out in front of you to the South (and out to Infinity).
6. Next send another one through your back to the North.
7. Next out your left side to the East.
8. And finally out the right side of your heart to the West.

Once you have your heart linked to the six directions, you are poised to perform your alchemical work and have it register more effectively. You can do this quickly and anywhere as a centering exercise. If you don't have a compass and are not oriented, simply say "South" in your mind's eye and your Shen will know what to do. Make sure you do all six directions with this as this is what literally parks our Shen at an exact coordinate point in the universe. The anchoring in the six directions is a critical component to all alchemical systems and is one that we will come back to (using the upper dantien) in our more advanced studies in the future.

What we need to do (in summary):

1. Recognize the pattern through mental awareness training and stop yourself before you do it again.

2. Forgive the perpetrator, situation, or conduct.

3. Withdraw your energy from the typical response pattern.

4. Bring balance to the Yin/Yang split by withdrawing your energy from the further creation of the field.

5. Continue to forgive and balance it in your mind's eye and watch the field around it lose its power.

6. Reabsorb this power into your lower dantien.

7. Link up with the Six Directions through the Middle Dantien.

8. Practice the Taoist Five Elemental Magic.

9. Go back to scanning with your awareness for any similar "threads" of discordant energy and apply the same practice to them.

Please remember that this is a process. Once you get into the game and start to understand it, you'll get better at it. It becomes fun and you will feel liberated the further you go with it. Keep releasing trapped energy and remember to absorb your power back into your field. Chaotic energy is not useful to us so bringing our unresolved charge back into the main energy system of our body is tantamount. With time, you'll have more life force and focus at your disposal to engage further into this process. Once you are feeling better, you will naturally notice imbalances and shadow energy trapped in others. When you see this, come back to your own center and heal the energy IN YOURSELF. Your connection with the Tao will facilitate this process. Allow your Heart to feel compassion for their plight and then heal whatever you see in yourself. There's never a dull moment for an alchemist and you'll discover that boredom will be a thing of the past.

※

CHAPTER TEN

SPIRITUaL PRACTICE

The Kingdom of Spirit is embodied in my flesh.
—*Hermes Trismegistus,* The Pattern on the Trestleboard

he essence of our Taoist spiritual practice is one of purification and reduction. We have mentioned that Qi Gong is a subtraction process that helps move away blockages that have propped up against the free flow of energy moving through us. This important understanding underscores our connection with Nature. We are One with all that is around us and the perception of separation can be likened to the proverbial Fall from the Garden of Eden. This intimate and personal interweaving of ourselves and our environment is the foundation of the Taoist understanding of Reality and is the source of our ultimate liberation.

Once we shake out faulty belief systems and trance-inspired ideas about ourselves, we begin to encounter the wonderment of Who we truly are and it is nothing less than amazing. The problem is, in line with polarity consciousness, we move away from our center to find ourselves. We ask around, and look up to an abstract concept of "Heaven" seeking peace and salvation from our miserable state. This is the exact opposite direction and marks the primordial disconnection from the Tao. Healing this is the most powerful act in which we can participate. It brings peace and understanding. It brings us back to our inner nature.

We are going to study the framework of the Five Elements as the model with which we are going to work. We are also going to learn a certain purification process under each element and I encourage you to practice these as often as possible. At first, things may seem awkward as we look through the goggles of our trance mentality. Keeping our focus on the practice, however, will allow us to discover that we are more and more interested in these practices of inner discovery and less inclined to seek out distractions and sedatives in our outer lives.

THE SPIRITUAL PURIFICATION PRACTICES OF THE FIVE ELEMENTS

Let's return to our original illustration of the relationship of the Five Elements and then study each of them individually.

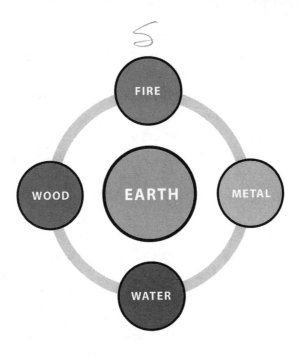

Five Element Chart

Earth

The purification practice for the Earth element is intimately related to the food that we eat. In previous chapters we've discussed the types, quantity, and timing of the food that we choose, but now we're going to examine the quality and source of these foods.

Everything that is material has an energetic and spiritual nature. We have already discussed this in Part One. Everything carries consciousness: animal, plants, even minerals. The source of our nutrition dictates the quality of energy we ingest. This was rarely a problem in the ancient world as food sources were directly extracted from a healthy environment. We now confront toxicity, hormones, and unhappy energy in what we eat. Livestock pumped-up with steroids and hormones and then brutally butchered for fast food needs carry a distinct energy pattern of a very low vibration. Grains mass-produced with pesticides then boxed and refortified, are devoid of life force and many of us are having trouble assimilating them. If we follow the axiom that "we are what we eat," then we need consume pure, natural, high quality, cruelty-free foods. It has a direct effect on our energy and spirit. If you do eat meat, never buy traditional meats that are not raised in healthy fashion.

An enormous concern is the amount of land and resources needed to raise cattle. We are losing our rain forests to fast food eaters stuck in a cultural trance, one that is threatening the future of our planet. There are healthier ways to grow and sustain beef but with a radically different approach that still may or may not work. We will discuss some of these in Part Three. Suffice to say, this entire argument speaks to one key concept: awareness. Anybody who consumes meat in this culture should be asked to go and kill the animal they'd like to eat, skin it, clean it, drain its blood, and then cut its flesh and prepare it. If you can't see what it takes to put that life form on your plate, you'll never develop the true reverence needed to appreciate its sacrifice for you. If you have never grown any food, it is hard to understand the time and effort and love that goes into sustaining this life form for your consumption.

Reverence becomes the centerpiece of our spiritual purification. Any time you ingest anything, stop and thank it for giving its life to sustain yours. Thank it and thank the Universe for providing for you. Don't over-eat and don't waste food. All these sentient entities are giving their lives to sustain us and we need to be both humbled and grateful by this incredible responsibility. With this ingested life force, it becomes our responsibility to wake up and spread grace and love on the planet.

GARDENING

A key spiritual practice that helps us align with the energy of the Earth is gardening. There is communion between us and the planet when we grow our own food. Growing our own produce is an important practice that helps fuse our positive karma (action) with our sustained development physically. We actually enter into the loop of feeding ourselves and have the opportunity to infuse the soil, the crops, and the entire garden with our good will and healthy energy before we eat the food. In fact, we can pro-gram specific goals or medicinal spells into the food and tell ourselves that we will take on those characteristics once we ingest this food. It is a way of entering into a live biofeedback loop with nature in how it connects and sustains us. Don't worry if you can produce enough in your house to feed your whole family: just get involved in the ritual.

ENVIRONMENTAL AWARENESS

My teachers taught me that nature usually provides a cure to whatever we are ailing from. Local botany is an important healing practice because it grounds us into the actual environment in which we live. Get outside and learn about the local trees, plants, and animals. Watch the birds and learn their calls. Become aware of the living biosphere in which you live. Getting involved in local hikes and learning about all the life around you is a powerful spiritual practice. Our return to our primordial home teaches us a great deal about ourselves, and should be treated with the reverence it deserves.

FASTING

Another key element to the Earth purification is an age-old tradition found in most spiritual lineages. Fasting is important when done correctly and it helps reinforce our understanding of nourishment and our relationship to the food chain here on the planet. Remember how we discussed the power of food as a trance and how most of us go unconscious while we eat? Fasting is the key to unlocking that energy and unleashing the freedom trapped in that trance.

I recommend a water-only fast one day per week. This means, from morning to night, simply sipping room temperature water all day. There is no reason to overdo it and it is important to not drink too much in one sitting (which will harm the kidneys). Make it a day where you can get away with exerting less energy and give yourself time for seated meditation or time in nature.

I understand this may be too much for many of you but I am again holding us to the gold standard in this book. If fasting once a week cannot be done, set aside one day a month. Water fasting is an excellent way to detoxify the body and give the digestive system a break. It helps clear the mind and allows us to understand our relationship with food in a deep way. Over the years, I've met a number of people who have done it for religious convictions or to prove that they can but they treated it like a monster that they had to overcome. Understand the nature of the reduction process and relax into self-discovery and liberation. Over time, you will find fasting to be liberating and enjoyable. I know people who have fasted on water for 21-40 days at a time. Now this is more challenging and should only be done under the supervision of a qualified healthcare professional.

It is important to note that many people are hypoglycemic and/or have unhealthy variations in their blood sugar levels. For these people, I recommend a modified juice cleanse instead (until they can fix their problem and go to water). This consists of:
• Filtered room temperature water.
• Freshly squeezed lemon or lime (use as much as you like).
• Grade B Maple Syrup (approximately 2 tablespoons per liter of water).
• A bag of organic green tea.

I have also recommended freshly-squeezed juices for a number of patients but the specific ingredients vary based on their condition. A good general recipe is:
• Kale
• Celery
• Apple
• Ginger
• Carrot

Try to use 50% of the bitter ingredients and 50% of the flavorful ones. Use organic ingredients and drink water throughout the day to flush out your system. It is a bit different for every person. I have listed some resources in the back of the book that will help you find a qualified healthcare professional if you need some help deciding how to fast.

One thing that I like to add to all liquid fasts that I find quite helpful for spiritual development is taking a vow of silence at the same time. This works particularly well because you tend to have less energy to engage in interactions with people on these days anyhow so you might as well do it all together! I find that most people spend the majority of their energy and Zhi (or creative willpower) just spewing wasted energy out of their mouths all day. We literally create our reality with our thoughts and our words so taking regular break from speaking is an excellent way to fix the leak here.

I WAS HEAVILY involved in my training while taking 24 units at UCLA. I had a three-week break and needed the time to practice some of the techniques I had learned. Finals week commanded my attention and I was committed to getting all A's, which I was able to do. The time had come for a mini sabbatical.

I booked a three week trip to Hawaii and spent the first week with my family in Maui. I then flew to Kauai where I spent one week alone in Waimea Canyon and another week on the Napali coast. Waimea Canyon was completely empty and I was the only person in there for the whole week. I found a nice campsite by the river and set up shop. I was to water fast for five days and go through a number of my spiritual purification exercises. I didn't speak a word and allowed my body to cleanse and purify while I focused white light into my field. I ran into a number a really uncomfortable feelings and memories and felt like pulling out a number of times.

The more I was able to let go and release, the easier it got and the lighter I felt. At one point, I was able to follow a family of goats and stay within ten feet of them without them seeing me. I felt like I had blended in with the natural environment so well that they couldn't detect my odor or energetic signature. The first couple of days were rough but it got easier and more rewarding the further I went. By day five, I was ready to slowly get back into juices as I would need more energy to hike several miles per day for the remainder of my trip. What was incredible to me was the amount of energy I felt during the fast. The more I cleaned my energy up, the lighter and more energized I felt. My meditations were incredibly clear and comfortable and several of the aches and pains I had been complaining about simply went away. When I was finally ready to eat solid food, I started with fruit. I picked a fresh mango off of a tree and I was in heaven. I was so thankful for that mango and it tasted so delicious that I spent almost an hour eating it as slowly and mindfully as I could.

Fire

Cleansing the Fire Element is very simple: cleanse Fire with Fire. Using fire to purify one's energy and renew one's light is an excellent way to quickly burn away impurities and raise the vibration of the light body. Fire purification requires one simple ingredient—a nice healthy fire.

We've all spent time in front of a fireplace or a campfire and have been captivated by its power and glow but how often do we engage the spirit of the fire to cleanse our energy and purify our fields? A campfire is a 3D reflection of the Universal archetype of Fire as an element and can be used for this purpose very well. Metaphorically, we can understand the nature of fire by examining its Gua (or Trigram from The Ancient Book or Oracles—The I Ching). [Ritsema, 1994]

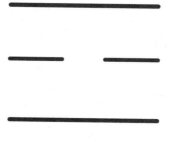

Fire Trigram

The upper and lower lines represent the energy of Yang and the broken line in the middle represents the energy of Yin. This is in the binary code system of the I Ching, the Chinese book of oracles, which uses this system of straight and broken lines that describe all of the phenomena in the whole Universe. Looking at a fire, we can notice the abundant yang energy of the actual flames that cannot exist without some form of substance, which in our case would be the Yin nature of the log. This becomes the microcosm of the metabolic processes that run in our bodies as well. We have our Essence which serves as the underlying basis for our material existence and that provides the substrate (tissues that efficiently collect and organize burnable calories) for the metabolic process of life to occur. This, in turn, kicks on the engines of the Spirit to have a foundation with which to explore and learn.

ENERGY / SPIRIT *Yang*

MATERIAL / BODY *Yin*

ENERGY / SPIRIT *Yang*

Fire Trigram Breakdown

FIRE RITUAL #1—FIRE CLEANSING
• Sit at a comfortable (and safe) distance from the fire and begin to breathe down to your lower dantien.
• Honor the fire by bowing to it and then allow its energy to permeate your field.
• State the following: "I give to you my impurities, my disharmonious energy, my sickness, and my sadness as fuel. Please purify these energies and cleanse my field by releasing the power in the darkness I've shared with you.
• Please continue to cleanse that which I cannot see in my shadow and help me return to the purity of my Original State."
• Sit for as long as comfortable and allow the fire to cleanse your field.
• Thank the fire for the healing and sprinkle some Frankincense or sage in there to purify the room.

THE PERSIAN NEW Year comes from the ancient Zoroastrian religion of fire worship. They believed in a Universe that held a dualistic Godhead; one good and one evil. The New Year was set to be on the Spring Equinox when the energies of light (yang) finally overcame those of darkness (yin). Just before the celebration, people went through another holiday where one of the rituals was to jump over a fire. (I always enjoyed this tradition as a child.) When older, I was taught what was to be said while jumping and came to understand that it was a fire purification ceremony wherein the people cleansed their energies before they entered the New Year. This realization was eye opening because it simultaneously showed me the esoteric wisdom of the ancients and the foggy sleep we are stuck in today.

These holidays have turned into not much more than social outings for boys and girls to meet. Commercial interests have taken over the promotions of these events and people simply walk around and through them like they are at the carnival... just another night out... Where has all the depth gone? How could we have become so mindless that we simply go through the motions of such a powerful purification rite? How did we fall asleep to something that was set up as a safeguard to keep us awake?

FIRE RITUAL #2—THE TAOIST CANDLE MEDITATION
• Find a comfortable place in a dark room without any breeze and have a seat.
• Light a candle that is about 6-12 inches off of the ground and sit about two feet away from it.
• Place your hands on your knees, cupping the knee caps with thumbs and index fingers touching.
• Breathe in nose and out nose with the tip of the tongue touching the roof of the mouth.
• Softly gaze at the blue part of the flame as you continue to breathe.
• Try to avoid blinking your eyes and soften your gaze.

- Sit here for as long as is comfortable (allow yourself to build up tolerance to this).
- Allow the flame to really link up with your third eye and cleanse your spiritual vision.
- Stay here as long as comfortable and simply observe what you see.
- When ready to close, pick up your hands and bring into chest (palms facing the flame) on the inhale and push hands straight out on the exhale towards the flame.
- Mentally pull your consciousness away from the flame on the inhale and separate or cut your consciousness from the flame on the exhale. Do this for five breaths in nose and out mouth.
- Close your eyes and sit in silent meditation for a while.

Metal

Metal is the element of autumn and represents the declining cycle of nature. It is the energy of shedding off excess and giving back what is superfluous in our lives. A healthy tree sheds its leaves in the fall and even loses excess branches that are weak in order to be stronger the year after. It is important to understand that the excess which sheds from a tree gets mulched into the ground and becomes a powerful fertilizer that helps the tree's positive growth into the future. The compost also becomes the fuel and nutritional base for the seeds of its offspring into future generations. This is how life grows in nature and is exactly how we grow on all levels. Again, there is no distinction between mental, spiritual, emotional, and physical in Reality. It's all One but, coming from the perspective of polarity, we see the entire spectrum of this experience as distinct and different. Yin and Yang help us to see the unity in all things by creating a counterpoint perspective.

Our spiritual purification practice for the metal element takes on the theme of release and renewal. We are going to learn this practice in a more formalized standing form with some visualizations, but once you gain proficiency in the ritual (the same as with all the other concepts shared in this book) you can let this process work for you at any given time. It is important to learn the essentials, however, so that some key components are built into your practice. This particular exercise can be quite cathartic and intense at times so make sure you are in a private, safe place for a couple of reasons. First of all, you will be in a very "exposed" position so allow yourself the space to be raw and molt. Secondly, there's a lot of chaotic energy going to be spewing off of you so you want to make sure that gets grounded into the earth and gets recycled. Some people who are very empathic can absorb vibrations easily and we want to make sure we take out our own trash.

THE VIBRATORY STATE

Thanks to the pioneering work of Rev. John Davidson, professor Stanislav Graf, Leonard Orr, and Master Hong Liu, we have come to understand a profound method of release and renewal that encourages letting go in a very primordial way. Rev. John Davidson (working intimately with the innovations of Alfred Korzybski) speaks of it succinctly:

"The degree of strain in the nervous system which results from the conflict of language attempting to encompass feeling is the measure of 'happiness and harmony'. The degree of strain is determined, not through language, but through the 'vibratory state', the body's reaction to language… (and) It is in the vibratory state that original symbol selection can be demonstrated through resultant abreaction, and that 'new symbols may be substituted for the old'." [Davidson, 2000, pp. 2-3]

Language, an artificial construct, often has trouble communicating personal feelings. Communication with our conscious mind gets processed through the imperfect language we have at our disposal. Not only do we lose so much in translation, we also use language to create levels of abstraction away from what Korzybski calls the "original event" which further separates us from Reality. The vibratory state is the disharmonious charge left in our systems from the energy trapped in our shadows. This energy, trapped in our shadow, coagulates in our energy fields until we're able to reabsorb or discharge it.

All things want to grow toward the light. This is an important point to consider: the trapped energies of our shadow would naturally release and come to light if we were to leave things alone. In fact, if it were not for the perpetual reinforcement and polarization of our energy fields, all things would self-correct naturally. We are the ones putting energy into this disarray and we are the ones keeping it that way. We spend our energy fighting with reality and swimming upstream. The vibratory state is a perfectly natural reaction to energy trying to release. The more we allow the trapped energies to be released through acknowledgement of the original event, the more settled and less tumultuous our vibratory state becomes.

The vibratory state feels like a mild trembling feeling. It can become full convulsions or just a mild rocking or swinging back and forth. Our practice involves passive scanning of the body/energy field for disharmonious energies and then an "allowance" that frees these energies to finally express and release. The critical mindset needed to perform this successfully is acceptance. Simply acknowledge this energy, let it be and express itself. Much like a small child that is being fussy and cries, ignoring it will not help… and neither will hostility. See what it wants. Allow it to move through your system in its own way until it express itself. We must breathe into the area. An infusion of fresh energy with breath and the light of awareness will dislodge trapped energy and set it free.

All kinds of crazy stuff gets dislodged during this practice and it is common to look like you're almost having a seizure while in the vibratory state. Just breathe through it and let it be until it passes. Remember that it was the suppression of these energies that created the problem in the first place so, be accepting of whatever comes up and just let it pass through. That would have happened at the Original Event had we not polarized, charged, encapsulated, and stored it so long ago. It would have come and gone like everything else but we were the ones who froze it in time and held onto it. This time, we've learned our lesson. Just let it be—whatever it is.

If the vibratory motions get too tumultuous, take a few attempts at releasing given energies. Chip away at it if you will. Oftentimes, people feel like they are dying. That's not really the case. What is dying is the energetic "life form" you've created, almost like a monster or demon kicking and screaming for its last breath. Stop feeding it your power and lovingly let it reabsorb into the Universe. These are your falling leaves. See them getting reabsorbed by the earth and pushing up flowers. Do it with a smile on our face.

PRELIMINARY STEPS

• Find yourself a private room where you can be for a good 20-40 minutes, preferably on the first floor. Out in nature alone is ideal although impractical for most city dwellers.

• Stand in wu chi posture with feet shoulder width apart and knees slightly bent.

• Put your hands into the "Post Position" which looks like you are hugging a tree.

• Have the tip of the tongue touch the roof of the mouth and breathe in nose and out nose to the lower dantien.

• Allow your shoulders to relax and settle into the posture.

• Make the following statement to the Earth (in your mind or out loud): "Please absorb all of the energies that I am about to release to you. Let them be the food for tomorrow's flowers. Thank you".

THE PRACTICE

• Begin to scan your body from head to toe for any discordant energies.

• If you can't feel this in your body yet, simply think of an issue that is bothering you and observe the first body part that comes to mind...start there. It may take several passes to detect anything when you first start.

• When you sense one, simply acknowledge it and then allow your consciousness to tune into its vibration and let it resonate within you.

• Keep your breath focused on your lower dantien.

• Begin to allow your body to move with it (stay in the structure of the Post Position but move within this framework),side-to-side, front to back, bouncing up and down, hands trembling. Do whatever naturally happens.

• Keep breathing down to your lower dantien and focus your attention on the vibratory state that you have just uncovered.

• Stay with this energy and keep breathing (and moving) with it until you feel like you have adequately discharged it.

• Again, allow any chaotic energy released to be absorbed into the Earth.

• You will find that the breathing becomes very erratic once in the vibratory state and you can exhale out your mouth as need be but always return to your cyclic lower dantien breathing. The constant flow of breath and life force to this process is what brings enough power in to dislodge stuck energies.

• You will also finds the parts of the body that are holding trapped energy and can often isolate precisely where the particular vibration is originating. Just keep breathing to that specific area and let the vibratory state continue to molt and unfold until it is done. Remember that these may be energies that have been trapped and reinforced for decades. Be patient with the process.

• Thank the energy for releasing and apologize to it for trapping it for so long.

• Move back into scanning for the next vibration if you still have an alchemical appetite and repeat this sequence or move to the closing sequence.

CLOSING SEQUENCE

• Exhale out the mouth and let the hands drop down to the sides.

• Inhale and circle the arms with palms up along the sides all the way to above your head (palms up), and then exhale with palms down in front of your body.

• Do this for three cycles, gathering energy up and smoothing the energy field on the way down.

• Give thanks to the Earth and visualize in your mind's eye all of the energy you discharged being absorbed in the ground. The further down it goes, the more flowers you seeing springing up all around your feet all around you.

• Drink some water and relax for at least 15 minutes. This would be a great time to go into some silent seated meditation and see inside. You'll be amazed at how clear the internal vision becomes when unhealthy energy is allowed to discharge.

In closing, you may go to taoistpath.com to see a video sample of what this practice looks like. This is very powerful stuff and it will change your life so treat it with reverence and patience. We do not live in a culture that accepts loss well. If you have a history of severe depression, psychosis, or any major mental illness, it is appropriate to proceed with caution in this process. Work with your therapist to move through these techniques. In these cases, it is important to have someone there to deal with the fallout as things get shaken up.

Water

Water is the element of winter. It represents the energy of consolidation, nourishment, and regeneration. It is the rest and the gathering of Qi and Jing that allows us to fully express energy outwardly. It is the good night's sleep that gives us energy for the next day. It is the dark, peaceful silence that balances all of the noise. Water is 60% of our bodies, and is the "soup" in which all of the processes of life work. In fact, water is the "currency" of life in many ways. It's our basis for growth and the driving force of all energy currents. There is a tremendous amount of energy traveling through water, and this "liquid" energy flows throughout our bodies and is carried through all life forms on the planet. Here is the Trigram for water:

—— ——

————

—— ——

Water Trigram

Notice how this Trigram is the inversion of the Trigram for Fire. The Trigram for Water consists of a single Yang bar between two Yin bars. It conveys a soft external appearance that houses a tremendous Yang power within. After all, it is water that carved the Grand Canyon. It is water that carries that same power through every cell of our bodies.

The spiritual purification practice for the Water Element involves a good amount of time in submersion in a clean source of water. Before you grab your swim trunks, know that chlorinated pools do not count, as chlorine can seep through the skin and create problems in our system. Natural and unpolluted bodies of water are the best to swim in but, in this particular practice, we will conduct our practice in a very convenient place- our bathtub.

Before we get into the instruction here, though, it is important to say a word about water quality in the house. Most of us live in urban environments where water is pumped from far away to get to our houses. A number of chemicals are added to the water to assure its safety from contamination. Millions of people die annually in the Third World because of polluted water so it is quite a blessing to be able to have clean water at our disposal in our homes. Modernity has its drawbacks, however, as a number of health issues have arisen in regards to the additives. It is important to not only have a filter for drinking water but also to have a good shower filter. There are a number of resources I have listed at taoistpath.com but, suffice it to say, our skin absorbs chemicals very effectively and these create problems that include free radical damage and the weakening of gut flora colonies.

WATER PURIFICATION EXERCISE #1
—SUBMERGED REJUVENATION

• Fill your tub with filtered water and get it as hot as you can comfortably tolerate.
• You can add a pure source of sea salts or Epsom salts if desired.
• Light a single candle within reach and then get into the tub. Submerge as much of your body as you can.
• Close your eyes and relax for a few minutes, allowing your body and mind to settle.
• Begin a series of connected breathing, which means connecting the inhale with the exhale without any pause in between. Do this for 20 continuous breaths.

• After 20 breaths, relax and breathe down to the lower dantien for a number of breaths and observe what comes up.

• Just like the Metal exercise listed above, find whatever vibratory frequencies that arise in your body and simply acknowledge them and allow them to be.

• Allow the water to purify and cleanse your energy body and absorb any chaotic Qi.

• Once you feel like you have cleared a layer, move back into 20 more breaths of your Circular Breathing.

• Repeat this cycle for at least an hour.

• You may feel discomfort that will not always be fun. Be with it and allow yourself to molt. The discomfort will pass and you will then cleanse through to the next item in your shadow.

• When you finally sense you are done for this session, slowly drain the water and take a lukewarm to cold shower. This will seal the energy centers that you just worked on.

• Thank the water for helping you cleanse and return your breath to your lower dantien before exiting the shower.

This practice is quite rejuvenating and can be done daily. But there is a trade-off between our personal needs and the state of the environment. Heating water for a bath requires a lot of energy and so I tend to do this practice as a treat every now and again. If you have managed to work your way off the grid and have solar heating and can reclaim the water for irrigation, then, by all means, do it more often. Natural hot springs are an excellent place to conduct this practice as well. This is inspired by Leonard Orr's purification process which I have found to be quite effective. Orr is the founder of Rebirthing and has contributed much to this subject. [Orr, 1998]

I HAD A PATIENT a few years back who had studied a variety of healing techniques and had put a lot of energy into learning how to heal. She displayed a variety of imbalanced Fire element signs (mania, insomnia, canker sores…) and her entire demeanor pointed to this clearly. She had run into some health concerns while working as a busy executive and decided to quit everything and study massage. She went from high-powered business woman to a crystal wearing shamanic healer in the matter of two months. Her possessions were all put away or given away and she was searching for answers everywhere.

Now this sounds good in theory, but what I found in front of me was a truly miserable person. She was running to the Light and away from her life and her family. The flame of her Heart Fire had gone out of control and she was making reckless decisions while compromising her relationships with a new judgmental "spiritual" attitude. This wasn't liberation for her, it was just rebellion.

After some discussion, I was able to convince her to try a balanced approach. I guided her to commune with the Water element (which balances a Fire disharmony) and gave her specific programming instructions for the water that she blessed and drank daily. It only took a month before she came to her senses. We were able to get her to take her keen business acumen and apply it to a new "green" business she had in mind. She went from spinning out of control and blowing through her life's savings to making great money while doing some real good for the world. She surrounded herself with good people and found a career that meant something. Her ailments had been cured and she had her life back…all because we were able to balance her energy.

WATER PURIFICATION EXERCISE #2
—BLESSING YOUR WATER

My Grandmaster taught us a special Taoist invocation to charge a spell or idea using Shen in a glass of water. This charged water can be given to a patient as medicine or taken for oneself. A good deal of excellent work has been done in the field of water research and I feel that, with a healthy understanding of the principles taught in this book and the premise of Dr. Emoto's work on water, that anybody can now practice this Taoist magic. [Emoto, 2004]

The process is simple:

• Take a glass of filtered water and place it on a table in front of you.

• Put both your hands around the glass and simply breathe white light through your palms into the glass.

• Drop into your Heart and say, "I love you" and "Thank You" to the water and hold that feeling in your heart.

• Allow that feeling to pass through your palms into the glass of water.

• Once the water is blessed, you can add any other frequency you want to the glass. For example, penicillin, vitamin C, cough suppressant, caffeine—whatever you implant with your Shen will be tuned into the water. Everything has an energetic signature so simply think of the substance you may need in your system and infuse its waveform into the water.

• Drink the water or give it to someone who needs it.

With practice, you will get better at this. It will suit you to read about the pioneering work of Dr. Emoto at some point. You will find that you can perform resonant tuning with any frequency pattern and do so quite effectively. High power microscopes have proven the stating of "I love you" and "Thank you" miraculously structures the water into beautiful crystals. This, in turn, positively affects the alignment of water molecules in our bodies. This is an excellent practice to do when in the bathtub. Simply turn your attention to the tub water and bless it before getting in. You can also implant a specific therapeutic intention into the tub water for your session

WATER PURIFICATION EXERCISE #3—DARK RETREAT

This advanced practice, taught in both Chinese Taoist and Tibetan Dzogchen traditions, , , , can be done for three weeks or more (senior students only) but is very helpful in shorter durations as well. The goal is to spend a period of time in complete darkness without any outside light or stimulation in general. This is an ancient method of rejuvenating the body and mind and accessing an incredible connection to Spirit. It is very challenging for students and should be done with caution. Try it at first for a two-hour segment—not around bedtime. From there, you can work your way up to multiple hours with people bringing you food and having access to a toilet that you have to feel your way to.

Again, this is a profound practice that restores Yin and Jing back to the system. In fact, it seems that people undergo interesting neurochemical changes with the high doses of melatonin that are released in the brain [Pierpaoli, 1995)] Melatonin acts as one of the body's most powerful immune-modulators and it also converts to dimethyl-tryptamine (DMT) which is associated with out-of-body experiences and intense feelings of spiritual connection. Fascinating studies have been done on this subject. [Strassman, 2001] Master Mantak Chia has had great success treating "incurable" illnesses with a dark retreat in Thailand. The pioneering work of Dr. Rick Strassman can help walk you through the various spiritual implications of this work. When you're ready, Dark Retreat is an important practice in the cultivation of the Light Body.

Wood

Wood energy carries with it enthusiasm and expansion. It is the emergent life force arising out of the restful winter, pushing to grow and thrive into the summer to come. This energy is easily detected and is almost contagious when "spring is in the air." It helps us fulfill our dreams and carries us forward with our ambitions. Syncing up with the Wood energy is easiest in the springtime but possible in any season by going out into nature.

WOOD PURIFICATION EXERCISE #1
—COMMUNING WITH A LEAF

Famous wilderness survival teacher and holder of the Apache tracking lineage, Tom Brown Jr., states that if you ever have a question about anything, simply go meditate on a leaf and the answer will present itself. [Brown, 1997] Anything. I can get into fractal mathematics and attempt to explain why that makes sense with the new quantum science, but I'm not here to bridge that gap and plenty of people can do that better than me. Instead, I'm here to show you how to do this and open up its endless possibilities. The practice follows:

• Go out into a natural environment (if possible) and find a freshly-sprouting leaf to meditate on—try not to pluck it off!

• Sit comfortably and take 10 breaths down to your lower dantien.

• Focus your attention on your heart and then focus your eyes intently on the leaf (softly gaze without "bug eyes").

• Connect up with the leaf through your heart and then continue to breathe in and out while focusing on the leaf.

• Allow yourself to quiet the mind and see the leaf and all of the intricacies in it while you continue to breathe and connect.

• Pose your question(s) to the leaf.

• Stay here for at least 20 minutes and breathe through any feelings of frustration, boredom, or general discomfort you may feel.

• When you are ready to close, return your breath and awareness to your lower dantien for another 10 breaths.

• Wish the leaf well and bow to it before getting up.

Find a young healthy leaf to practice this on. Once you are able to communicate with the sentience of the leaf and the language of its underlying life force speaking to you, then the fun really starts. Remember: all of life emerges through the same Universal fractal pattern, so any part of the whole contains all of the information of the Universe—past, present, and future. The leaf is a budding snapshot of that pattern which places it right in your face. Actually, it is always right in your face all of the time! Once you bite into the Mystery of Mysteries, you'll realize why the great masters are always laughing.

WOOD PURIFICATION EXERCISE #2
—RANDOM ACTS OF KINDNESS

The Spiritual attribute of the Wood element is that of benevolence, which acts as a counterweight to the disharmony expressed in anger, frustration, and depression. The Wood element is the General of our systems. It takes the heart's desires and carries them throughout the body. Subsequently, the Wood element is our body's "doer," the element that gets things done. If we examine the mental/emotional pathologies that emerge with a disharmonious Wood element, we see problems with wrongful action. Anger is an aggressive energy responding to something we have an aversion to. Frustration is a sense of pent-up energy from action that didn't quite manifest in a desired end result. Depression is the energy of giving up on action that has been frustrated. They are all tied into how we move towards our desires or away from things we can't tolerate. Most people in the West have Wood element pathologies because we feel like we always have to "do something" to fix things or change reality to our liking.

The ancient Taoist teachings tell us that once we have come back to balance and harmony with the Tao, then all action becomes spontaneously-inspired and driven from the power within versus mental reactions to emotional charge. This is a wonderful place to be and cultivate but we need to bridge that gap by taking the edge off of this deep-seated pathology of finding a problem and attempting to do something about it. We are fighting imbalanced action with more imbalanced action.

The nature of this next exercise is very similar to the Mental Practice meditation we discussed earlier. If you recall, that practice asked us to observe any and all action in our minds and simply stop doing it. The only action that is acceptable in that practice is asking the question: "What am I doing right now?" Then stopping whatever mess you found yourself in, calmly returning to your state of inaction.

In this practice, we are going to follow that same line but, instead of practicing inaction, we are going to practice the only karmically healthy form of action out there: benevolence.

This means performing good deeds for the benefit of all life.

I HAD PURCHASED a *mala* prayer bead necklace in India and had taken it along with me wherever I went. Every great master I encountered and studied with, including the Dalai Lama and Karmapa Lama, had blessed it for me. These particular prayer beads are built with a counting system wherein you slide a disc to one side for every time you say a prayer. You slide another one over for every hundred. There was another counter that I slid over for every time a finished ten sets of one hundred, which made a thousand. I was told I needed to say the Tibetan prayer *"Om mani padme hum"* (Hail to the jewel of the Lotus) into this *mala* ten thousand times to activate it. It took dozens of bus rides and hundreds of hours of patiently praying into this thing for over six months until I had finally reached ten thousand. This relic was the single most valuable thing I possessed and was so proud to have prayed into it and have it been blessed by so many Saints. I guarded it with my life and never took it off.

Here I was reveling in the beauty of my new toy when my inner voice came in loud and clear. I was instructed to give it to a friend of mine back in Los Angeles. I tried to pretend I didn't hear it but the feeling was unavoidable. When I returned to the States, I simply handed it over to this person as a souvenir and carried on about my business. I never told this individual about the remarkable value of this gift as something made me stop every time I came to disclose it. I just felt that it wasn't for him to know. I thought about it often and occasionally still do. It was like Bilbo Baggins (*Lord of the Rings*) giving away his precious ring of power to Frodo. It was a powerful lesson in non-attachment and it has taught me much about externalizing spirituality. It was the act of doing the prayers that meant everything. The material object... that was a shiny trap!

Part of the pathology of our Western Creation Myth is that we should do good deeds for other humans, and that we may do so at the expense of the environment…which God has told us is under our dominion anyhow. Not anymore! Make sure your definition includes all Life/all sentient beings/ anything you see or don't see/all that exists. We are all One and part of the same Life Force, so excluding anything in your benevolence creates polarity and separation in the very fabric of the Universe.

The practice is a simple one. Perform five random good deeds every day. Do more if you can. It could range from helping a person in need, to picking up trash on the beach when you see it. Maybe it is giving a compliment to a stranger who looks like they need it. You decide, but the quickest way to heal a Wood Element pathology is to start inundating the world with genuine good deeds.

On that point, I'd like to emphasize the importance of anonymity in this work (as much as is possible). We are not performing these acts for the cultural accolades but just because. Our egos would love to take credit for these actions, but drop it! Simply do good deeds without conditions or strings attached. Let your Higher Self perform the good deed, not your ego.

WOOD PURIFICATION EXERCISE #3—CLEANSING ANGER

As mentioned earlier, pent-up anger leads to frustration. We become depressed when we unplug and don't do anything about it, and we become full of rage if we let it swell up for too long. The Taoist perspective is to release or discharge repressed emotional energy in a controlled and meaningful fashion. I am always surprised at how much repressed anger I see in our society. People are overflowing with it. For me, I have spent a good deal of time in the martial arts where we have an organized and effective platform to work out aggression. Some of the nicest people I have met are seasoned martial artists who have come full circle and found inner peace through a deep understanding of their anger and pent-up frustrations. I also meet "spiritual" teachers who look like they are about to explode.

The conscious act of moving anger through us and allowing it to express in a controlled setting is both liberating and empowering. Holding onto anger is like having a gong go off in your head and being unable to do anything about it. I highly recommend an organized martial arts discipline if it is possible for you. If not, a great way to work out some aggression is to put on some gloves and lay into a punching bag or a pillow. Do it somewhere in a safe environment and really allow yourself to open up the floodgates and let the anger move through you. Remember, all energies want to move and express naturally. Allow the anger to release and move through you and out into the punching bag. Hanging onto it gives it more charge and it eventually consumes us. Once you are done, (or exhausted), sit in silent meditation and visualize a green light around your body. Bring your attention back into your lower dantien and notice what has changed inside.

This is an excellent way to siphon off pressure that has been building up for years. It may take several attempts to clear yourself of these pent-up feelings but stay with it. This does not fix the problem, though. The problem with anger is usually the swallowing of words when a boundary is violated. Sometimes it is appropriate to be upset about a certain thing. For instance, if an elderly woman is trying to cross the street and no cars are stopping for her at the crosswalk, it is perfectly appropriate to get out there and help her cross while sharply signaling the violators to stop. Standing up for what is right and just is critical and it is usually when we swallow our words and keep them inside that they turn into anger and frustration. Speak your truth and be honest and raw in life and there is less to swallow. When boundaries are crossed, we feel violated. If that keeps happening to you, work on strengthening your boundaries. Do this with the relationships in your life and also do this by strengthening your Wei Qi using the Qi Gong exercises we learned earlier.

Anger is just another emotion and it has received a very negative connotation in our culture because we judge it as bad. What is truly bad is our reluctance to be real and raw in the moment. We feel like we are not being good people when we feel angry, so we hide it. We bottle it up and store it for years and then one day we snap at our spouse for something silly they do and it blows up into an explosion of dramatic proportions. When we speak our truth in the moment and let people know that a certain action/comment/behavior bothers us when we first encounter it, we help establish healthy boundaries and prevent the creation of yet another internal demon.

This concludes Part Two of this book. Practice what you've learned and keep your focus on using these techniques to subtract or to simplify your life and clear blockages in your field. You will soon begin to feel more energy and clarity available to you on a day-to-day basis. This energy has always been there but we are too busy creating that mess we call our lives to actually feel all of that power moving through us.

Part Three has us exploring what we can now do with this information and what that means for our personal growth and development. We'll look directly into the light at the end of this tunnel and get our bearings straight. Our sleepy trances would like to convince us that we're not worthy or that this course of action is not for us. But we now know better! We are going to boldly push through and claim our birthright!

✳

PART THREE
Coming Home

CHAPTER ELEVEN

THE PREDATORY UNIVERSE

Light drives out darkness. This simple truth is the practical key to the problem of how to combat demons. A demon perceived, i.e. on whom the light of consciousness is thrown, is already a demon rendered impotent.

—*Valentin Tomberg,* Meditations on the Tarot

N ow that we have laid the groundwork for what is going to clean our energy fields, it is time to look directly into the face of the monster and gain some appreciation for the magnitude of the problem as it relates to the world we live in. We have developed an understanding of how we interface with Reality and, through our reactions, how it is we leak energy into our shadows. We have learned that this is what creates the trance mentality which makes us walk around like zombies, 90% asleep and constantly suffering on all levels. It is this leaking of our energy that opens us up to the "black market" of energy exchange. This is the predatory reality that has us feeding off each other and allows other entities to live off of us all. Let's go back to our Five Elements diagram and take a look:

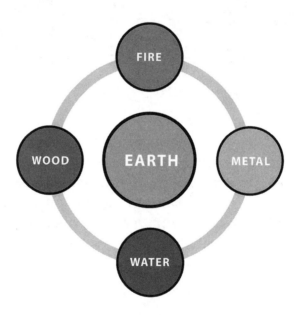

The Five Elements

Recall that we have a vertical spiritual axis of Fire and Water. This fuses Attention and Intention with the central Intellect that serves as the basis of our major alchemical work. Then we have the horizontal soul axis of Wood and Metal through which the Intellect tries to process the rising and falling circumstances of our lives. It is through this horizontal axis where the Intellect develops the ego, which in turn serves as a fortified identity to help us deal with day-to-day life. This is also where we leak a great deal of our energy through our aversions and cravings. We bleed into our shadows on this horizontal axis. We pump energy into the opposite polarity of whatever makes us uncomfortable, while we also reinforce beliefs and characteristics in our ego that help protect us from the way we feel about these things. Over time, we create clusters or families of these reactions that thematically join together and form our fear-inspired beliefs and subconscious behaviors. These behaviors are subconscious by nature because they come from our shadows; the light of conscious awareness doesn't see them and so they go unchecked. We, in turn, walk around in trance most of the time. Then, we run into each other.

It's bad enough having one zombie around…but what happens when there are more? What if almost everyone is asleep? Take a look around you. Since we are all truly One, the perception of separation is part of our ignorant sleep. We have a permanent spiritual flu that keeps being passed around because everyone is unaware of the cure. The way thought aversions bundle together and create subconscious belief in my shadow is the same way it happens within the shadows of others. We tend to attract like-minded people into our fields for good reason. Think about it this way:

John has a single bad experience with a schoolmate who happens to be black. That created an aversion against that particular boy. Then he saw that boy hanging out with a couple other black children so he extended his judgment against "those boys." He'd avoid them in the halls and at lunch. He tells his friend about this dislike, and his friend says that his father told him to watch out for black people because they steal. John can't help but to feel vindicated. The energy in his shadow which has already taken life from his own aversions before has now taken on a new belief system—black people steal. Now, John and his friend find vindication in their belief by talking to a few other boys and suddenly they all have created a hostile environment for the black boys, who can't even figure out why this is all going on. Twenty years later, John has moved into a safe neighborhood where they don't let "those" people in and he talks about how inner city people are all lazy and that need more prisons to contain them. Somehow he has lumped Arabs, Mexican immigrants, and a few other races of people into his belief system over the years. These people are not to be trusted...I'm buying a gun.

Every time John has an aversion to anything that corresponds to the race theme, it gets filed into this folder and feeds the monster in his shadow. He develops a huge array of subconscious behaviors that he simply accepts as self-evident truths but he has no real rational or conscious foundation for any of it. Does this guy sound familiar?

The fact of the matter is that we're all involved in this game all of the time unless we wake up and understand how it functions within us. We do it with everything. We recruit people who share our likes or dislikes into our lives subconsciously and we help each other reinforce these beliefs through "mob mentality".

• *I agree not to mention anything about the affair that you're having if you keep quiet about my alcoholism.*

• *I won't make comments about the dark circles under your eyes if you stop looking at my bald spot.*

This goes on in every walk of life and we help serve each other's shadows with cooperative behavior.

• *I'm willing to give you the compliments you need and bring you along into my social circle so long as you help me with my homework and let me cheat off of you.*

• *You keep dressing up and looking pretty on my arm at cocktail parties and I'll give you all the money and security you need in life.*

Or my favorite: the "Guru":

• *I will give you the spiritual liberation you seek and promote you in my church or organization if you sleep with me and/or transfer all of your possessions to me.*

Puppeteers

There are the billions of people walking around this planet who are completely ignorant of their behavior, and then there are those others who have finally discovered the cure and woken up, but merely to a certain degree. There are only two ways to go once you wake up from trance: either you see the plight of your fellow humans and feel compassion, or you see the inherent weakness in their vulnerable state and figure that you have leverage over them.

People interested in awakening and embracing the love of the Life Force are the great Saints and teachers who have come and gone. They are also the millions of people committed to helping humanity to some degree and on some level. These people don't have to be fully awakened to have their hearts in the right place. I see this in most Americans: good God-loving people. Sadly, the great majority of them still carry a polarized charge in their shadows. Because of the nature of the shadow, these things are unconscious by definition, and it leaves this whole class of people open to being manipulated and coerced.

The other category are people who can (to varying degrees) see through the behaviors of others and who understand how to invoke archetypal arguments and "mob mentality" in order to leverage people into fulfilling their desires. There are people skilled in the esoteric arts who are quite active in this realm, but they are not alone. We all do it unconsciously. Like a good Judo fighter, we learn to see weakness in each other in our subconscious processes. We throw and get thrown—always engaged in some wrestling match most of the time. Those who are good at this are often the ones who are the most successful in worldly affairs because they comprehend and execute this manipulation the best.

If you create a monetary system and lend it to governments of the world, and that money is valued as the currency of freedom, power, and abundance, then he with the most rises to the top. Who is the one with the most? How about the one who created the game and issues the money in the first place? There are a number of individuals who have gotten this game down and have billions of people globally buying into their way of living life. Because people are completely asleep, they can't even question things—"it's just how things are." When a car dealer sees a middle aged guy on his lot staring at a red Corvette, he knows the exact angle to leverage this guy into getting his money. Let's see…wants to feel desirable again…has some money…wants to impress girls…is feeling insecure…" Easy—convince him that this car will make him feel better and fulfill his myriad desires.

The advertising industry is essentially built on the exploitation of human emotions—fears, desires, insecurities, and beliefs. You have to buy this home alarm system because the world is not safe and someone is going to get you! Because we don't have conscious awareness of what is going on within ourselves, there are many people all around us that have learned to feed off the energy in our shadows and get what they want. The black market of energy is where most people go to get their daily fix. The great majority of their conscious energy has been ripped off so they need to get into the game and get more. Either you become a predator or you lock yourself up with depression and anxiety to avoid people and the rat race. Because we have lost so much of our personal power to our shadows, we feel tired and drained. Because we need to keep functioning in our day-to-day jobs and lives, we need to get the lost energy from somewhere. So we drink stimulants and start to drain energy from each other. We have become a culture of vampires sucking life force from wherever we can every day, just to get by.

Personal Journeys—High Finance Parasites

I'VE ALWAYS KEPT in contact with old friends from the past. I called one guy who I had a history with back in high school to see how he was doing. I'd heard he'd had a couple of kids and it turned out that he was doing really well for himself. He had an enormous house on top of a hill and was raking in the dough. Apparently, he had been riding the crest of the home equity loan trend and had made a bundle. What he (and others in his field) did was to convince people to borrow against the perceived value of their homes in a market that promised to keep expanding. He was adept at getting into the emotional undercurrents of his customers and help them to imagine what it would be like to have an endless supply of excess cash in their hands. These people usually went for the deal and then rushed out to buy the SUVs, boats, and 4 wheelers they had always wanted. But now with the collapse of the housing bubble, all these toys have been repossessed, and these people, who were manipulated through the weaknesses of their shadows, are hurting terribly.

And my adept "friend"?

He now makes a living by convincing people to stop paying their mortgages in order to get the principal of their loans reduced by the banks he once *represented*. This guy still has his nice house and still drives big cars…

Money and Sex

Money and sex are two of the biggest hang-ups for people in our culture when it comes to leaking out vital energy. They hold pivotal spots in people's consciousness and carry deep-seated anxiety and fear-inspired beliefs that lead to harmful behaviors. Let's start with money…

We live in a culture where there has been a strange juxtaposition of beliefs on the subject of money. The religious heritage of many people has inserted a deep-seated "money is evil" program which is always running in the background. Along with this come thoughts like "rich people all gain their wealth unethically," or "I don't want money to corrupt me. This type of programming gets superimposed on the reality of the economic system in which we live. In the US, money talks. Commercials are constantly prodding us to buy new products or change our look in order to be desirable. Forces pull on us from all sides trying to get us to spend our hard-earned cash, and, in the end, most of us do. "I need this new car because I deserve it" or "this purse is so outdated…I need a new one" are common types of thoughts. These things cost money and we are happy to pay or finance our way into getting the stuff that we desire. Fine. Make money and buy what you desire. The problem is that most Americans are too happy to borrow and get into deficit spending. Everyone is stressed about money and the subject occupies way too much of our daily mental energy. In order to be free of this pathology, we really need to balance our personal budgets and be more mindful about our expenditures. If you want more things, fine, go make more money. However, do not spend more than you should on "stuff" and then complain about being stressed about money all of the time. There is nothing inherently wrong or evil with money but our relationship with money creates profound stress and anxiety in our daily lives.

Sex is the driving force behind so much of our culture and consumption-based economy that it is seen everywhere. Makeup, clothing, cars, music...you name it, there's some aspect of sales that ties in sex. Why? Sex is the fundamental energy that drives our species. Sex is our connection to our immortality and all of our life force. It defines who we are and our egos are often driven by it. People are so lost in their mental sexual meanderings that they can be leveraged in any way by people who understand what's going on. We are talking about powerful stuff and people are putty when their loins explode with no amount mental reasoning that can stop them.

The solution to this pathology is actually quite easy: learn Tantra which is the ancient spiritual art of personal cultivation teaching the practitioner to harness, control, and work with their sexual energy. The aim is to raise and refine this energy to the spiritual centers of the brain and to learn to harness and control this force. This is the path to an ultimate source of power and realization which cannot even be described. The leaking of sexual energy is equal to spiritual suicide in the Tantric sense. This energy must be understood, cultivated, and more importantly, celebrated once one realizes the beauty and magnitude of it. Again, please refer to taoist-path.com for resources and teachers of Tantra.

Vampires and Demons

It's not hard to create an artificial demon. Here's an excerpt from Meditations on the Tarot which is from the Western Hermetic tradition:

> *"How are demons engendered? As with all generation, that of demons is the result of the cooperation of the male principle and the female principle. i.e. the will and the imagination, in the case of generation through the psychic life of an individual. A desire that is perverse or contrary to nature, followed by the corresponding imagination, together constitute the act of generation of a demon." [Tomberg, 1993, p. 408]*

Let's look at this excerpt closely and piece it together in the language we have learned in this book.

1. A desire that is perverse or contrary to nature is a reaction to a thought or emotion that reflects an aversion or a craving. In essence, nature unfolds for us in a particular way and our reaction results in a desire "away" from this flow.

2. The male and female principles are the will which is the Zhi housed in our kidneys (female, water, yin) and the imagination is the Attention or Shen housed in the heart (male, fire, yang).

3. We have a desire or reaction on the horizontal axis and use the vertical axis to Create in accordance with this. Therefore, when we have an unnatural desire, we then use our creative principle to create an artificial demon.

4. This is exactly what we have been talking about since the beginning of this book but I have avoided using the aggressive nomenclature until now. The energy we pump into our shadows that breathes "life" into our aversions and cravings actually creates artificial demons which take on a life of their own and begin to influence our mind/activities.

Let's examine this mechanism in a diagram to understand it better.

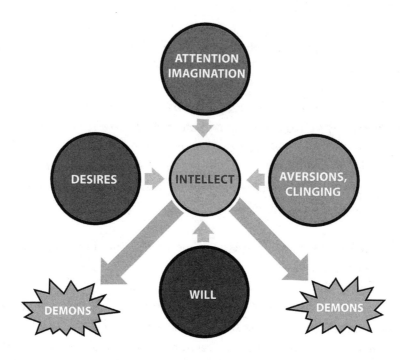

How We Create Demons

In this faulty model, our mind and emotions have an abreaction to whatever reality is presenting and, using our Creative faculty, we polarize the energy and literally breathe life into demons we have created that live in our shadows. These demons then influence our thoughts and create similar situations for us in life that draw us into similar abreactions which in turn continue to feed these demons. This is what is called an "internal possession" in Taoism. The way we would conduct an exorcism in this situation is exactly how you have been taught already.

1. You acknowledge the behavior and bring the light of consciousness to it.
2. You stop engaging in your habitual pattern of reinforcement through aversions and cravings.
3. You drop into your heart and forgive the person, situation, thing that is causing your internal reaction.

4. You watch as the energy deflates and dissipates while you hold it in love and withdraw the power you have put into its opposite polarity.

5. You search your consciousness for similar energies/demons and perform the same process.

If we don't exorcize our internal demons they will keep drawing us into unhealthy behavior until our last moment in our earthly bodies. In fact, once our demons have enough power in our shadows, they constantly drain us of our vitality. This, however, starts to diminish their source of energy, so one of three things happens at this point.

1. We continue to get drained and at a certain point, devoid of essential vitality, our Ying Qi is compromised and we get ill and eventually die if an intervention is not sought.

2. We learn to import energy from the outside world. At first we do this through stimulants and drugs- anything to squeeze more energy out of our present situation. Eventually, we learn to take energy from others, and then become vampires (unconsciously) as our internal demons find ways of having other people give us their power.

3. We gain awareness of this cancerous cycle and stop feeding our demons. They kick and scream for a short time and then wither and die off. The more Qi Gong we practice and mental awareness we have, the easier we clear ourselves of these parasites.

Unfortunately, we have a lot of people in the first two categories listed above and precious few in the third. Now that you are this far into this book, it is your responsibility to step up and clear your parasites. By bringing vitality and awareness to your energy field, you will dispel all of your own internal demons and then become very aware of the vampirical/predatory nature of the world around you. You can then illuminate this behavior and help the people around you snap out of it. With enough people waking up, the cycle is broken and humanity is freed from this zombie/vampire trance.

Human Transference

This is the most common form of possession out there. It is rampant in the United States and is one that gets carried through from generation to generation. We see it in sexual predators and pedophiles as well as in those with addictions and perpetrators of domestic violence. It is when someone's internal demons are so empowered that they draw them into an action that they otherwise would not do. Many of these people often claim that "something came over me" or that "I just couldn't stop myself even when I knew better." This is a classic example of the shadow having more energy than the conscious part of the energy field… when we are no longer in control. A person who has left their psyche and their energy field "unchecked" for years infects another person (or group of people) through their actions. We know that the majority of sexual predators were molested in their past. Like a mental virus, it carries on from the perpetrator to the recipient/victim and plants the seeds for further growth. If the victim does not heal the trauma and forgive the situation, then they harbor this infection in their own shadow. When they are weakened at some point, they may find themselves expressing this demon—much to their own surprise.

We transfer belief systems and ideas into each other's subconscious minds because we are unaware of their existence. (This is how advertising and political campaigns work, and these two professions have it down to a science…) People are unaware of their demons and have unexamined shadows so when in a "sleepy moment," one's shadow is able to overpower conscious actions allowing these demons to express themselves. Like a virus, they have taken on a life of their own and feed off our energy. To survive, they must infect the next person they come in contact with. The more culturally appealing these demons might be, the quicker they can spread into more host bodies. They are also called memes in popular culture. [Brodie, 1996] We are unconscious to this transference and become the willing agents of this process through our ignorance. We gave birth to our own monsters and we have fed them and nourished them, and now, being the proud parents that we are, we spread them to others. Whoops, there goes the neighborhood.

OVER THE YEARS I have become brutally aware of the significant impact our families have on our subconscious processing. When someone comes in with a particular neurosis, I drill into their family and cultural history immediately. This often leads us to the larger storylines that they had unknowingly bought into growing up. Because most people try to sort out their life's problems for the next generation, most of us have a number of memories where our parents were being unreasonable about certain things. They were so picky about some crazy little detail that we couldn't understand…

The emotional charge associated with family issues that many patients hold is what I find suppresses much of their vitality. Sometimes it takes a few months to unravel as people cannot even see the way they are leaking their power away.

When I was a monk, my master taught me how to look into a person's energy field and observe the connections tapping into their power. After I was finally able to see what he was talking about, I became both shocked and depressed for a while. Too many people are walking around with their energy fields tied down. It almost appears like a series of umbilical cords that are piped into the lower dantien. I was taught to follow those cords or threads of energy back to where they attached. Most of the time I found the other side of the cord attached to a parent or family member. When teaching the patients how to cut these cords and seal them off, they start to wake up as their energy stores become available to them for the first time in a while. At this point we can see how enmeshed they were with their families. There is love and there is codependency…and leaking of our vital energy is not healthy love.

External Demons

We have spoken of people manipulating each other for personal gains and of internal demons manipulating behavior for their own survival and proliferation, but now, we must talk about a more insidious energy; that of disembodied external entities. This is a subject that has received attention from ancient traditions ranging from Ayurveda in India to Shamanism in Peru. I draw my experience from the Taoist and Chinese medical traditions, which both go into this subject in some detail.

According to Taoist and Chinese conceptions, many of the entities that fall into this category are former humans that, for one reason or another, were trapped in our dimension after losing their bodies. They either had something that held them back from willingly leaving, or more frequently, their death was so jarring or quick that they don't believe that they truly died. These are often ghosts of relatives that are reported in house hauntings around the world. They are not actually "demons" per se. Their consciousness remains trapped in this dimension and their energy attaches to a known place or to known people. There are thousands of these stories all over and anybody who has actually encountered one of these entities will not be convinced by anyone that they don't exist. These entities are actually relatively easy to deal with because, just like the internal demons, they need a source of energy to live off for survival. If we stop feeding them, they lose their power and must move along. Now, very much like the feeding of our internal shadow energies, we feed these entities through our minds and our emotions.

Having a human body is the ultimate source of infinite power—once you know how to tap into it. Disembodied entities can latch onto us or our ideas and live off of them for long periods of time. Haunted houses are a good example because the entity there often inspires fear, which is a powerful, raw energy. The more people acknowledge that the house is haunted and that this entity exists, the more energy becomes available to it. In my experience, dead relatives also will provoke such strong emotions as they have to stoke the fire of their own memory in their living loved ones in order to drink the energy that is given off from the ensuing grief or fond feelings aroused. It is important to remember that most of these entities do not want to be trapped here and that we can release them by acknowledging what they are and then creating a portal for them to return back to the Source. These entities have no power outside of the power we give them unconsciously and please remember, they are us. Love them and give them the space to find their way back home.

Insidious Demons

There are also more insidious energies out there that come from other planets or dimensions, or are created by dark masters here on the planet. They have been called Archons by the early Gnostics, Jen by the Persians, have been classified into many subclasses by various cultures around the world. In fact, every culture somehow alludes to them in some way. These entities often have far more dangerous intentions and are to be avoided at all costs. It is important to remember that all of these entities feed off of the energy of fear and so it is critical for us to stay in our hearts and bring the energy of love and grace into the room.

"The greatest trick the Devil ever pulled was convincing the world he didn't exist."
—*Kaiser Soze,* The Usual Suspects

There is very special training that goes into Taoist exorcisms and that is beyond the scope of this book, but I'd like to take this opportunity to make an important point. It is very easy to try to blame some outside agency/energy for the way we feel, or possibly closer to home, mom and dad might be the culprits- but this is not the way to fix anything! Again, we are responsible for our own awareness and we are the only ones capable of cleansing our energy fields. Even the intervention of a shaman requires the subject's will and participation in the ritual to be effective. The more we reclaim our own power back and return to our center, the less our internal demons have leverage over us, which means the less we are in trance and the more we will be able to move towards positive energies and opportunities in our lives. When you wake up to your true potential, there is no demon, internal or external, that will be able to influence you or get in your way ever again.

Farmers vs. Hunters

Taking into account all of this predatory activity and our horizontal leeching off of one another, it becomes important to hold a new frame of mind when encountering people and engaging in the outside world. We are surrounded by millions of people who the Buddhists call "hungry ghosts." They are devoid of their own power and are seeking to partake of some of yours in order to get through their day. They are lost to their internal demons and are trying to enroll you in their dramas. They are being led by the puppeteers into voting and buying the way they are told and they are also after your money. They are....wait. They are you and you are they! Before we get into a reactive polarized "us vs. them" mentality, let's realize that these are our brothers and sisters and that we are all in this mess together. The good news about waking up is that it can happen rather quickly and that it is the birthright of every human being on this planet. So, before we start to build walls around us and freak out about vampires and zombies attacking at the gates, let's gather ourselves and get to work.

When I was younger and had just created my integrated medical group, there was a great deal to learn and lots of different models to emulate. I hired a business consultant whose "vibe" I liked (he also came well recommended) and we got to setting up systems so that we could efficiently help as many people as possible. One thing that he taught me early on was that most business people in the U.S. act like hunters nowadays. They are out to pull down their daily feast, thinking that tomorrow is a new day with new quotas. Their lives are filled with lots of excitement and lots of stress—always trying to win the sale and win people over. Farmers, on the other hand, take the time to develop their relationships (crops) and water and nourish them. At first, things start off slowly but then, the yields get greater and the farmer has an abundance of crops that keep rolling in. In regards to a healthcare practice, this meant creating a "family practice" environment where we cultivated our relationships with people and established rapport and trust for years to come. In the perspective of the conversation at hand, it means moving out of the predatory frenzy of the horizontal axis and literally farming our energy field—tilling the soil and pulling weeds constantly.

Now that we have conducted a semantic full circle, let's take a moment to examine the words we are using in this practice. "Energy Field" denotes a space that is fertile and is to be cultivated. The field is Yin in nature, taking seeds (Yang) and nurturing them to grow. It is the space where water and nutrients mix to hold the space for life forms to grow and evolve when activated by sunlight. The healthier the field, the better the yield. That said, some fields are more fertile than others being endowed with rich nutrients from a volcano or sitting in a river delta where water and silt are abundant. This is much like our bodies. Some of us are born with strong Jing/Essence and have a lot to work with and others, like a barren desert, have more challenges to keep things growing. Either way though, after a number of seasons, if there is abuse or neglect from the farmer, the field starts to get compromised and cannot support the life and growth it is used to. The soil needs to be turned and weeds need to be extracted. It takes a good amount of work to keep a field healthy but the rewards are immeasurable. This is the same with our bodies.

Our energy fields are a direct reflection of the state of health of the Jing, Qi, and Shen. If the energy is flowing smoothly and the diet and lifestyle are healthy, then there is a strong energy field and the Light Body begins to take hold. If there is a disconnect in any of these parameters and the person involved is being drained by ignorance, then their shadow demons become fast growing weeds in their fields.

The crops we choose to grow are the dreams and aspirations of our heart but the ones we end up growing are a result of the noise in the shadow. All it takes is fear-inspired desire or the charging of an aversion and there we have it—another weed we just planted. The more we water it with our leaky energy, the more of our field we lose and the more of a mess we have to deal with. Most people, even when they muster the courage to look inside, see such a mess, they turn and run, asking for their doctor to supply them a pill. The majority shy away from the gardening that they need to do—the very thing that will give them their life back. They revert to the predatory black market of energy exchange discussed earlier. They develop a charge around their dramas and entrench themselves behind the ego's battle lines. "I'm upset with so and so because they won't give me what I need..." These people let the weeds in their own field grow rampant and go off to plunder their needs from friends, neighbors, or clients instead.

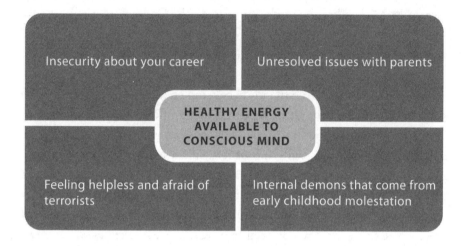

Unhealthy Energy Field

In this mockup of a flat energy field, we see that we have very little of our total energy available to us when the energies of the shadow are still being fed. Once we begin the Great Work and start to tend to our fields daily, then we pull the energy out of the unconscious shadow processes and allow it to nurture our healthy core. Once this happens, the field starts to look more like this:

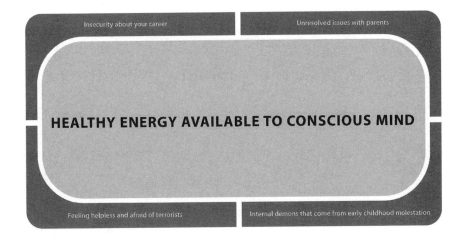

Healthy Energy Field

As we gather more and more personal power back within our conscious grasp, we are able to use more of it to pull weeds and exorcise our demons. At this point, we are feeling better about ourselves and have the energy and vitality to meet life head-on. With our continued practice of Qi Gong and the mental/emotional/and spiritual practices we have learned here, we continue to refine and clean until The Great Tao is in the driver seat instead of all of the noise. The "I" that was created by the ego as a defense mechanism gets softened and dissipates in charge and we surrender ourselves to the joyful manifestation of Reality as it unfolds in front of us and we watch ourselves unfold with it.

We have defined the problems and from the next chapter on, it is time to delve into the essence and meaning of this esoteric practice. It is time to set our sights for nothing short of complete enlightenment and the full activation of our Light Body.

✳

CHAPTER TWELVE

THE TAO of MANIFES-TaTION

Turning the light around is the secret of dissolving dark-ness and controlling the lower soul. There is no exercise to restore the creative, only the secret of turning the light around. The light itself is the creative; to turn it around is to restore it.

—*Lu Tung Pin,* The Secret of the Golden Flower

Throughout this book, we have learned what happens when we ignore the natural processes around us. We see how internal demons are created in our shadows that in turn begin to influence our behavior. We have also noted how this phenomena leads to a culture of vampirism, codependency, and mind control. We see how suffering creates a rift in our awareness of Nature and how this fundamental split sends us down a dark and sleepy path towards further ignorance and deterioration. In short, we have circled around the problem and now it is time to focus on the correction.

We have studied the energetic, mental, emotional, physical, and spiritual exercises that are designed to bring balance to our energy and help increase the flow of vitality in our fields. Now we must take control of the very system that has gotten us into so much trouble: it is time to program our subconscious minds and restore the powerful Trinity that allows us to be masters of our own Universe.

We have examined the mental and emotional aspects of our affliction, as these are the processes that channel our vitality into the shadow. We have learned that it is by the very nature of this subconscious programming that we embed energies into the shadow which then take on a life of their own. These "demons," if you will, suck off our vital force and live off of our energy fields like parasites. It is the lack of clarity and conscious communication between our conscious minds and our subconscious minds that allow this to be possible. It is this fundamental disconnect that allows there to be a leak in the first place. Once we begin the process of pulling weeds from our energy fields, we reclaim more and more of our conscious awareness.

The major function of the Taoist alchemical tradition is to turn the light of awareness inward so that we can examine ourselves. Our alchemical work creates the environment for us to take control of the seeds we plant and have more of an active role in the unfolding of our lives. Let's take a look at our familiar diagrams again:

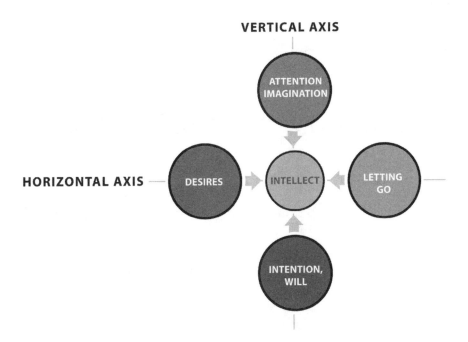

The Five Element Spirit/Soul Axis

We see that the horizontal axis and the vertical axis all meet and communicate at the central level of the Intellect (Yi). This is the birthplace of the ego where we create coping mechanisms for the energies we feel along the horizontal axis. This is what we call our Self Consciousness. It is the conscious aspect of our self-understanding and is the self-aware aspect of our energy field. This level of consciousness sits balanced between the poles of Super Consciousness (Yang Heaven Aspect) and Sub Consciousness (Yin Earth Aspect). It can be viewed like this:

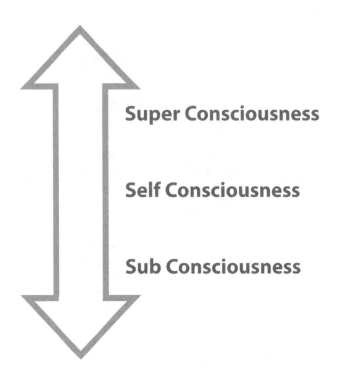

Consciousness Gradient

Just like when the polarization of the Tao created a spectrum between the extremes of Yin and Yang in every particular thing/concept, we can view our consciousness under the same light. We can say that the Super Conscious Yang awareness is associated with Heaven and the Sub Conscious Yin awareness is associated with Earth. The Trigrams of HEAVEN and EARTH (note that the capitalization is being used to differentiate the primordial concept of EARTH as related to HEAVEN from the element Earth in the Five Elements) in the I Ching are the following:

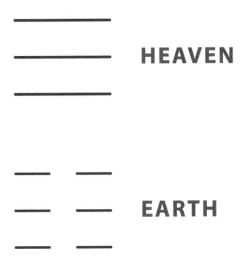

The Pure Trigrams

Notice how the Trigram for HEAVEN is three solid Yang lines which reflect the ultimate pure state of Yang (as an archetype of the original split of the Tao) and how the EARTH Trigram has three Yin lines which represent the pure state of Yin. These are the symbolic representations of the ultimate states of these two poles. Now, when we take a look at how they interact in humans, we get the Trigrams for Fire and Water.

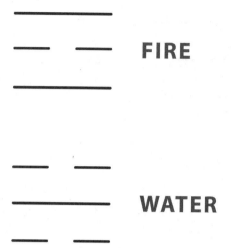

FIRE

WATER

How Heaven and Earth Manifest in Humans Before Alchemy

The Fire Trigram resembles that of HEAVEN except with a single Yin line in the middle which functions as the substance it needs to burn as fuel. The Water Trigram looks like the EARTH Trigram except for a single Yang line in the middle which gives it its power and dynamic life-carrying energy in our world. Bringing Fire and Water into balance with our Intellect creates an environment for HEAVEN and EARTH to coexist in balance within our bodies. This becomes the fundamental basis of our alchemical work.

When we go back and examine our diagram, let's take this information and overlay it to get to our next level of understanding of this system:

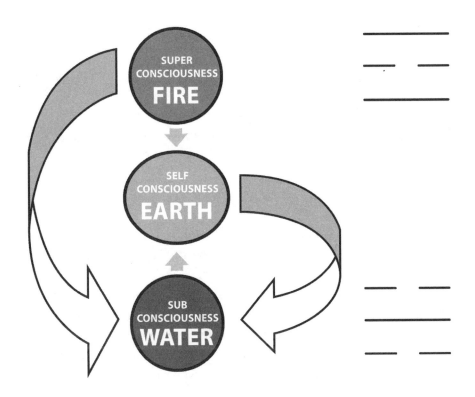

How Information Transfers in Human Consciousness

The fusion of Yin and Yang takes place in the central Earth element of the Intellect which acts as the pivot of the entire axis. They can come together if the space is clear in the center. Now, if we have not cleared an ample amount of the shadow noise in the Intellect and/or Self Consciousness is afflicted by this, then we have a problem. You will notice an interesting phenomena: namely that our Self Consciousness and Super Consciousness both feed suggestions into our Sub Consciousness. If we are constantly wrestling with aversions and cravings, we keep channeling negative energy into the defense mechanisms we've created in our Sub Conscious reasoning. These processes become programmed, and in turn, feed belief systems and fear-inspired thoughts back into our Self Conscious realm. This is the downward force-feeding that has gotten us into a real mess.

To better understand the differentiation of these levels, we can examine some of their characteristics in the following chart:

Aspect	Super Consciousness	Self Consciousness	Sub Consciousness
Element	Fire	Earth	Water
Manifesting Principle	Inspiration	Intellect	Intuition
Power	Attention/Focus	Reasoning/Integration	Intention/Will Power
Feeds Info to:	Sub and Self Consciousness	Sub Consciousness	Self Consciousness
Gets Info from:	The Great Tao/ Universal Intelligence	Super and Sub Consciousness	Super and Self Consciousness

Consciousness Roadmap

The most important concept to hold in mind here is that:
THE SUB CONSCIOUS MIND IS AMENABLE TO SUGGESTION.

These suggestions will either form into shadow charges from a misunderstanding of life or come from conscious programming. Your Sub Conscious is being programmed either way, so unless we are constantly engaged in what is passing through to it, someone, some insanity, or some demon is doing it for us instead. This is where our involvement comes in. It is imperative that we program what we want to see in our lives directly into our Sub Consciousness. At first, when we are primarily concerned with pulling weeds, it will come in the form of basic cognitive behavioral changes. This involves putting in healthy suggestions to override old bad habits that have been haunting us and becomes a vital part of the process of deflating the energy of our shadow fields and pulling back our personal power.

Say that every time we see a car accident on the side of the road, we have a full panic attack because we remember the terrible accident that killed our parents. In this case, our internal healing work drives us to:

1. Feel that energy once the thought field is invoked.
2. Watch it with an open heart while pulling back all of the power we've pumped into the fear of this event.
3. Do our mental, emotional, and spiritual cleansing on the energy of this topic.
4. Place a suggestion into our Sub Conscious minds to be thankful for, in our example, having our parents as long as we did. We do this whenever we

see an accident and to automatically relax our systems and secrete endorphins into our bloodstream.

In essence, we place an "overlay" suggestion on top of the old one. We teach ourselves to be aware of these patterns and then we place healthier habits into the Sub Conscious minds as the programming that is replacing the old faulty "code." A word of caution though—there is a Yin and Yang principle to everything (as we have learned) and this Yang principle of actively reprogramming the mind has become quite fashionable in self-help circles lately. It is important to maintain balance and this means doing the reconciliation work. The Yin aspect of this principle is the act of allowing us to feel and heal the traumas of the past. This leads to the deflation of the shadow energy. This work, by its very nature, is not particularly comfortable because if it was, then this content would never have been stuffed down into the shadow in the first place. A proper healing perspective requires both sides in order to accomplish the Great Work. We must heal our wounds and reclaim our power while also implanting new behaviors and positive suggestions. Balance is the Way.

The Sub Conscious mind will put into play anything we program into it. Once we become more adept at this game we essentially create a blank canvas of our spiritual energy upon which to play. Working through the murky waters of our current Sub Conscious shadow habits becomes quite fun when we finally get a grasp of this principle and start to literally reprogram our response patterns and habits. As we pull the weeds out of the dark corners of our energy fields, we get more and more Self Conscious clarity and we can use this to implant our Sub Consciousness with whatever goals, dreams, or aspirations we want. This is where the exciting part comes in.

With this knowledge we can become active Co-Creators on the planet. We can picture the world and the life we want to see and help it take form and shape. The more we connect with our own internal power, the easier this process becomes and the quicker it continues to happen. I have met many people who are venerable wizards. They live the life of their dreams and enjoy all the world has to offer. The ones that stay happy are the ones who keep growing and evolving personally.

It has recently been popularized that people can learn this system and crack the code of manifestation. They see themselves driving Bentleys to their boats and having several houses all around the planet with servants in them. Whatever the material fantasy is, it is a small portion of the entirety of the human birthright and there is great danger in using this system only as a means to these ends. Sure, having material possessions is not inherently bad. In fact, go ahead and enjoy what the world has to offer you but, and here's the big but, to what end? What many of these systems have failed to impart is the most important aspect of this entire axis—the one that takes us from the realm of wizardry into that of enlightenment and inner peace.

Personal Journeys —Hungry Ghosts and Ancient Wisdom

I HAD JUST moved to a new area in Southern California and was out to meet people in my field: doctors, psychologists, chiropractors, and personal trainers. I'm always interested in meeting people in the community and see who is doing good work and whom I can trust my patients with. I ran across a fellow in charge of a local "Law of Attraction" group and had made plans for a face-to-face. I felt that particular body of work had a great deal to offer so I was excited to exchange knowledge with this gentleman. We managed to fit in a lunch on a day I wasn't scheduling any patients. I arrived 10 minutes early, got a table and waited. I finally called him when he was 15 minutes late.

He was surprised to hear from me and had totally forgotten about our meeting after confirming it himself. He urged me to stay— just a quick shower and he'd be there in 15 minutes. I was annoyed but enjoy people watching so I hung out. His 15 minutes turned into 25, and as he rushed in and was full of empty apologies. Within five minutes of pleasantries he told me that he had just left a crazy career in the mortgage industry where he was doing ecstasy and cocaine all the time. He was tired of the hookers and the blow—well, actually, the money had dried up and he didn't manage to save any.

The "Law of Attraction" bit was going to be his new thing and he was excited to make a bunch of money out of memberships. I almost choked on my food. This guy didn't have a pot to piss in, could barely make a lunch appointment, was just sobering up from a 10- year party, and was now being looked up to by some poor, lost people who were searching for a shepherd! He insisted that I join his group and learn all about how to attract great things into my life…do what I say—not what I do. I paid for lunch and respectfully declined.

There is nothing inherently wrong with the "Law of Attraction" as channeled through Esther and Jerry Hicks. In fact, this body of work represents a profound and unique contribution to the body of knowledge available to spiritual seekers in our time. Let's take a look at where this system fits into the Taoist model that we are learning in this book:

The Law of Attraction Using the Taoist Framework

The Law of Attraction teaches us to focus on and manifest our desires. It cautions us about where to focus our attention because anything that we plant will grow. From a Taoist alchemical perspective, it teaches us to take the Desires of the Wood Element and tie our Attention (Fire) and Intention (Water) to them in order to make them happen. It's about the fulfillment of dreams and the empowerment of people through Universal laws. Human suffering, in this theory, is the result of focusing our attention on what we do not want or on the lack of a certain thing we desire. Welcome to aversions and cravings. Essentially, this system explains the spiritual science we are learning here, albeit in truncated form. When we put energy into the lack or the opposite of a particular desire, we are feeding a cycle of suffering. Clarity and understanding of this system leads to liberation.

This law liberates our desires and, helps us understand how to pattern our lives in a successful way, but it does not address other elements of the human experience adequately. First of all, the opposite pole of the horizontal axis is the Metal Element, which is responsible for the balancing and checking of decline and reduction energies. Again, we have the story of the World being the Western cultural oyster, of which we have every right to ravish and enjoy. But balance is the key, and tempering our desires and letting go of the past is apt counterpoint to a perpetual desire-driven mentality. Yes, human desire backed by strong emotion is a very powerful catalyst to manifest things on the planet for ourselves, but if we are not careful, it can lead us away from Self-Realization and evolution of our consciousness. As usually taught today, The Law of Attraction is still a system based on imbalance. Always remember what the Great Tao wishes from its two offspring, Yin and Yang: balance and equality. In my opinion, the Law of Attraction needs to be tempered with a much grander motive—that of ultimate awakening.

In previous chapters we spoke of individuals who had gained a certain amount of understanding of the esoteric sciences and had begun to use this knowledge to their advantage. These are people who have learned to manifest objects through their understanding of Sub Conscious programming and also taught themselves to leverage fellow humans by the weaknesses they see in their shadows. These people may have learned a few interesting tricks but they may or may not have tuned into the main channel—that of the Super Consciousness.

The Super Conscious Influence

The Western tradition speaks of the concept of Revelation. This is how God reveals Himself to us in every instant and how it is our job to accept this Reality gracefully and without judgment because it is perfect exactly how it is. This is a very good example of Super Conscious influence and our relationship to it. The Great Tao is all things and places and times, and all at once. It is unfolding and spiraling in and out of existence in every instant. It accounts for all of the cycles within cycles within cycles that account for the movement of the largest clusters of galaxies to the subatomic interactions going on in every cell of our bodies. The Universe is so big that it is impossible to comprehend the scale—down from infinity and up to infinity. It seems that the farther (or deeper) we look, we keep finding more levels on larger and smaller scales. It is absolutely beautiful and awe inspiring. We have recently ascertained that the Universe follows a specific type of mathematics that reveals everything follows a fractal pattern. [Joyce, 2000] Like a hologram, any small part of the Universe that we look at has encoded in it the blueprint of the whole. We see this same phenomenon in the DNA of human beings. All of the code from the start of life on this planet—and some would argue it came from another plane—is encoded in every cell in your DNA. That means, we have all of the information within us that encodes our cells to become a fish, a tree, an ape, or a carrot.

Jeremy Narby, an anthropologist who studied the spiritual ceremonies of Amazonian tribes, explains how native shamans make the claim that the plants told them the whys and wherefores of herbalism. Narby discovered that by ingesting a hallucinogenic brew called ayahuasca (DMT), natives communicate with a "coiled serpent" that tells them how to prepare the plants. He postulates that there is a subconscious level of communication in our own DNA that is driving us to evolve and become more self-aware. [Narby, 1999] By ingesting the brew, we put ourselves into a state where Self Conscious reasoning can observe the conversation that is always taking place between the Super Conscious realm and our Sub Conscious realm (in this case via our own DNA). The Sub Conscious mind somehow understands this information and changes the way we express ourselves by switching certain genetic sequences on and off based on the messaging it receives.

It is fascinating how we have recently discovered a whole internal system of language that involves the release of photons (particles of light) when our DNA zips and unzips. [Rattemeyer, 1981] The photons somehow communicate with the DNA in our cells and there is a system of coordination that instantly orchestrates our growth and direction based on this information. In other words, Super Consciousness somehow relays information to us via our DNA, and our Sub Consciousness takes this information and encodes it into a photon-based language that instantly communicates to all of the cells in our body. We instantly shift what we are doing and "create" a new reality based on this new encoding. This is where the magic happens.

Once we learn to listen to Super Consciousness, we begin our resonant tuning with the Primal Will to Good of the entire universe. It seems that there is a definite direction in our evolution and that this has been encoded through our DNA. [Sherwood, 2006] The first moment we became self-aware as humans also ushered us into polarity consciousness. Through the resultant reactions to our aversions and cravings were born from this "fall," we began to create noise in the channel. We began feeding energy into the shadows of our Sub Consciousness reasoning and distorting the message or the light-based language that flows from Super to Sub Consciousness. We stopped hearing the Inner Voice and fell further into confusion. We became convinced that "this is it" and deluded ourselves that we had attained the highest level of evolution possible on the planet. This forced us to invent tools and technologies to make up for the inherent powers we had forsaken. We thought we lost Eden, but all we really lost was our ability to see it.

We fell asleep and have been living a dream ever since.

So let's now look at the Taoist model that corrects this deviant mentality and puts us back on the fast track to evolution and freedom. To walk with the Tao is like a hot knife through butter. It is like flowing down the stream of all that is effortless because we are in sync with the Super Conscious fractal of which we are a central part. This model for manifestation is the correction for our human pathology and when properly understood and practiced, will result in nothing short of illumination and true self-realization.

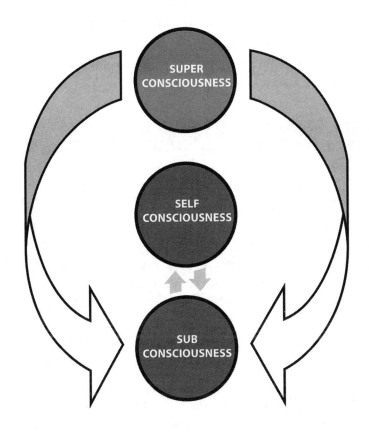

Letting the Tao / Super Consciousness Guide our Actions

Our correct understanding of the nature of our existence leads us to dissolve the egos of our Self Conscious identities and allow Super Consciousness to feed information directly into our Sub Consciousness. This, in turn, makes our Self Consciousness the willing agent of the Universal Mind. Notice how the information of the Sub Conscious mind channels directly into the Self Conscious mind and vice/versa. The master along the path is selfless and takes inspiration from the living currents of the Tao and acts in harmony with these currents. He is, however, capable of communicating and interacting with the Super Consciousness through his Sub Conscious mind. He can still implant seeds for growth and manifest his intentions in Reality because of his access and understanding of the internal language. His renewed understanding of the relationship of the Self and Sub Conscious minds creates a "rebirth" of sorts as he shakes off the heavy influences of the shadow and wakes up to his true potential and place in the Universe. Life then becomes a dynamic act of playing like a child does out in nature; full of wonderment and magic.

Personal Journeys—Fireflies in Machu Pichu

I HAD SPENT a number of days hiking the *Camino Inca* which was the original trail from the city of Cuzco into Machu Picchu, Peru. It was quite the adventure and the ruins of Machu Picchu were absolutely incredible. I had spent an entire day wandering around as it is an enormous site with plenty to see. After having made friends with a local guide, I was told that the park would re-open at night for visitors. I found some food and waited around for several hours before I could go back in. There were only two sets of couples and myself waiting when the gates opened that night. We paid our money and I let the others work their way into the park with their flashlights first. I wanted to go in the dark and see with my Shen.

Once I was all alone, there was an eerie silence. Machu Picchu is a big place and here I was standing alone in the dark with an uncomfortable feeling rising up. I asked God to guide me: "you brought me here, now tell me what to do!" I couldn't believe my eyes. A firefly had lit up right in front of me and then started floating along the path. I followed dutifully until the light flickered out. Here I was standing in complete darkness again…now what? Another firefly lit up and continued to travel away from me. Again I followed.

I followed a chain of a few dozen of these until they stopped lighting up, and found myself in the center of the central temple on the main hill! There was an incredible glow to the night sky, almost as if it was flashing. I could hear and actually feel voices and a dull chant permeating the air. I sat with my back against one wall of the temple and began to meditate. I was 23-years-old, then and felt overwhelmed by the whole experience. I kept telling myself to trust in Higher Power. I could sense that a stream of information was being dumped into my head. A voice in my head that I distinctly recognized simply told me not to worry about it...that this information was to unlock and open up for me at some point in the future...I was too young to grasp it all then.

This was the same inner voice I heard while trapped in the dark cave as a child. I relaxed and settled into be passive about the whole thing. My Super Consciousness was in a serious dialogue with my Sub Consciousness and I was not allowed to hear the details. It was as if my Self Conscious mind did not have the expanded sense of Self or the capacity enough to deal with the information that was being transmitted. There was too much of "me," or who I thought I was, in the way. I sat silently and allowed; part in curiosity and part in utter terror.

To this day I don't quite know what happened when I woke up. I felt a jolt and found myself lying on my back as if I had just fallen backwards. I got up and was perplexed about where I was. It took me a couple of minutes of exploring to realize that I was on the other side of the wall I was leaning against. Did I actually fall through that wall? Did I get up and wander around but not remember it? Either way, I felt strongly that it was time to go. My work there was done...or Machu Picchu was done with me. I was told that I'd be back a few years later but it was now time for me to move on. Right then, there was a flash of a firefly in front of me. I dutifully followed the chain of lights and eventually found myself back outside by the gate. They guided me into the ruins and then out. The night guard gave me a smirk and asked if I had enjoyed myself. I tried to crack a smile but simply kept walking...I had a lot to think about.

It is important to remember that this level of mastery is born out of our understanding that comes from our reconciliation of the primordial split of Yin and Yang. We are still talking of uniting poles along a spectrum with Super and Sub Consciousness coming together in a synergistic relationship. This is the essence of the Tao of Manifestation and it is the mark of liberation. The system does not stop here, however. The Great Work of Taoist alchemy specifically takes this level of understanding to its natural conclusion. We are to literally become the understanding of this phenomenon. Having a mental understanding of a concept in a theoretical form is wonderful, but it will eventually lead to disharmony as it is a still a polarization of the Tao. We must learn to fully embody this understanding and become this understanding in a very real sense, so we may then fully bring balance to our realization and not depart off into levels of abstraction.

The Fusion of Fire and Water

When we look at our stylized diagram of the vertical axis, we can see a symbolic depiction of how these concepts work and, consequently, we can come to understand how to use this system for our own liberation. This split is wonderful for our third dimensional brains to understand but it is important to note that the central premise of the Great Work is the union of Fire and Water—the dissolution of the perception of duality. The Tao is One. In our path of return to the Source, we must reconcile all understanding of the alchemical science and, in the end, dissolve all levels of duality and become what we are practicing.

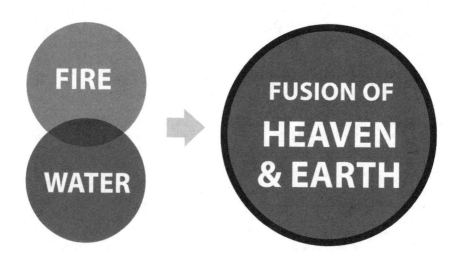

The Taoist Alchemical Path

With the artificial construct of the "self" (ego) dissolved, the fusion of Fire and Water becomes the fusion of Super and Sub Consciousness. This means there is no separation between us and the Great Tao. There is no interference or noise that disrupts this flow and we are fully connected all of the time. We become the very embodiment of the Life Force that moves through all things. The ways we used to identify ourselves—defense mechanisms, fear-inspired behavior, material desires, all wash away as the light of awareness is turned inward. As we illuminate the dark corners of our shadows, we remove all the skeletons from our closets and come clean by seeing Reality for what it is in the current moment. At this point, we become the agents for the Universal Will which flows through us and are connected to it from within. At this stage, our realization of what we truly are is no longer jaded by self-doubt or self-aggrandizement. We finally realize what Reality truly is and where we belong within it. We no longer embody the primordial separation but the union that culminates the Great Work. We don't lose our identity but we actually find our true identity. Our unique identity is an important part of how the Tao manifests so don't worry about that part—all the good stuff that makes you special remains!

This Great Work becomes the subject of the next chapter which is about the Light Body. This is the "homecoming," or the full-circle understanding of the alchemical process. This new understanding is the ultimate step, the realization of our greater aim—to become the realization of which we speak. The Great Work applies the principles of this chapter to our physical bodies. Remember, our bodies are only separate from our minds, emotions, and spirit because of polarity consciousness. The wax of the candle and the aura of the flame are simply opposite poles of the same realization and one needs the other to complete the cycle. The fusion of the Five Elements and the reformation of Yin and Yang is the process by which we literally work and clean our bodies until we are fully linked up and healed. The more we connect our Sub Conscious and Super Conscious minds by listening internally and clearing away the noise, the more we become that very realization.

✳

CHAPTER THIRTEEN

THE BIRTH OF THE LIGHT BODY

The light is neither inside nor outside the self...
once you turn the light around,
everything in the world is turned around.
—Lu Tung Pin, The Secret of the Golden Flower, Ch. 3

amed Inca shaman and scholar Alberto Villoldo coined the term *homoluminous* to describe the next level of humanity's advancement from homo sapiens. [Villoldo, 2000] This coming progression is the birthright of all humans as taught by a number of worldly traditions, but has been a lost spiritual technology for many centuries. However, this knowledge has fortunately re-emerged just recently. Homoluminous is the end result of the practice of all Yoga (which means union) and is the natural consequence to our illumination. The more aware we become, the clearer the light body practice continues to be for us. The more we wake up, the more we can see the energy fields and luminous bodies of others and eventually ignite our eternal Light Bodies.

While science now reveals that consciousness is the central aspect of everything, the expansion and collapse of our Universe from the Big Bang Theory looks remarkably like the Hindu story of Lord Brahma breathing in and out, contracting and expanding the whole Universe in this cycle. So if there is no real concept of time except in how it relates to the space it is associated with within the fractal, then what's 15 billion years amongst friends? It's all a big dream. These vast expanses of time and space that we calculate outward (towards the edge of the Universe) and inward (looking into the subatomic world) are simply scales that blow our rational and ordered 3D minds away, but mean absolutely nothing to our consciousness which is in all places at all times.

As we start to wake up to the many mysteries of our Universe that exist both outside and inside our bodies, we learn that each of us has a critical and central role to play in the grand scheme of this shared existence. We are intimately connected to all that is and we are the willful agents of the natural patterns of the One Life Force and yet we feel trapped. Trapped within these physical bodies and further trapped in the dramas of our shadow energies. We feel drained and disconnected and always wonder why we are so lost...until now.

We have studied the essence of the Taoist Alchemical teaching and have come to understand the nature of suffering, but more importantly, we have learned to clean up our energy fields and free our minds from the turmoil of our shadow energies. We have learned to unblock our energy flow and to return the powers of our Sub Conscious minds back to their intimate connection with Super Consciousness. In short, we have gleaned the knowledge to identify our problems, correct the disharmonies that exist within us, and tune into the pure energies of nature while reprogramming healthy habits into our energy fields. We should finally be complete, right? Not exactly. For within this newfound ability to awaken ourselves, there exists a paradoxical void. Soon after we have learned the tools to break from our trance state and plot our own course, we are being told to surrender to the Super Conscious Will and become a participating agent of this consciousness. We then discover that we must do this work and dissolve our egos so that the Intelligence of the Tao guides us freely through the world as conscious co-creators of Reality. This sounds very good but...well, what do I do now?

We have now arrived at the fundamental paradox of the Taoist teachings.

We learned early on that it is our doing that creates most of our problems, and we have been taught to practice "non-doing" or "being" in our mental meditations. This practice is helpful in showing us:

1. The insanity under which we operate daily ...
2. How we needn't engage in it, and ...
3. How liberating it is to passively "be" without reacting to myriad events and circumstances all of the time....

When we practice non-action and are comfortable there, eventually we get hungry or have to go to the bathroom. Maybe our legs start to hurt from sitting and we need to walk around and stretch. We get up to do so and we see a hummingbird outside so we watch it and smile. While in the garden a neighbor says hello and invites us to watch a DVD they just got from a friend and we do so. The DVD is about polar bears dying in the arctic and we are moved. The following week a cousin asks us to get involved in a group that helps raise awareness about global warming and we attend. There we meet the love of our lives and get married. Now together, we travel to exotic places and try to make a difference. Again, the Western concept of Revelation comes through here. The Great Tao has placed our path in front of us right here and right now. We are so mentally abstract about the meaning of life and what we're supposed to do that we fail to see the path right in front of us. We wear out our brake pads and drain our vitality instead of enjoying the ride.

So the first aspect of "non-doing" is freeing the mind and energy from the grips of the shadow and really enjoying the present moment for what it truly is. All the grace and beauty in the world presents itself to us when we do. This does not, however, account for the paradoxical effort required to complete the Great Work. So how do we reconcile the laissez-faire Taoist approach of non-effort with the dedicated work ethic of "The Way is the Training"?

Taoist Monastery life in China involves a great deal of physical labor and chores along with several hours a day of Horse Stance. This is a deep Kung Fu stance that helps drop the energy down to the lower dantien while strengthening the legs and building resolve—Zhi in the Kidneys. This is part of the very tedious training that is done for at least one year before the young monks were even allowed to learn to throw their first punch. The tradition of Kung Fu literally translates to "hard work" or "eat bitter" in Chinese. So how were these high level Taoist adepts conducting such rigorous physical training with incredible dedication and still learning to relax? How did they deal with the two axioms of "Taoist Way Not Forced" and "The Way is the Training" in the same curriculum? Again, here we have the central paradox of Taoist training and one that needs to be teased out before we go any further.

There is an inherent level of distortion that we humans begin with when we incarnate here on Earth. Assuming we have perfectly adjusted families and very little drama growing up, we still have the essential human mental pathology to deal with—the nature of suffering and our leaking of energy to our shadows through aversions and cravings. This is why monasteries like to take children in before a certain age. There is less junk to deal with. So let's assume that most of us didn't grow up in a temple setting deep in the Himalayas somewhere and that we grew up in the West with all the insanity that comes with it. At this point, we have a good amount of emotional charge and mental aversions that have fed our power into our shadows. We have done our damage and have a good deal of work to complete in order to undo what has been done.

If you recall in the chapter about the nature of suffering, we discussed the notion of Karma and how this equates simply to "action," then you might concede that a good amount of action has filtered into your shadow processes over the years. In fact, we've come a long way to create an enormous mess (unconsciously). Although we can practice non-action for several years to dissipate the charge we have stored there, Taoist Masters have found that a fusion works better for the majority of the people they encounter, especially in the West. Sure, an occasional student has a sudden flash of insight and through this enlightenment instantly clears themselves of all of the junk they were carrying, but this is rare and too few people experience this. What about the rest of us? Well, we get to work. The same aspect of Karma comes in as we instill positive karma into our lives. We develop rituals and habits that help remind us every day—actually several times a day—to do one simple thing: WAKE UP! We keep falling asleep to the deep trances burned into our shadows and so must set constant reminders and perform practices that illuminate our awareness of this phenomenon. This is a powerful and effective way for us to attain real results in a short amount of time.

In this realization the paradox is resolved. We work hard in the training in order to erase previous damage that we have done and to function as a failsafe against falling back asleep. We simultaneously practice "non-action" as related to our mental and emotional attachments while we develop our strong energy fields. We must also clear the power trapped in our shadows while we learn to observe Reality for what it truly is. We comprehend what it means to relax in our effort—we fuse action and inaction just as we balance Yin and Yang. We train to relax in a deep horse stance and we study to stay relaxed until the moment of a necessary strike…or until we actually have to stand in front of those people at that presentation. We understand to be aware of our energy flow and stop the leaking. Doing so, we gather more personal power and cultivate further awareness of the living breathing currents of the Tao flowing through us. We essentially wake up to a deep understanding of who we truly are and continue cultivating and refining our energy towards the ultimate aim which is the development of the Light Body and its eventual Ignition.

Personal Journeys—Your Pet Can See Energy

ONE OF MY favorite times to practice Qi Gong is at night in the yard. I love the silence and the sphere of stars above making it a perfect way to close down a busy day. I've always marveled at how my dogs have loved to accompany me out there. As soon as I start my practice, they stop playing and they sit there and watch me move the energy. I've experimented with them by projecting energy into a nearby object with my mind (no body or eye movements to lead them on) and I watch how they then fixate on where the energy has moved. I've also expanded my field to envelop the dog and, depending on the type of set I'm practicing, they get excited or tranquil.

It seems our pets have retained the ability to see the Light Body while most humans have fallen asleep to this.

THE LIGHT BODY IN DIFFERENT TRADITIONS

In this section, we are going to conduct a brief overview of the various cultures on the planet that have a Light Body tradition. This is in no way a complete list but serves as a sampling of the range and thoroughness of this body of knowledge across the globe. The take home message here is that there are dozens of cultures that have been involved in this type of training for thousands of years. This field of study has a rich history. It has slipped under the cultural radar in the modern age for reasons we have discussed earlier but is now in resurgence. The more we wake up, the more we become interested in this spiritual science again. We are slowly remembering what we thought had been lost.

(I have chosen small excerpts from each and have kept it brief as this book is not intended to be a cross-cultural analysis of the intricacies of the varying practices. Consider it a primer covering differing views of the same subject with an open invitation for you to delve deeper into whichever tradition appeals to you the most.)

Egypt

The Egyptian tradition of the Light Body is one we wish we had more information about. There are a number of living cultures that have preserved the Light Body tradition around the world but the Egyptian and Mayan cultures of antiquity have all but disappeared and are being reconstructed by historians and anthropologists. We do, however, have a powerful vision left behind by the priesthood of this ancient tradition and it is that of the ascending light body and the nature of "star fields" located in interstellar space.

Here is an excerpt from a manual on Egyptian magic:

> *The Egyptians divided man's constitution into a graduated series of parts. First was the physical body, or khat. Overshadowing, or enveloping, this body was a series of subtle bodies, each more ethereal than the last. The first of these, and the most dense of the subtle bodies, was the shadow, or khaibit. The next was the ka, the body of emotions. This was followed by the heart, ab (or hati-ab, which can be translated "outer heart"). The next was the ba (soul), which was linked to the ka through the ab. The ba rested in the spirit-body, or sah (sometimes sahu), which was presided over by the spirit, or khu… These and other designations for man's components were all governed by the highest, the khabs, the divine component which means star…*
>
> *The magician's Subtle Body, or Body of Light, is the chief tool used in some Low Magick operations and in almost all High Magick operations. Essentially, it is the living aura that pervades the physical body and extends slightly beyond it. It is shaped somewhat like and oval or egg… and it contains colorful swirling forces of energy that express thoughts and emotions… [Schueler, 1994, pp. 26-28]*

We can obviously see some similarities in the conceptual framework with that of the Taoist system we have been discussing. The Egyptians were known to have a very cohesive system with a strong underground order that preserved this information for centuries. Much of this Egyptian knowledge has been preserved through a number of present-day orders in the West.

Tibet

The Tibetans have one of the best-documented and clear-cut histories of the Light Body practice. There are a number of practitioners alive to this day that are intimately involved in this work and are living bearers of this tradition. Although there has been a great deal of chaos and destruction that has been inflicted on the country of Tibet, much of the tradition has been preserved outside the country and for this we are eternally grateful.

The following are some excerpts for Norbu Rinpoche:

> *The Jalu (in Tibetan), or Body of Light, realized through the practice of Dzogchen is different from the Gyulu, or Illusory Body, realized through the practices of the Higher Tantras. The Gyulu is dependent on the subtle prana of the individual, and thus, since prana is always considered to be of the relative dimension in Dzogchen, this Gyulu is not considered to be Total Realization. The Jalu, or Body of Light, itself, is a way of manifesting realization that is particular to the masters who have carried the practice of the Longde or of the Mennagde to their ultimate level, and with only very short breaks in the lineage, it has continued to be manifested right up to the present day. [Norbu, 2000, p. 158]*

Master Norbu then proceeds to tell a tale of a certain master who had decided that it was time to die and asked his disciples to seal him in a tent and leave him in peace for seven days:

> *The disciples went down the mountain, and waited, camped at the foot of it for seven days, during which time it rained a great deal and there were many rainbows. Then they went back up and opened the tent, which was sewn up just as they had left it. All that they found inside was the master's clothes, his hair, and his fingernails and toenails. His clothes were the clothes of a lay person, and they remained there in a heap where he has been sitting, with the belt still wrapped around the middle. He had left them just like a snake sheds a skin. [Norbu, 2000, pp. 158-159]*

The Tibetans have a long history of cultivation of what they call the Rainbow Body. They have a number of dedicated practices devoted to this with thousands of aspirants who train in these systems. Their great masters were said to have been able to consciously shed the remnants of their physical bodies and to evolve into a body of pure light.

China

The Taoists of China have one of the longest standing traditions of Alchemy and Light Body work in the world. Much like Tibet, much of this work has been diligently documented in the Taoist Canon and a great deal of this information still lives in the oral tradition. Masters impart this wisdom on their students only when they are ready and can finally undergo the final illumination processes.

There is an extraordinary level of detail that has been transferred along these lines within the Chinese tradition where there certainly is no shortage of words. Here is an example of an excerpt in the preparation of the "immortal fetus":

> *Gather the five vitalities and return them to the source (the upper tan t'ien in the brain) where the union of (positive and negative) vitalities will produce the immortal foetus…If the five vitalities are full a golden light will soar up to unite with the light of (essential) nature to become a single light which is the union of the radiant vitality of the positive principle (yang) in the head and the bright light of the negative principle (yin) in the abdomen into one single light which will result in the egress from the immortal foetus. The practiser should then lower his eyes slowly to look down before closing them with the combined force of his heart and intellect as if to make a jump. [Yu, 1973, pp. 163-171]*

There are volumes of specific instruction on how to go through this process and what pitfalls to avoid. Needless to say, this is the primary tradition from which I teach and this excerpt is not to be taken out of context. It serves merely as an illustration of the depth of scholarship that has gone into this very specific field by thousands of practitioners.

It is important to remember that there is one Light Body and the various traditions of the world have come to describe it in slightly different ways. I personally found the Taoist path to be very well laid out and easy to follow as a student. This in no way should take away from the validity of the other systems that exist. In fact, I have studied many of them and each has a special piece of the puzzle in my opinion. With a history of secrecy and distortion in some of these traditions, bits and pieces of this vast body of knowledge are often missing. In fact, there is a great deal of this in the Chinese culture as everybody tries to preserve their turf of this "ancient Chinese secret." In the old days, this knowledge was supreme power for your clan/tribe and the secrets were carefully guarded. One of my teachers who is a traditionally trained Chinese man without a hippie bone in his body had an interesting response to a student when asked who the originator of our knowledge was. His answer: "Atlantis." All of the jaws dropped in the room but with further thought, it made sense. Each of these spheres of understanding that sprang up around the world when looked at as a whole, point to a previous era when we allegedly had a cohesive body of knowledge that revolved around these practices before we fell into darker times. We are now waking up to this knowledge again.

India

The Hindu tradition is also noted for its exceptional scholarship in this field and its priceless contribution to the yogic arts. Hindu scholars represent an unbroken line of Vedic scholarship and research and are another of the "flame holder" traditions of the world. They have an extensive understanding of the energy systems that operate in the body and their knowledge of yoga and breath work speaks for itself.

From Paramahansa Yogananda's autobiography:

> *So long as the soul of man is encased in one, two, or three body-containers, sealed tightly with the corks of ignorance and desires, he cannot merge with the Sea of Spirit. When the gross physical receptacle is destroyed by the hammer of death, the other two coverings—astral and causal—still remain to prevent the soul from consciously joining the Omnipresent Life. When desirelessness is attained through wisdom, its power disintegrates the two remaining vessels. The tiny human soul emerges, free at last; it is one with the Measureless Amplitude... When a soul is out of the cocoon of the three bodies it escapes forever from the law of relativity and becomes the ineffable Ever-Existent. Behold the butterfly of Omnipresence, its wings etched with stars and moons and suns! [Yogananda, 1946, p. 489]*

When one first starts to study these systems, one thing becomes quite apparent from the start: there's a lot going on here! There are people (very intelligent ones I may add) that devote their entire lives to the study of these systems. There are precious few, however, that combine such rigorous intellectual study with the actual practice of these arts. That being said, a great number of the most famous Ascended Masters that have walked the Earth in this past cycle have come from India. India, to this day, remains the world's treasure chest of spiritual knowledge and the holy men and women who practice it. This is a country where God permeates all daily activities and colors all traditions.

Inca

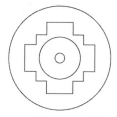

There is very little left of the living Inca tradition thanks to the Spanish conquest. This once-great empire was known for its stargazers and medicine men along with the incredible architecture of its monuments. There are a small number of shamans that have come down from the high Andes recently and have begun teaching the knowledge of the ancient Inca. They feel that with the coming earth changes, it is time for us to come together and re-learn what we once knew about the luminous body. Dr. Alberto Villoldo has played an integral part of bringing this knowledge to the West. Here is an excerpt from one of his books on the subject:

> *The Luminous Energy Field is shaped like a doughnut (known in geometry as a torus) with a narrow axis or tunnel, less than a molecule thick, in the center. In the Inka language it is known as the popo, or luminous bubble. Persons who have had near-death experiences report traveling through this tunnel in their return voyage to the light. The human energy field is a mirror of the Earth's magnetic field, which streams*

*out of the North Pole and circumnavigates the planet to reenter again
through the South Pole. Similarly, the flux lines or cekes of the Luminous
Energy Field travel out the top of the head and stream around the luminous body, forming a great oval the width of our outstretched arms. Our
energy fields penetrate the Earth about twelve inches, then reenter the
body through the feet. [Villoldo, 2000, pp. 48-49]*

It amazes me how similar this all sounds! The Inca tradition is having a
resurgence with the teaching of this knowledge by a small number of Elders
who have recently descended from their mountains to share this information with us once again.

Judaic-Christian-Islamic Traditions

The origins of the religions of The Book of Abraham come from the an-
cient Zoroastrian and Egyptian traditions and their contemporaries. The
early Judaic mystical knowledge fell under the umbrella of the study of the
Kabala which was essentially borrowed from earlier Egyptian knowledge.
Much of the essence of this tradition carried over into Christianity and
Islam which were have maintained their own Secret Societies, such as the
Rosicrucians, Builders of the Adytum, Golden Dawn, and others. The use
of the halo as a device to convey association with Divinity is described in
the following quote:

*The whole-body image of radiance is sometimes called the aureole or
glory; it is shown radiating from all round the body, most often of Christ*

or Mary, occasionally of saints (especially those reported to have been seen surrounded by one). Such an aueola is often a mandorla ("almond-shaped" vesica piscis), especially around Christ in Majesty, who may well have a halo as well. In depictions of the Transfiguration a more compli-cated shape is often seen, especially in the Eastern Orthodox tradition, as in the famous 15th century icon in the Tretyakov Gallery in Moscow. [Didron, 1851]

The artistic depictions always show enlightened Saints in their Light Bodies emanating Divine Light through their mere presence. The story of the Transfiguration of Enoch serves as a great example of this: "In the Book of Enoch, when Enoch returns to Earth, he tells his children that although they see him as the earthly, human Enoch, there is likewise an angelic Enoch (Metatron) that has stood in the Lord's Presence." [Schodde, 1882] Enoch's developed Light Body allows him to present in human form to his counterparts while being able to stand in the "Lord's presence." In this story, Enoch had been able to cross the bounds of three-dimensional reality with his understanding and development of a Luminous Body.

Much Christian iconography portrays Jesus in the central role of the central figure, or sun, amongst our zodiac. This can be seen in images of Jesus as the guiding hub for his twelve disciples. In fact, there are thousands of references to Jesus being the living embodiment of the Guiding Light. There is also a growing body of research that is pointing to the parallels be-tween Jesus, the Son of God and our central star, the Sun of God. [Massey, 1900] It seems that much has been borrowed from the older Egyptian idea of Sun worship and the notion of Star Seeding. If Jesus is to serve as an example for us in life, then the cultivation and ignition of the Light Body becomes the central goal of our religious practice. The understanding of our essential nature leads to the enlightenment of our energy fields and the activation of our Light Body.

COMING HOME

If Jesus Christ was to be understood as the "Sun" vs. the "Son" of God, then what does that story mean to us? If the Egyptian Mystery traditions speak of the Earth being a literal "star seed," then where do we go from here? The emergence of an enlightened human is a spectacular thing. It bends time and space and creates something special. If Earth were a school and we were students, well, there are too few graduates right now. What does graduation from the Earth school mean? How can we understand what all of these traditions are saying and how can we relate to this information? The answer is simple.

You already know.

If we look at the concepts and principles we have studied thus far in this book, we can come to realize that there is a certain energy exchange that we deal with every day of our lives. We have learned to maximize the flow of that energy through our fields and to minimize the impedance or the blocked flow of that energy. We have learned to reclaim the power we, and only we, have trapped in our shadows and we have come to understand the process by which our demons are created and shared them with one-another. Now, the reversal of this process leads us to an interesting place. Jesus teaches his disciples to "Be a Light unto thyselves" and we see similar language in several biblical passages:

> "Let your light so shine before men, that they may see your good works, and glorify your Father which is in heaven." *Matthew 5:16*
> "While ye have light, believe in the light, that ye may be the children of light." *John 12:36*
> "For ye were sometimes darkness, but now are ye light in the Lord: walk as children of light" *Ephesians 5:8*

And we also hear the same theme from the Buddha:

> "Be a light unto yourself, betake yourselves to no external refuge. Hold fast to the Truth. Look not for refuge to anyone but yourselves."
> —*The Buddha upon his deathbed*

This is exactly what we are heading towards. By turning the light of awareness inward, we are able to experience the wonderment and mysteries of the universe through our alchemical process. We are able to free up more and more energy and to refine it into a better understanding of Reality as it is. This refinement process frees up the smooth flow of energy in our outer meridians and also opens up our 8 Extraordinary meridians which lead to greater psychic intuition and inner vision. This level of attainment prepares us for the next step of our process which is the fusion of Yin and Yang at every level of our energy system.

We begin by developing and balancing the lower dantien. Once consolidated and strong, we then use this energy to open, refine, and balance the energy of the middle dantien whose place is around the heart. Again, after more practice we do the same at the upper dantien (third eye) and then the crown. From here, there is very specific breath work that allows us to create what is called in Taoist lore "the Immortal Fetus." This is an energy field that we cultivate and nurture daily within our abdomen. With rigorous effort and focused attention, we energetically birth this new body from within. Once created, we effectively molt off our physical attachment with the third dimension and allow for this new vehicle to become the trans-dimensional house for our expanded consciousness. At this point, many masters have been able to perform miraculous feats because they are no longer bound by the laws of the third dimension. Babaji and Lu Tung Pin among many other ascended masters have the ability to incarnate as they wish and take on any physical form that suits them. These ascended masters have no filter or distortion between what they wish and what is instantly manifest. They have literally evolved into our birthright... they have become examples of homoluminous.

Now, the cultivation of the Light Body is a life-long process that entails refinement and consolidation of energy in different dantiens or energy centers of the body. It requires us to consciously clear our obstructions and open ourselves up to Source energy. Once we have done so, our perception shifts and we understand the true "I" or our eternal identity. Our understanding of time and space dramatically shifts and as our newfound radiance renders us unbound. I will devote a future book to the subject of time and its central role in the alchemical process.

All of the groundwork that we have laid out here must be mastered and the student should have a great deal of proficiency in Qi Gong and internal awareness. Once the light of awareness is turned inward and the mysteries unlocked, then the path to the Light Body further reveals itself to the student. There is never a time when we are not being guided internally by our Super Conscious minds via our DNA. It seems that evolution has a trajectory and we are the canvas. The Light Body is the next level in our growth and, this is important to remember, it keeps going on from there. The initial step is to become self-aware and develop a vehicle that immortalizes our consciousness. Remember, in an ever-moving fractal, there really is no end—finite thinking is a mark of our polarity consciousness. Evolution gets more interesting but unfortunately, most humans don't even know the game.

The statement "immortalizes our consciousness" is an important one. It is said in the Hindu tradition that when we incarnate here on Earth, we agree to have our perfect memories "wiped" so that we can experience finding ourselves all over again. With each successive reincarnation, we take on new lessons and work towards a self-awareness until we are finally "there." When we break through and realize our true nature we are then enlightened. With the evolution of homoluminous, we essentially break the cycle of birth and death as we no longer need our physical bodies to exist on the dimensional Earth anymore. We, in essence, have come full circle and have married Yin and Yang to become an active constituent of the Great Tao. It is said that an ascended human is a sight for sore eyes in other dimensional realms. This may have something to do with the low number of graduates we've had in the past 5000 years of maybe because this is the central proving ground for everything. We have a small window to wake up and evolve or we shall perish and take the ecosystem down with us.

Personal Journeys—An Early Glimpse

THERE WERE A number of intense experiences I was subjected to as a monk. Many of which involved delving deeply into my inner realms and freeing trapped energy from my past. After one particular episode of heavy rebirthing type breathing with my teacher, I had pulled through a very difficult memory from my childhood. I had felt as if I were dying and wanted anything other than what I was feeling come up...talk about aversions and cravings! After some initial struggle, I relaxed through it and simply let the feelings, memories, and thoughts be as they were and pass. Instead of dying, I felt liberated on the other side of this experience. It was as if I had shed spiritual poundage in that moment. I laid there for a while before opening my eyes and orienting myself to the room. What I saw startled me. Not only could I see a fully-developed luminous egg around my teacher, but also orbs of light around the other students on the far side of the room. As I squinted my eyes and looked at the details of their light bodies, I noticed that one was brighter and somewhat different than the others. As I tried to recognize his face, I realized that it wasn't one of my fellow monks. He had the glowing face of an old Chinese master. My teacher whispered to me that he was here to oversee our work and was a friend from the lineage. The Master smiled at me and then walked right through the wall. I turned to my fellow students in awe and noticed that I could still see their light bodies. I thought that it was a hallucination. Little did I know that this was just the beginning of an adventure I am still happily on...

Unless you start by building your foundations and working from the core upwards, you will not be able to activate your Light Body. It simply will not work. We cannot ignore any aspect of ourselves and move on to the shiny, fuzzy stuff. We cannot avert the pain we sense lurking in our shadows and leap ahead to a Light Body without crashing. In trance consciousness, the instant success storyline is fed to us by the demons that feed off of our energy field. They, like all other life, seek self-preservation and resist annihilation. The light of consciousness washes them away. It illuminates the shadows in which they hide and helps us regain our personal power. Remember, the Devil is the Trickster. Don't fall for the shiny shortcuts. We need to let the directionality of the Life Force guide us internally to grow and evolve and literally transform into the next iteration of our species.

I'd like to speak to critical minds: if there are guys/gals out there with Light Bodies, then why don't they come show themselves? Through personal communication with the great immortals of my lineage I have come to understand that there is a profound psychological flaw in the West that keeps them from appearing in this age. In the East, there are constant visitations and stories of people being accosted by masters. Even in the West, many are approached in the dream state and given instruction but seldom in person and hardly ever in the public arena. I have been told that this is due to a flaw in Western thinking—the savior complex. There was a great break in the tradition of the Gnostics of antiquity and the thinking of a certain extremist sect of Judaism from the Dead Sea called the Zaddikim back at the turn of the millennium. [Lash, 2006, pp. 65-66] The ancient and age-old methodology for transference of information and enlightenment was through, what John Lamb Lash calls "The Revealers." These masters of the Great Mystery were the embodiment of the secret practices they taught and helped people find their own way there by patient teaching and regular study. In opposition, were "The Redeemers," as Lash named them, who were born out of an apocalyptic mentality that asserted that the messiah was coming and that we would all be saved by this individual.

We find that much of this thinking had transferred to early Christian ideologies and, carried by the sword of the Romans, has infected Western culture. Before this time people were not encouraged to kill in the name of God and be forgiven for "saving" the souls of those they enslaved. Never before did our creation myth pull us out of the Garden and place us in the position of dominating the natural world. The great ascended masters will not show up on prime-time TV and do that dance for you because, chances are, we'll expect them to fix all of our problems and put them up on a cross. The ascended masters will not contribute to this insanity. But it is common for them to communicate with those who begin doing the work and learn to listen. The trap is this: they can help you find your own way, but have already left us wonderful systems to follow. Once we start to wake up, they and the entire rest of the Universe are right here waiting to celebrate with us. If you are one of those people who say you'll believe it when you see it, well, I hate to break it to you, but that is coming from the deep trance you're trapped within.

The greatest delusion that humanity has taken upon its collective consciousness is the idea that everything is random and that we are powerless in the chaos of the universe. This is the perfect belief system to enslave a race. If you are such a person, do yourself a favor and read some articles on quantum physics.

The role of the master is to illuminate the Way for those around them by a simple principle—their actual presence illuminates the darkness of ignorance. It is for us to become the Light and literally "ignite" our Light Bodies into being. From here, our singular presence helps dispel the shadows around us and to shine away ignorance. The breeding ground of vampires and zombies goes away when the Light shines all around. The more people wake up, the easier the task of illumination gets and the more pleasant our world becomes. We are in need of beacons of Light who will lead their lives by example and serve as Inspiration for the family and friends around them. Shine into your world and make it a better place. The only way that happens is to change yourself. When we become homoluminous we set an example for the world around us…our mere presence will serve as an example of what liberated humanity looks like.

✳

CHAPTER FOURTEEN

WHERE WE GO FROM HERE

We must be the change we wish to see in the world.

—Gandhi

verything is already here and now. Coming full circle is the Taoist way. So the question becomes, why do we start the journey to begin with? Why do we do anything or go anywhere if there's really nothing to do or nowhere to go? The answer is simple. As Yin and Yang represent the primal split of Tao, this perceived split created all movement in the Universe. With polarity comes spin, with the spin comes the movement and the breath of life in its myriad forms and faces. Coming home is our opportunity to finally let go of our self-created dramas and fortified shadow energy and to move with the flow of the Tao. This is where we encounter the paradox of inaction versus action.

It's like saying a surfer is doing nothing once they've caught a wave or that a sailboat is doing nothing when it is lined up behind a strong tailwind. The Universe moves. The Great Tao moves. Being silent and still gives us a chance to harmonize with this movement and literally "ride the wave." With this, we become eternal players in an eternal game. The difference being, however, that there is no stress and no strife when we are in sync with the patterns of Nature. When we stop putting in chaotic noise we can peacefully listen to and dance with the orchestra of all Creation. It moves us. It drives our action. It becomes the guiding force for all of our motives in goodness and in grace. However, like the surfer who sees a wave coming, we have to paddle hard sometimes to catch it. Once we do, it is a great ride. We catch the tailwind and it is smooth sailing from there.

Where we go from here should be apparent. To create the environment for personal growth and healing and to do so starting right now. Effective practice is where the rubber hits the road. In Part Two, we have been introduced to a number of practices to help us reconcile our energy losses and to correct the imbalances. We have spent a lot of time getting into a mess and we may well require a number of steps to clean it up. Not to worry. Now comes the practice. After years of dedicated training, the one thing that I find helps build the Zhi or the power of Intention better than anything is the practice of Gongs. These are personal agreements or rituals that we commit ourselves to in order to push our practice forward. We will discuss these at the end of this chapter but it is first important to get a global view of the action we need to take. This involves looking at the world around us and our relationship to the notion of global citizenry. We need to create a healthy environment for cohabitation so that we have the necessary foundations for our practice.

Global Green Citizenry

In the Creation Myth of the ancient Gnostic tradition, the planet Earth was formed when the Goddess Sophia "morphs into terrestrial form, becoming a planet herself, but an organic one, sentient and aware: the earth…The terrestrial globe solidifies and life arises in rampant forms… Sophia awakens to the world of her solitary dreaming, the template of the Anthropos and proceeds to live out a divine experiment: the unfolding of human novelty." [Lash, 2006, p. 160] This becomes the basis of the Gnostic story of Creation which speaks of a sentient being from the center of the galaxy who comes out to the galactic arms in order to experiment with how life can emanate through her dream. Human beings, in the Gnostic understanding of Reality, are the living acting agents of Divine emanations that comes to us through our connection with Sophia, the planet earth. We are to co-create and evolve together as we are intimately tied to one another. Like neurons in the human brain, we are each like neuronal extensions of Sophia and she experiences herself through our senses. The more aware and conscious we become, the more self-aware She becomes…waking up as a fully sentient being. This is an important counterpoint to the Judeo-Christian version that places us in dominion over the Earth and attributes Divinity as coming from above somewhere. It gives Divinity a characteristic male voice and, by deduction, places the feminine in an inferior position.

Taoism can apply the magic of the rational way of looking at life to our Western notion of Divinity. A male (Yang) God alone is a fundamental state of imbalance. There can be no Yang without Yin and anything other than a perfect balance of the two cannot speak for the Ultimate Source. The West's male-oriented view of Divinity is, in my opinion, is a major contributor to the way we see ourselves, and the way we relate to Mother Earth. Our imbalanced grasp of the Highest Aspect—or the Holiest of Holies, if you like—has created a cultural imbalance that has passively allowed for the raping of the Earth and the destruction of our ecosystem.

We measure progress not by how we cohabitate but by how well we can amass resources and pull commodities out of the natural environment. This way of thinking makes it perfectly okay to tear through a forest to pull out timber or to blast through a beautiful hillside in order to pull out coal. We draw fences and fight over terrain as if we own Her—versus the Native American view in which we belong to Her. Our relationship with the Mother Earth is totally symbiotic. She needs us to evolve and wake up into a fully sentient Light Body, and we need her as a nurturing home. To lose this connection, to allow mass extinctions, would be catastrophic.

In our postmodern era, we need to act together as a species to defend our natural habitat. Lack of fresh water, overproduction of sewage, strip mining, desertification due to global warming, pollution in the seas, over-fishing, deforestation, and overpopulation are issues that affect all of us. If we continue thinking that we are the "chosen people," then we will continue to draw our lines and fight over resources until it is too late.

The polarization of our minds is fully reflected by the American political system. You are either Red or Blue- for taxes or against them, an imperialist or an isolationist, pro life or pro choice. This simplistic approach to political discourse reflects the insanity of our times and the state of our collective consciousness. Enlightened citizenry begins with awareness. This means we need to be awake enough to participate in our political processes. The people running the show now are puppeteers for specific economic interests. It seems that the planet and the environment have suffered irremediably as a result.

Waking up to our inner truth is the necessary first step to changing the outside world. Once awake however, it is time to get involved and take our planet back for our children's children. Wake up and get involved.

I WAS ON a guided hike with a cultural anthropologist and ethno-botanist on the island of Bora Bora in Tahiti. We were interested in the local plants and traditions and wanted to see the real culture behind all of the tourism. The guide was a passionate man who had devoted himself to the study of the Polynesian culture. We had parked the car in a rural neighborhood and were walking through an area full of houses. The guide explained the history of Tahiti to us while we were still walking in the world he called the "present."

Tahiti is a former French colony that was taken during the land grab days of European Imperialism. With the ships came Jesuit priests and diseases from the Old World. The guide explained that the population of the Islands decreased from nearly 250,000 to 20,000 people in just a few short years because of the plague. The local king asked the head Jesuit priest on the island why his relatives were dying and the French remained unharmed. The answer was simple and devious: "Obviously my God is better than yours." The king agreed to do whatever it took to protect his people. He didn't see what was coming.

The priest demanded that all of the Tahitians come down to the coast and leave the interior of the island where they had lived for thousands of years. Their entire culture was founded on the crops and temples that existed in the hills. In one broad stroke, they were cut from their heritage. They were told that the French "God" could see them if they went into the hills and He would punish them and their relatives for it. To this day there is a Taboo Line on Bora Bora that most of the natives will not cross.

When the locals came to the coast, they were instructed to tear down their old pagan temples and use the stones to build a church. Then they got hungry. They were told that they needed this thing called money in order to buy food. How were they to get money? Simple—they needed a job. However, jobs were only available to people who had an education from the church… and then the chasm began. Today, the biggest health concerns amongst the islanders are heart disease and diabetes. They have taken on a carb and fat-rich Western diet and can't afford fruits and vegetables, as they are imported from New Zealand.

We crossed the Taboo Line into the "past," as our guide called it, and I was floored. There were fruit trees (mango, papaya, banana, passion fruit, grapefruit, and coconut) as far as the eye could see along with ginger root, vanilla bean, and many other items. The fruit was rotting on the ground as nobody was willing to risk crossing the Taboo line to get it. It was the King's family land open to the public.

Here I was, standing in a microcosm of the Garden of Eden separated from the rest of the world only by an imaginary line that people were terrified of. A tear came to my eye. It wasn't bad enough for us to be separated from the garden but we then raced around the globe finding cultures that were perfectly happy in their coexistence with the planet and we had to eject them too. All they had to do was reach up and grab their fruit or cast a line and pull a fish from the beautiful sea all around them and they were at peace. Now, they are bound by the financial systems and diseases of lifestyle that infect Western civilization. They no longer go up the mountain to claim their birthright but they wait on tourists and go home to their TVs and stagnant lives. Our guide was hell-bent on educating them and changing this trend and I wish him the best. I feel that healing that wound will have global repercussions. We all have a stake in this healing.

The Plan

A practice is only as good as its implementation and there is only one person that can sit in that saddle—you. At this point we know what the problem is and how we got into this mess. Since we've identified the mechanism of pathology and we've have learned specific practices, we can start correcting the disharmonies in our energy fields. Armed with the solution to the problem: let's get to work!

In the Taoist tradition we have two main branches: Mountain Taoists and Fire Taoists.

The Mountain variety live in secluded enclaves of distant, nearly inaccessible ranges and lead lives of rigorous regimented practice and ritual observation. This is a very dedicated lifestyle that is a fast track to clearing obstructions which gives us plenty of time daily to work on our Light Body. Very few people I know have the luxury of living this lifestyle.

The Fire Taoists live amongst the people. They hold worldly professions but are committed to their practice and their energetic cultivation. They make their daily life the basis of their Qi Gong. The world is their practice and they diligently work on turning the daily "lead" of experience into the "gold" of illumination. These are the people that the world needs right now. For every monk holding the light up in the mountains, we need ten thousand performing the Great Work right here. There is no Garden apart from where we live—it's all One. This leaves us with the empowering knowledge that we are in the unique position to evolve and practice right here in our current lives without shaving our heads or getting into a funny wardrobe.

This does not, however, preclude us from spending some time in nature, especially at first. Resonant tuning with the pure vibrations of nature is critical for us to be able to calibrate to the energy curve of the Great Tao. The hikes I take every week I call "gathering the Nectar." and they are an extremely rejuvenating practice. This is all part of the life of a Fire Taoist.

Review of Practices

Let's now summarize the battery of practices we have learned in this book and, more importantly, create a personal plan to begin our own practice and start the Great Work. In order to keep it simple and keep it digestible, I have outlined the major points under each category here in this chapter.

I've also put together resources and tools that can be accessed at taoist-path.com. Please know that much of the information shared with you here been kept secret for thousands of years. It required decades of study and practice to reach the higher levels of these practices. Secrecy is no longer a value in these internet times, but just because the information is available, don't shortchange their immense value. I've organized online forums, web-based lectures, online video demos, retreats and much more in order to provide you with all of the tools necessary for your growth and continued development.

PHYSICAL PRACTICE
As mentioned earlier, the health of the physical vehicle is the underlying basis of this entire practice. Negligence of the body will deter your ultimate growth and keep you from developing the correct awareness of the Tao within you. The four major aspects of this practice are:

1. Diet
2. Exercise
3. Sleep
4. Mindset

Please review the chapter on physical health in Part Two and, when ready for more resources please refer to the following websites:
well.org
vitalityhealthcare.com

QI GONG

The practices outlined in Part Two are designed to build a strong foundation in your energy field and help enhance the flow of your Wei (Defensive) Qi and your Ying (Nutritive) Qi. Altogether, to do all three would take just under 45 minutes per day. If this is too much to start with, try doing one or two a day and cycling between them on different days. This will allow you to grow and develop the different skills and to fortify different aspects of your energy field as you go.

Daily practice of Qi Gong is essential as it is the fastest way to clear your energy field and to dispel shadow energy charge. It frees up the underlying power we need to really delve into the Great Work. Again, the third exercise is available to view at taoistpath.com. There is little point in trying to learn moving exercises from a book. Watch the video clips and learn the exercise. The other two are in the book because they are static postures that can be captured in pictures. After your first hundred days of practice, you will be able to learn the next level of exercises via DVDs and I have created an online correspondence system that allows you to video yourself performing the different practices and submit them for review. This way we can make sure you are doing the exercises correctly and keep moving you up in the training.

The first hundred days are critical. This is what is going to burn in a good habit and start the awakening process. I highly advise you to commit to a schedule you can uphold and practice this daily.

MENTAL

The mental practice that we have learned will function as the central operating system for our minds for years to come. Constantly asking ourselves the question: "What am I doing right now?" is a conscious act of injecting Self Awareness into the dreamy sleep of our unconscious days. With continued practice, we begin to feel the freedom and liberation of simply being instead of constantly doing and reacting. We can't feed our shadows when we do nothing and, better yet, we can finally hear the undertones of our Super Consciousness through our DNA when we finally stop jumping in with our incessant mental activities.

EMOTIONAL

The cleansing of emotional attachments is an incredibly liberating practice that frees up enormous reserves of energy for us. Emotions are powerful and, when repressed, can compound into an explosive force. Learning to harmonize our emotional currents is critical. It is important to note that emotions are perfectly natural expressions we have to events and that it is the imbalanced state of these emotions that creates suffering. If we allow them to naturally come and go, they are raw and real and they are the very flavors of life. It is important to remember this because there is nothing wrong with passion. Naturally emerging desires are a huge catalyst for growth, evolution, and change. It is the imbalanced reflection of our aversions and cravings that cause the trouble and bring on our suffering.

The emotional cleansing practices in Part Two of this book can be liberating. Like a virus scanner, program your Sub Conscious mind to smooth out and heal imbalanced emotional charges as they arise. It will become obvious when we are getting carried away with an emotional charge. We can first of all stop engaging in it any further (mental practice), and having illuminated it with our conscious minds, we can proceed to heal it with the emotional practices we have learned. As things pop up, we forgive, heal, and clean the energies. Don't get frustrated because you have years worth of stuff that you will start becoming aware of and it'll take time to heal and clear it all. You will feel a thousand pounds lighter on the other side and wonder how you ever lived carrying all of that lead around!

SPIRITUAL

In Part Two, techniques have been provided you to serve as a battery of tools to help you continually clean and purify your energy field. There is nothing more amazing than the feeling of being totally clear of "gunk" and being able to simply be, see, and hear the Love of the Universe coursing through you. There is nothing left to do at this point. You are fully complete and have no wants. You are in ecstasy—just elated to be alive. This feeling is your birthright and getting there is not an addition process. The more you subtract, the closer you come to Source, and the more your Light Body becomes activated. The more you cleanse and heal the more whole you become. There is less of "you" and yet All of You.

Take your time and cycle through all of these practices and you will find a rhythm that makes sense for you in your lifestyle. Do a minimum of one of these per week, however. Especially at first, we need to take a number of dedicated acts of self-love to break out of our trances and wake up to the alchemical process. The task at hand is waiting for you but you have to see the benefits before you fall back asleep.

MANIFESTATION PRACTICE

The Manifestation practice becomes an important part of our work in that it allows us to understand the mechanism through which we can create the exact surroundings and circumstances we need in order to perform the Great Work. When we get a sense of how to silence our reactive minds and how to stop feeding energy into our shadows, then we have a clear channel for Super Consciousness to fuse with our Sub Consciousness and guide us effortlessly in life. We can also learn to plant mental seeds via our Self Consciousness directly into our Sub Consciousness in order to optimize our lives and to help quicken the healing process. We can learn to use this Manifestation process to gain a profound understanding of our critically important role in the Universe. It empowers us to shine the light of awareness on the shadows that house our mental, emotional, physical, and spiritual afflictions. A critical piece of the puzzle is learning the rules by which the Universe operates and to become a master of this knowledge.

The manifestation practice is based on a proper understanding of Reality. Once we get a sense of how things operate in our Universe, then we are empowered to play a more active role in the embedding of our own Sub Conscious minds. We then learn to "get out of the way" and let the currents of the Great Tao (or the Voice of God or whatever you want to call it) speak directly to us and guide our actions in life. We learn to move naturally with the waves of Creation and become co-creators.

To build this understanding into your daily life, it is important to pick a certain set of suggestions or goals that we would like to program into our Sub Consciousness and then do so on a daily basis in our Gong (described below). We can simultaneously learn to listen to Super Consciousness and program Sub Consciousness. Work on creating a set of reasonable goals and beliefs you would like to adopt. I have included a number of forms and pages to help you clarify your goals for yourself on the website. With these, we can help identify your negative patterns and replace them with positive ones. You can also set your 30/60/100 day goals for your gong and reinforce them daily. I highly recommend using these tools as they will help solidify your intention and focus your attention on your personal goals.

Now, let's move on to the next section where we'll engage in the actual implementation of a program for you.

Gongs

A Gong in Chinese is a designated amount of time that you allot to perform a specific task daily. For example, knowing that it takes at least 90 days for a particular good habit to burn into your nervous system, I have found that the Hundred Day Gong is the most appropriate length to practice. This means that we pick a particular practice (or set of practices) and designate them as our Gong and we diligently practice them every day for 100 days without fail. This means that if you miss a day, even if its day 99, you start over. Not only does this build resolve, it forces us to wake up and pay attention to our day-to-day routines. It is incredibly painful when you miss day 46, for instance (I did!) and have to start over. At first you try to make excuses to yourself about how it was okay and how you'll just keep going, but then, a deal is a deal…you start over. Next round, you pay attention! It is a wonderful way of not only building focus and determination, but also to ensure that you train regularly. It is a dedicated act of self-love that snaps you out of your daily trance and brings the light of awareness to your consciousness. The more we practice, the more we wake up and the better off we are.

I do these all of the time in my personal life and development. I set goals for myself for the next 100 days (physical, mental, spiritual) and I look at them daily and I reinforce my Sub Conscious mind every day for those hundred days. When it is over, I assess where I am and take a few days of introspection and meditation before I set my next gong. In essence, I allow my Super Conscious mind to guide me into the next series of programs for the Sub Conscious mind. This is a wonderful method for bringing the Self Conscious mind into the equation and tie all aspects together—again, harmonizing Yin and Yang.

Depending on how dedicated you are and where you think you'd like to start, you can put in something simple, like one Qi Gong set for starters and do that for a hundred days or you can get far more involved. I usually have eight exercises or meditations per day in a given gong but that's me— I've been a monk. Start where you feel like you can realistically manage it with your current time allowances and get the first hundred days under your belt. I assure you that afterwards, you will do more of them and add more goals and practices as you go along. This practice really helps get you on track and creates an environment for growth and personal development that is self-inspired and easy to follow.

Please go to taoistpath.com and start this practice today. Now that you have read this book, you have been equipped with the tools that you need to start your practice and work towards full liberation and the ignition of the Light Body. This is all abstract knowledge, however, unless you actually engage in the daily practice and work towards this end. I have been commissioned by my Grand Master to share this information with you and, more importantly, I am here to support you. You are a central piece to the growth and evolution of our species and you play a critically vital role in this process. I am committed to your evolution and enlightenment and will support you along the way. The more people who wake up, the faster and easier this process will be and the world becomes a better and better place.

SAMPLE GONGS

Let's take a look at a couple of sample gongs for you to consider for your first hundred days. Again, I've created a number of interactive tools on the website for you but if you are less computer savvy, simply create a Gong for yourself using one of these as an example.

SAMPLE GONG #1—PRACTICE ALL OF THESE DAILY

Silk Weaver's Exercise
Shaolin Standing Form
Triple Burner Exercise
10 minutes of Emotional clearing daily
15 minutes of Mental practice daily
Minimum 30 minutes of exercise 5 days per week with 2 recovery days
Read through and focus on manifestation sheets daily (you can download these from the website)

SAMPLE GONG #2—PRACTICE ALL OF THESE DAILY

Alternate between one of the following daily:
    Silk Weaver's Exercise
    Shaolin Standing Form
    Triple Burner Exercise
30 minutes (in one sitting) of Emotional clearing once per week
10 minutes of Mental practice daily
Minimum 30 minutes of exercise 5 days per week with 2 recovery days
Read through and focus on manifestation sheets daily (available online)

Conclusion

We now have all of the tools we need to get started on our alchemical path. You understand the science behind how your problems are created and you understand how to stop creating these problems. You understand where all of the energy you feel you lack has gone and how to reclaim it from your shadow. You understand the principles of manifestation and are now equipped with the tools and resources to reprogram your Sub Consciousness and tune into the inner voice of Super Consciousness. You have learned about the Light Body and have been given the powerful tools for the commencement of your journey to this level of awakening and understanding. You have learned a lot but I would like to take this opportunity to drive home the most important concept in this book and that is:

Do not sell yourself short.

You are amazing and a critically-important part of the whole Universe. Wake up from your trances and wake up to the present moment. Wake up to your power and wake up to your potential. You are so incredibly special and you will never cease to be amazed once you embark on the alchemical journey. I have laid out the necessary steps for you and have put together a number of tools and resources to help you at all stages along your path. Now, it is time to take that step.

The word Namaste in Sanskrit means "The Light within me respectfully bows to the Light within you"

Welcome home and Namaste.

In Loving Service,
Pedram Shojai

Resources

Acupuncture/Natural Medicine
Chinese Medicine—nccaom.org
Natural News—naturalnews.com
The Well Channel—well.org

Diet/Nutrition
Organic Foods—livingbeyondorganic.com
Nutritional Coaching—vitalityhealthcare.com
World's Healthiest Foods—whfoods.org

Economics
The Solari Report—solari.com

Esoteric Studies
Sacred Mysteries Productions—sacredmysteries.com
Builders of the Adytum—bota.org
Alchemical Texts—levity.com/alchemy

Exercise
Functional Training—athleticism.com
Cross Training—crossfit.com
Getting Outdoors—sierraclub.org
Heart Rate Monitors—suunto.com

Green/Alternative Energy
Resource—treehugger.com
Products—realgoods.com
Alternative Housing—http://earthship.org
Environmental Products—ewg.org

Qi Gong
Video, Online, and Seminar format training—taoistpath.com

Martial Arts
The Taoist Institute—taoistinstitute.com

Meditation
Vipassana Meditation—dhamma.org
Brainwave Technologies—monroeinstitute.org

COMPLETE LIST AT:
taoistpath.com with multiple resources available for free at: well.org

A Brief Overview of the Systems I Teach

LEVEL ONE—HEALTH QI GONG
These sets have been selected from various traditions because of their ability to free up and open the energy flow in the system. They are very safe and serve as the groundwork for further development. These have been compiled in the "Yellow" DVD that you will find on the website. I highly recommend one hundred days of practice on this level before moving up to the next level.

LEVEL TWO—SHAOLIN BASICS
This is the "Red" DVD from the website. This includes a number of energy sets from the Shaolin Qi Gong system of Bodymind development. This series can be practiced along with the "Yellow" series. It is more "Yang" in nature and it really drives a great deal of power through our systems. The second exercise in this section (Square Horse standing form) comes from this tradition. This level will help you develop more focus and physical stamina/power. It will help bring up the charge of your conscious energy field and help you cultivate the Zhi or the willpower needed to dispel the energies trapped in your shadow.

LEVEL THREE—ADVANCE SHAOLIN

This bridges us into the alchemical practices from the Shaolin tradition that help unite the polarities of Body and Mind. These exercises specifically help charge the tendons, muscles, and bone marrow with energy and help us integrate our physical vehicles with our energy fields—all tied through attention and intention. These are found on the "Orange" DVD and are to be practiced once you have become proficient in the first two.

LEVEL FOUR—TRANSFORMATIVE SHAOLIN

This is the final stage of the Shaolin cultivation and it is extremely powerful in its ability to integrate the Five Elements (through the Shaolin Five Animals) and develop higher levels of understanding of Reality through enhanced meditation. I have arranged to produce this one in the future.

LEVEL FIVE—TAOIST ALCHEMICAL PRACTICE

The Grandmaster of my Taoist tradition has imposed a strict policy on the instruction of this powerful system and it centers around direct transmission. There are six levels in this system which go through the entire spectrum of the training needed to develop a healthy Light Body. I teach this system in seminar format and am happy to teach any serious student. Please refer to taoistpath.com for information on upcoming seminars on the Taoist alchemical teaching.

*

Bibliography

Arguelles, J. (2002). Time and the Technosphere. Rochester: Bear & Company.

Batmanghelidj, F. (2003). You're Not Sick, You're Thirsty. New York: Warner Books.

Bellis, M. D. (2005). The Psychobiology of Neglect. Child Maltreatment , 150-72.

Braden, G. (2009). Fractal Time. New York: Hay House.

Brown, T. (1997). Way of the Scout. New York: Berkeley Publishing Co.

Campbell, N. (2008). Gut and Psychology Syndrome. Cambridge: Medinform Publishing.

CDC. (1996). Surgeon General's Report on Physical Activity and Health. Washington DC: U.S. DEPARTMENT OF HEALTH AND HUMAN SERVICES.

Ch'an, O. o. (2004). The Shaolin Grandmaster's Text. Beaverton: Order of Shaolin Ch'an.

Cox, R. (1997). The Pillar of Celestial Fire. Fairfield: Sunstar Publishing.

Danielou, A. (1987). While the Gods Play. Rochester: Inner Traditions.

Diamond, J. (2005). Guns, Germs, and Steel. New York: W.W Norton & Compnay, Inc.

Didron, A. N. (1851). The History of Christian Art in the Middle Ages. Boston: Harvard University Press.

Dong-Yuan, L. (2002). Treatise on the Spleen & Stomach. Boulder: Blue Poppy Press.

Emoto, M. (2004). The Hidden Messages in Water. Hillsboro: Beyond Words Publishing.

Fitts, C. A. (2009, 1 22). The Solari Report. Retrieved 7 15, 2009, from The Solari Report: solari.com

His Majesty King Khesar, T. 5. (2008, November 7). Gross National Happiness - The Center for Bhutan Studies. Retrieved July 1, 2009, from Gross National Happiness - The Center for Bhutan Studies: http://grossnationalhappiness.com/

Kalus, S. (2009). A new strategy to analyze possible association structures between dynamic nocturnal hormone activities and sleep alterations in humans. American Journal of Physiology , 1216-1227.

Kalus, S. (2009). A new strategy to analyze possible association structures between dynamic nocturnal hormone activities and sleep alterations in humans. American Journal of Physiology , 1216-1227.

Korzybski, A. (1948). Science and Sanity. London: Charlotte Schuchardt Read.

Kukolja, J. (2009). Ageing-related changes of neural activity associated with spatial contextual memory. Neurobiology of Aging , 630-645.

Lash, J. L. (2006). Not in HIS Image. White River Junction: Chelsea Green Publishing Company.

Lash, J. L. (2006). Not in HIS Image. White River Junction: Chelsea Green Publishing.

Lash, J. L. (2006). Not in HIS Image. White River Junction: Chelsea Green Publishing.

Lawlor, R. (1991). Voices of the First Day. Rochester: Inner Traditions International, Ltd.

Lipton, B. (2005). The Biology of Belief. New York: Hay House.

Loehr, J. (2003). The Power of Full Engagement. New York: The Free Press.

Maharshi. R. (2004). The Spiritual Teachings of Ramana Maharshi. Boston: Shambala.

Mandelbrot, B. B. (1982). The fractal geometry of nature. Boston: W.H. Freeman and Company.

Massey, G. (1900). Luniolatry, Ancient and Modern. Private , 175-187.

Mastorakos. (2005). Exercise and the stress system. Hormones (Athens) , 73-89.

Melchizedek, D. (2000). The Ancient Secret of the Flower of Life. Flagstaff: Light Technology Publishing.

Narby, J. (1999). The Cosmic Serpent. New York: Tarcher/Putnam.

Norbu, C. N. (2000). The Crystal and the Way of Light. Snow Lion: Ithaca.

Norbu, C.N. (1996). Dzogchen—The Self Perfected State. Snow Lion: Ithaca.

Orr, L. (1998). Breaking the Death Habit. Berkeley: Frog Ltd.

Orr, L. (1998). Breaking the Death Habit. Berkeley: Frog, Ltd.

Pert, C. (1997). Molecule of Emotion. New York: Touchstone.

Pierpaoli,W. (1995). The Melatonin Miracle. New York: Pocket Books.

Rattemeyer, M. (1981). Evidence of photon emission from DNA in living systems. Naturwissenschaften , 572-573.

Ritsema, R. (1994). I Ching. Rockport: Element.

Schodde, G. (1882). The Book of Enoch. Columbus: Andover.

Schueler, G. (1994). Egyptian Magick. St. Paul: Llewellyn Publications.

Shapely, D. (2007, May 4). CIA Considers Global Warming Threat. Retrieved July 1, 2009, from The Daily Green: http://thedailygreen.com/environmental-news/latest/1350

Shier, D. (1996). Hole's Anatomy and Physiology. Chicago: Wm. C. Brown Publishers.

Strassman, R. (2001). DMT - The Spirit Molecule. Rochester: Park Street Press.

Thompson, W. I. (1996). The Time Falling Bodies Take to Light. New York: St. Martin's Press.

Tomberg, V. (1993). Meditations on the Tarot. New York: Penguin Putnam, Inc.

Villoldo, A. (2000). Shaman, Healer, Sage. New York: Harmony Books.

Villoldo, A. (2000). Shaman, Healer, Sage. New York: Harmony Books.

Vitale, J. (2007). Zero Limits. New Jersey: John Wiley & Sons, Inc.

Yogananda, P. (1946). Autobiography of a Yogi. Los Angeles : Self Realization Fellowship.

Yu, L. K. (1973). Taoist Yoga. York Beach: Samuel Weiser, Inc.

✳

Glossary

Alchemy

The ancient art of transmutation which is the foundation of esoteric spiritual work. The premise is the transformation of lead to gold which, in the human experience is taken metaphorically as the refinement of our internal energy and our life's processes into coherent white light and full Self Realization. This practice is the basis of our work here and we return to this concept throughout the book.

Chakra

Spiritual energy center or hub for the vital energy (prana) of the body. These come from the Indian Yogic system and are located on vital plexus points along the central channel of the body. There are seven of them which start at the perineum and end at the crown of the head. Each have a different color, vibration, orientation, and mental association attributed to them. There are also a number of centers above the head as described in other systems.

Dantien

Energy reserve area where Qi energies come together, gather, condense, and rarify. There are three main dantiens along the central channel of the human body according to the ancient Taoists. The lower dantien in located three fingers below the naval and spans from the front of the body to the spine. The middle dantien is centered in the chest at heart level and the upper dantien in located slightly above the eye level in the center of the forehead. The lower dantien is the primary reserve center from which we breathe and cultivate energy during our Qi Gong practice. Each of these centers need to be cultivated slightly differently and need to be unlocked in sequence in order to attain true enlightenment and liberation.

Defensive Qi

Also called "Wei Qi," this is the type of energy that circulates around the exterior of the body and is in charge of protecting our systems from exterior attack. It can be likened to the functions of the immune system. It helps open and close pores on the skin and helps maintain smooth flow of energy along our exterior "force field". Healthy Wei Qi is critical for one's practice to progress.

Energy Field

Term used to connote the shell of energy surrounding our physical bodies. All life forms have energy fields. These tend to be the tangential reflection of the state of overall flow of energy throughout our systems. The purpose of the Qi Gong practitioner or the Yogi is to cultivate the flow and quality of this energy field in order to remove blockages or impedance in them. The cleaner and clearer they are, the closer we are to Source energy and the more power and grace can run through us.

Essence

Also called "Vitality," this is the level of energy/substance which represents the core genetic makeup of who we are. Our Essence is tied to our sexuality and comes through to us from our parents. It is the reserve system or battery for the Qi energy which runs through our bodies and is to be guarded and cultivated by the advanced practitioner.

Five Elements

The Chinese medical system breaks all of reality down into five flavors or elements of emanation. These are Fire, Wood, Water, Metal, and Earth. They represent the movement of energy in nature through the cycles of Yin and Yang. Each have particular organ correspondences with colors, sounds, flavors, emotions, internal organs, and tissues they are associated with.

Food Qi

This is the energy we extract from food. It mixes with the energy we draw from the air in order to pool in the center of the chest and become usable in a metabolic sense.

Gathering Qi

This energy forms when Air and Food Qi combine in the chest. With the help of the Original Qi coming from the Kidney Essence, this form of energy makes the "True Qi" which then feeds into the Nutritive and Defensive energies of the body.

Gong

A designated set of activities that one signs up to doing for a set period of time. These are set of as conscious acts of self love and dedicated attention to self care. The typical gong recommended in this book is for 100 days as it takes at least 90 days of behavioral re-patterning to take place. One should choose a reasonable set of practices to perform daily and must not miss a day for 100 days. Any slip up and one must start over. This helps develop focus and willpower while creating good habits and enhancing the overall health of the system.

Hermes Trismegistus

Famed Alchemist of the Western tradition who is believed to be the reincarnation (or same incarnation) of Thoth the Egyptian (or Thoth the Atlantean). Hermes is famous for his alchemical doctrines and esoteric texts left behind.

Homoluminous

Term coined by Inca scholar and teacher Alberto Villoldo. This state represents the next level of evolution of the human species from homo sapiens. The premise is that our next level of growth bridges into self-discovery and the understanding of the energetic matrix around us. From here we wake up and activate our Light Body and literally evolve into the next stage of our growth, Homoluminous.

Hun

The "ethereal soul" which is housed in the Liver and is attributed to the Wood Element. The Hun is responsible for the body's connection to Spirit. It can be best described as the Astral body. It must be properly rooted and anchored in the blood or one feels restless at night and has strange dreams. An unrooted Hun also leads to a loss of direction in life. Upon dying, this soul is released upwards to Heaven.

I Ching

The ancient Chinese book of changes. This miraculous work breaks all reality into a series of trigrams and hexagrams based on a binary linear code of Yin and Yang expressions. A solid line is Yang and a broken one is Yin. These trigram and hexagrams code into 64 different possibilities which mirror our genetic code and describe all emanations of reality. The book is also used to cast fortunes and foretell the future through divination.

Jing

Also called "Vitality" or "Essence," this is the level of energy/substance which represents the core genetic makeup of who we are. Our Essence is tied to our sexuality and comes through to us from our parents. It is the reserve system or battery for the Qi energy which runs through our bodies and is to be guarded and cultivated by the advanced practitioner. Jing, Qi, and Shen are considered the "Three Treasures" of the body and are to be cultivated daily.

Kung Fu

The ancient martial art of China practiced by thousands of monks for centuries. The literal translation is "Hard Work" or "Eat Bitter." Kung Fu is grounded in deep Qi Gong knowledge and uses the meridian system of Qi flow to potentiate power and direct lethal strikes. Many of the Qi Gong systems we study are grounded in Kung Fu as the two were inextricable in the temple systems through which they were preserved. Deep Kung Fu stances are important to cultivate in order to ground our energy and harness our internal power via Qi Gong.

Light Body

The luminous glowing field of energy that is activated once we have properly cultivated and refined our Qi. There are Light Body traditions all over the world and they all allude to a luminous glowing field around the physical body. Once activated, the practitioner can slough off their physical body and maintain continuous consciousness as they are free from the cycle of birth and re-birth. The Light Body cultivation becomes the central theme of our work once we have removed blockages in our energy fields and are ready for the transformation of our "lead" to this spiritual "gold".

Meridians

The network of channels or pathways for the flow of Qi energy through the human body. There are twelve primary meridians along with eight "extraordinary" ones. These represent each of the internal organs along with certain metabolic functions and psychic channels. The smooth flow of Qi along these meridians is critical for the maintenance of good health and Vitality.

Nei Gong

The internal form of Qi Gong which focuses on the alchemical aspects of the practice. Here, the practitioner gathers and concentrates energy in the dantiens and works to refine and cultivate awareness. The expansion and refinement of consciousness are natural components to this practice as the Light Body is activated and the flow and coherence of energy and light are optimized and tuned to Source energy.

Nutritive Qi

After the energy of Food and Air come together, they are infused with the Original Qi derived from the Essence. This True Qi then differentiates into Nutritive and Defensive Qi. The Nutritive Qi is the raw energy the body uses to maintain, heal, and restore the internal organs. This is the energy we run off of for our day-to-day needs. It must be maintained and cultivated so that we are in relative abundance so as to not deprive our vital organs of the energy they need to thrive.

Original Qi

This is the energy derived from the Essence which is stored in the Kidneys. This vital energy comes from our genetic "bank account" and is used to infuse the energy we derive from food and air. The Original Qi is stored in the lower dantien and is a vital force in the overall energy system of a human. In our Qi Gong, we work to nourish, maintain, and maximize the Original Qi by nourishing the essence and optimizing efficiency in the system.

Po

The "Corporeal" soul which is houses in the Lungs. This is the most physical and material part of a human's soul and is intimately connected with our breathing. Giovanni Maciocia calls it "a direct manifestation of the breath of life." The Po returns back to the earth upon death and is related to constrained feelings of sadness and grief.

Prana

The vital energy which is tied to breath in the Indian Yogic system. The prana flows through "nadi," or channels of energy (much like the Meridians in the Chinese system) throughout the body. There are nodes of greater concentration and the goal of the practitioner is to breathe awareness and attention to blocked regions in the body and allow the prana to flow in and heal.

Qi

The vital energy that circulates through all life. It is the currency of exchange amongst all life forms and is the moving aspect of sentience. Its refined form is Spirit and its substantiated form in Essence. Qi circulates through Meridians (energy pathways) throughout the human body and is attained through air and food. The state of our Qi flow directly influences our health. Qi is to be cultivated, refined, and moved in order to wake up. Stagnant Qi is the cause all many disease processes.

Qi Gong

The ancient practice of energy cultivation from China. Literally translated as "Energy Work," this practice, along with mediation, is the foundation of most temple arts. Kung Fu, Tai Qi, and Chinese Medicine all have forms of Qi Gong as it is the cultivation of the vital Qi energy in our systems that is tantamount to the activation of our Light Body.

Shaolin

The famous Chinese school of martial arts and Buddhism. Shaolin was an existing Buddhist temple before being visited by Do Ma (Bodhidarhma) the famous monk who transformed the school with his introduction of Qi Gong. Da Mo created the famous "warrior monks" of the Shaolin Temple and trained them to be the defenders of good in ancient China.

Shen

The Spirit which is housed in our hearts. Shen is one of the "Three Treasures" in Chinese medicine (Qi-energy, Jing-Essence, and Shen-Spirit). Shen is the awakened understanding of Who we truly are and the manifestation of that existence here in our bodies. We are to cultivate and refine our Shen and our awareness through our practice of Qi Gong and mediation. A clear mind leads to clear Shen. Clear Shen leads to Enlightenment.

Shen Gong

The practice of cultivating Spirit or Shen. This practice is not to be confused with devotional prayer because the Chinese translation here uses the meaning of "mind" here for Shen. In this light, Shen Gong is the cultivation of psychic perception, ESP, clairvoyance, and other mental powers through specific practices. One of the early Shen Gong exercises a student learns is to see the energy between their fingertips in a certain stance or to see the aura of a person. Shen gong is useful for healers and is a powerful tool for awareness but should be only practiced as part of an overall balanced curriculum.

Tai Chi Chuan

The martial art which is become very popular in the West. Translated as "The Grand Ultimate Fist," it is revered for its slow movements and graceful appearance. Done correctly, Tai Chi is a sophisticated martial art with an underlying foundation in Qi Gong and energy awareness. In essence, it allows the practitioner to become the stage wherein Yin and Yang dance in their interplay. Known for its many health benefits, Tai Chi has become quite a hit in the US.

Tantra

The ancient spiritual practice of energy cultivation through sexual co-stimulation. Tantra is a high art wherein the practitioners tap into their powerful Essence energy and use Qi and Shen to fuse, ignite, and raise the Kundalini energy which is stored at the base of the spine. It is extremely powerful and should be done carefully. Done right, Tantra liberations one's mind from sexual aberration and brings forth deep understanding of our essential Divine nature.

Taoism

The ancient Chinese philosophy of balance and harmony with nature. Based on the principle of the mutual enhancement and interaction of Yin (passive) and Yang (active) forces in nature, Taoism teaches the student to find balance in every facet of their lives. There is also religious Taoism which bridges into the various Deity worship traditions of ancient China. Note: this is not the variety which is represented in this book. Here, we are talking about the life philosophy/mastery as developed by the ancient Taoist sages: Lao Tzu and Chuang Tzu. We use those as our base and work to develop a modern understanding of them as applied to today's world.

Wei Gong

The form of Qi Gong energy cultivation that works on the Wei Qi, or external defensive energy of the body. Wei Gong helps bolster the immunity and protects the body from external pathogens. It is always important to have some Wei Gong practice in one's regimen as this becomes a policy of health assurance in a world where health insurance does so little.

Yang

The active expression of the Universe/Tao which is the balanced counterpart to the Yin expression. In the example of hot and cold, hot would be the Yang attribute.

Yi

The central Intellect or the Mind which is housed in the Spleen. This is the Self Conscious aspect of the mind where we must learn to integrate and assimilate information. A calm mind and a healthy connection with one's Super Conscious aspects combined with a healthy relationship with one's Sub Conscious mind are all critical facets of having a healthy Yi.

Yin

The passive expression of the Universe/Tao which is the balanced counterpart to the Yang expression. In the example of hot and cold, cold would be the Yin attribute.

Yoga

The ancient Indian art of body/mind/spirit cultivation. The word means "union" and it serves as an alchemical vehicle for the development of the Light Body. The Yogi works to open up blockages in their nadi (energy pathways/meridians) through breathing into specific postures, asanas, while cultivating awareness and relaxing into their bodies. Self-awareness and enlightenment are the ultimate goals of this sophisticated system. We see a very watered down version in the West but the essence of this practice is quite noble and is a true pathway towards Liberation.

Zero Point Energy

The amount of energy associated with the vacuum of empty space. This is predicted to be infinite as it is the sum of the energy of all of the subatomic particle interactions of the Universe. Tapping into this field is the subject of much study in science. This is the field that has been proposed can be tapped into by ascended masters through their consciousness.

Zhi

The will power which is housed in the Kidneys. The Zhi is the Water element's "spirit" and is tantamount in a student's ongoing development. The Zhi of the Kidneys needs to work with the Shen and Attention of the Heart for us to be present and awake. The serious student builds and cultivates Zhi through practice (especially Gongs) in order to step into their personal power. From here, one's energy is properly activated and the Qi flow is robust and unblocked.

※

When you new big thing
law perfect every thing
is your will tilt your
head back and laugh@
the play! B-

ProcessMediaInc.com

Well.org

TaoistPath.com

✳